Industry, (
and the

For Mary

Industry, Children and the Nation

An analysis of national identity in school textbooks

John Ahier

The Falmer Press

(A member of the Taylor & Francis Group)
London • New York • Philadelphia

UK   The Falmer Press, Falmer House, Barcombe, Lewes, East Sussex, BN8 5DL

USA   The Falmer Press, Taylor & Francis Inc., 242 Cherry Street, Philadelphia, PA 19106-1906

© 1988 J. Ahier

First published 1988

British Library Cataloguing in Publication Data

Ahier, John
   Industry, Children and the Nation: an analysis of national identity in school textbooks.
   1. Great Britain. Education—Sociological perspectives
I. Title.
370.19′0941
ISBN 1 85000 408 0
ISBN 1 85000 409 9 (pbk.)

Jacket design by Caroline Archer

Typeset in 11/13 Bembo by
Imago Publishing Ltd, Thame, Oxon

Printed in Great Britain by Taylor & Francis (Printers) Ltd, Basingstoke

Contents

Acknowledgements

I should like to thank John Beck and Geoff Whitty for the help, guidance and advice they gave me during my research for this book.

Introduction

In 1981 Martin Wiener, an American academic, published a book which tried to help explain Britain's eighty years of comparative economic decline in terms of a cultural anti-industrialism and anti-urbanism (Wiener, 1981). According to Wiener, to blame for this failure was the way the ruralist culture and country pursuits of the aristocracy and gentry first infected the industrial middle class and then the whole cultural fabric of society. If 'rural myths' could be found in the United States, for example, (p. 6) they did not exemplify and resonate with anti-industrial values, as in the United Kingdom. Wiener argued that the very character of the 'English way of life' came to be seen as a country way of life, and the countryside was used as 'an integrating cultural symbol' (p. 49) for both the traditionalists and the social critics; an 'emollient, patriotic ruralism' was used by Stanley Baldwin and Ramsay Macdonald, or sometimes 'the myth of the changeless country supported a fervent utopian radicalism' (p. 58).

Published in the depths of a period of headlong economic descent Wiener's book received much public exposure. His ideas had a programme in the *World in Action* television series devoted to them (The Betrayal of British Industry, November 1982) in which the then future leader of the Labour Party and a Conservative Minister voiced support. Ralph Dahrendorf, too, relied heavily upon the Wiener thesis in his series *Dahrendorf on Britain* (BBC television, January 1983) to explain what was both possibly self-destructive to the British, yet also lovable to the German academic, about the English way of life. There was also exposure in the press of what Anthony Sampson called this 'traditional American criticism of the British' ('Gross national happiness', *The Observer*, 24 October 1982). The thesis fitted in well with the criticisms of the educational system and its role in the national decline. Wiener's book did not dwell for long on that educational system but did present the public schools (many situated well away from urban life, p. 21) as the institutions originally engaged in turning the sons of the industrialists into respectable, non-industrial gentlemen. He noted that even though sporadic attempts had been made to bring industry closer to the universities this had never succeeded because of the essential features of the culture. Elitist academics and ultimately radical students, as typical products of the English system, defended the apparently 'higher national values' against commerce (p. 134).

These were not new ideas about the English educational system and its history. D.C. Coleman, writing in 1973, had hinted at the role of the public schools in turning 'players' into 'gentlemen' and the possible economic effects and Corelli Barnett had made similar points with regard to Britain's military and economic decline (Barnett, 1972 and 1978). In the latter address Barnett presented an explanation of decline very similar to that of Wiener's, stating, 'In my analysis the values and outlook of British society, especially in the elite opinion-forming groups, and as expressed through British education, have been a key factor' (p. 7), and he charged the late- and post-Victorian elite with generally ignoring the national need for education 'at every level, from primary through secondary to technical and university, in order to secure competitive success against foreign economic rivals' (p. 7). When one comes to consider exactly *how* the content of state education may have displayed the anti-industrialism and anti-urbanism then Wiener himself makes some tentative suggestions. For example, he hints that a writer like Dickens had great influence on the middle class in the way his novels taught that class to detest the whole process of Victorian urbanization and industrialization and then the educators of that class wrote these messages into the content of school history. Wiener (1981) noted that,

> One of the most popular history text-books for children in the inter-war years (Humphrey House, The Dickens World, London, 1941) gave over its entire introductory chapter on the nineteenth century to Dickens, quoting his novels to illustrate virtually every aspect of the first half of the century, most of them 'abuses' that his 'protests' helped remove. (p. 40)

Similarly, he found that the black picture of industrialization which the Hammonds had painted in *The Town Labourer* (1917) had been of prime significance in forming the public images of industrialization via school text-books and other media (p. 85).

A simple, straightforward empirical research project could suggest itself — that is, to affirm or deny such a thesis with regard to educational content. Wiener's own methodology consisted of producing a multiplicity of examples from mostly non-educational areas of social life, seeking to confirm thereby the existence of an essential cultural quality. Would a parallel content analysis of school textbooks during the historical period studied by Wiener give a similar confirmation of anti-urbanism and/or anti-industrialism? There have been some precedents for such a project, whether from a similar concern for national economic advance or from other social interests. D.C. McClelland had attempted to look for 'achievement imagery' (p. 57) in different societies' reading schemes (McClelland, 1961) and other American researchers had looked at the lack of urban situations and characters depicted in American children's textbooks, and some explicit attempts had been made to correct that omission in books like *The Bank Street Readers* (Zimet, 1969: Niemeyer, 1965). R. Gordon Kelly's PhD thesis entitled 'Mother was a lady' (Kelly, 1970) had traced some details of children's fiction to the authors' desire to reassert the qualities of the small rural community and the so-called 'gentry ideal' (p. 223). By the time Wiener published his book the content of children's books had become a very serious concern. As Hoffman declared in 1981,

> on the literary and critical front, children's books have — if not come of age — at least been allowed to come down from the nursery, and be inspected by the grown-ups ... there is now an indisputable children's book world, in which serious people take seriously what children read. (p. 193)

Whilst certainly not concerned with anti-industrialism as a problem within the national culture many of these critical studies used a methodology and implicit theories of cultural transmission consistent with those in Wiener's work. In their exposure and critique of sexism, class bias and racism can be found standard forms of content analysis built upon theories of bias by misrepresentation, and internalization by repetition. Thus, for example, it was thought that children would come to have stereotypical and 'unreal' images of women because the text-books they used only portrayed women as mothers doing domestic work, viz *Sexism in Children's Books* by The Children's Rights Workshop (1976); *Sex-role Stereotyping and the Ladybird Books* by David Whiting (1981); *Sex-stereotyping in School and Children's Books* by The Publishing Association (1981); and J.B. Hurst's *Images in Children's Picture Books* (1981).

When the social class aspects of children's books have been considered then attention has been chiefly focused on the 'sins of omission' of the writers for children. Coming from the middle class themselves, and writing for acceptance by middle class teachers, it has been argued that they either grossly misrepresented or missed out altogether the lives and institutions of the working class (Leeson, 1977; Anyon, 1981; Purkis, 1980). Similar work has also been carried out on the racist imagery of children's books and the stereotypes of racial groups often found there along with the ethnocentric representations of the 'Third World' viz Broderick (1973); Milner (1975); Dixon (1977); Hicks (1980). But, on a number of accounts, the educational research project suggested by combining the Wiener thesis with the available and popular means of investigating children's books would have been a very problematic one. As will be shown in the following chapters the very approach to the isolation of a cultural value like anti-urbanism or anti-industrialism invites suspicion. Wiener's own implicit theory and methodology impelled him to identify and list the expressions of a national cultural essence (albeit of class origin) as an integral part to arguing for the significance of so-called non-economic factors in Britain's economic decline. Other historians like Hobsbawm, whose explanations included more obvious economic matters, were misunderstood or oversimplified by Wiener as, for example, when he mistakenly tried to present the Hobsbawm thesis about Britain as a generalization about the progress of all capitalist economies (J. Beck, unpublished manuscript, section 3.6–3.15). Wiener's concept of an all-embracing cultural anti-industrialism enabled him to overlook the differences between the criticisms of Victorian *capitalism* and criticisms of industrialism in general, and, because his key historical cause was a feature of the *national* culture, then he ignored the international nature and effects of capital, be it cultural or economic. Associated with that, Wiener's method of documenting instance after instance of a national ruralism, from new towns to gardening, relied upon holistic conceptions like 'world view' (found in the title of part 2 of his book) and 'world outlook' (p. 4), with all their presuppositions of unity. Finally, when it comes to considering what place education occupies in the Wiener thesis then the inadequacies are all too clear. There is a naive view of the relations between state education, national culture and the elite from which the cultural values are said to descend. The presupposition of a consensual national culture and a 'seepage' theory of elite influence is obvious, as in the following summary of his social theory:

'Elites' he wrote,

have disproportionate influence upon both the effective climate

of opinion and the conduct of affairs. The values of the direct-
ing strata, particularly in a stable, cohesive society like modern
Britain, tend to permeate society as a whole and to take on the
color of national values, and of a general mentalité. (p. 5)

Writing now, six years later, Wiener's suggestion of a national ruralism has certainly kept its superficial conviction. At one level one can
find numerous expressions of that national cultural essence. The
popularity of books like Flora Thompson's *Lark Rise to Candleford* and
the ubiquitous *Diary of an Edwardian Country Lady*, of cottage styles in
furniture and country clothes, the resurgence of artistic interest in the
English landscape tradition (viz for example, the Arts Council show
Landscape in Britain in 1983) may all be taken as instances of this. Yet
there are also contradictory suspicions and conflicts, as there may have
always been. Criticisms of the Common Market Agricultural Policy
and some of the messages from the emerging ecological movement
have undermined any straightforward positive images of national
farming and the farmer. The publication of Marion Shoard's *The
Theft of the Countryside* (Shoard, 1980), for example, was influential in
bringing into opposition the idea of a natural, national heritage and
the national farmer-hero. Henry Moore's foreword expressed perfectly the identification of England with its land, but a land faced with
destruction, and it ended with the plea: 'Please read it for your sake,
for the sake of your children, and for the sake of your country'.

It could be said that the countryside and some of the country
figures are being called into question from all sides. Conservative
Members of Parliament have attacked the absurdities of the supports
for British agriculture (Body, 1982) and some members of the Labour
Party have formed The Socialist Countryside Group to campaign on
both ecological matters and agricultural wages and conditions. Even if
it was once different it is now very difficult to accept a basic building
block of the Wiener thesis that the English countryside is available as
an unproblematic 'integrating cultural symbol' (Wiener, 1981, p.
49).

And if the *substance* of the Wiener thesis has come to look suspect,
then so have the conventional methods of approaching children's texts
suggested in the imaginary research project we have outlined above.
A preliminary exploration of the concept of 'stereotype' (Perkins,
1979), suggested that it had been used in an unthought-out way in
those conventional analyses. In that critical work on children's texts
stereotype had generally referred to negative, simplified and mis-

taken images which appeared to determine what the child-readers would come to believe and act upon. Perkins hinted that stereotypes were not simple misrepresentations of another reality but relate to and indeed depend upon social structure; they are, 'structurally supported' (*ibid*, p. 147). Useful observations were made about the dependence of negative on positive stereotypes (for example, the happy-go-lucky black on the white Anglo-Saxon Protestant) and about the way stereotypes enter subjective identity 'providing people with explanations and definitions of themselves and of others' (*ibid*). There were, however, many unresolved issues within the paper which was critical of the socialization models shared by functionalists and Marxists yet itself used quite simple ideas about the learning of contradictory values to develop an alternative.

At this time too there were some intellectual developments in the areas of literary and film criticism in particular which could ultimately have some considerable effects on the ways children's texts might be approached. These attempts to re-examine the whole relationship between reader, author and text, and to use semiotics and the psychoanalytically based work of Lacan in new forms of discourse analysis were not applied to *children's* texts in Britain until later, when a paper by Valerie Walkerdine posed some fundamental questions for the whole tradition of sociologically informed criticisms of children's books and other publications (Walkerdine, 1984b.) Her point was that all such work operated with simple, passive concepts of the pre-given child-subject who merely learns from the texts the distorted images and stereotypes of class, race and gender. Instead she analyzed the complex role of fantasy in young girls' comics. Breaking new ground in the application of concepts from psychoanalysis and semiotics to texts for children she changed the focus. Instead of seeing such texts as instruments for socializing passive individuals into the dominant values, they are presented as offering solutions and making places available for the contradictory and problematic child-subjects. Perhaps unfairly in some respects, Walkerdine compared the psychoanalytic account of gender to the sociological and argued that where

> for the latter the internalization of norms is assumed roughly to work, the basic premise and indeed the starting point of psychoanalysis is that it does not. (p. 181)

Even if we do not accept her characterization of sociology for, after all, the social itself can be characterized as a set of contradictory 'sites' or practices in which the contradictory subjects exist, this paper, and the developments in discourse analysis from which it comes, seems to problematize any approach to children's books which reduces them to repositories of an anti-industrial value or ruralism.

In the light of other criticisms, our imaginary, simple project seems doomed, so long as it is motivated and organized by notions of an essential national culture. Yet, as chapter 4 will show, an examination of English history books for young children during the period to which the Wiener thesis refers finds them dense with the images of an idealized country life and rural, childlike innocence. How can we acknowledge these persistent conventions of representing the country without being tempted to re-enter that dangerous problematic which combines an arrogant description of a whole national culture with a demeaning simplification of how child-readers become adult believers? To make some sense of what seems like an empirical and observable ruralism, and yet to reject the notions of an essential national culture, the *actual* research project has attempted to return to what was an interest of some much earlier critics of textbooks for children — an interest in nationalism. This is not to ignore the fact that those previous concerns were expressed with almost tragic naivite, as, for example, in the so-called Cesare Resolution to the League of Nations in 1926 and the subsequent Declaration in 1937 (reproduced in Heater, 1980). Also the early work in this area used the same approaches to national stereotypes as were subsequently used with regard to race and gender (viz Lawerys, 1953). Following the Falklands episode, however, it could hardly be denied that a return to some consideration of British nationalism is a necessity, and some new investigations of the cultural-ideological aspects of national identity have recently emerged as, for example, with *Formations of Nation and People* (1984); 'Charms of residence, the public and the past' by Bommes and Wright (1982); *Imagined Communities: Reflections on the Origin and Spread of Nationalism* by Anderson (1983); and *Capital and Class* no. 25 (spring 1985).[1] These studies suggest quite different ways of understanding the conventions of representing England's rural past to children, seeing, for example, the contemporary infatuation with 'heritage' and the countryside as part of a never-completed calling of 'the imaginary Briton' (CCCS, *Making Histories*, p. 264). With such an orientation, and along with a different conception of subjectivity, this book attempts to return critically to the whole notion of a national ruralist culture and textbooks as expressions. Instead of assuming that a psychologically and socially undifferentiated child-reader imbibes such a national world-view this project tries to suggest an ideological labouring of national construction, an ever-problematic enterprise of locating children and readers within the territory and boundaries of the nation-state. Instead of the idea that children become socialized into the (ruralist) values of the state the suggestion here is that some readers may 'find themselves', either within the national chronologies of the history books, or within the maps of the homeland in the geography texts, and others may not.

To return to the Wiener thesis, one may say that industrial decline can hardly be attributed to the expression of anti-industrial cultural values by the schools, partly, at least, because values do not influence behaviour in the ways that this explanation would demand. Similarly, educational programmes which might seek to present positive images of industry will fail to have any general effects. But there are, in the geography and history textbooks studied here, numerous clues, presuppositions, implicit theories and complex bodies of representations which do suggest, *indirectly*, why Britain's industrial decline has been so determined. For almost 100 years these books have struggled to represent Britain as the safe, benevolent homeland of a united race which, because it was the first country to industrialize, has been made to appear as the only one to achieve that condition.[2] The benefits of Britain's natural and imperial fortunes have been constantly emphasized at the expense of both labour and enterprise. With such an education in the 'social' subjects few alternative economic or political realities could have seemed as attractive for children as a nation at peace with nature and its people.

Finally by way of introduction and explanation I should say something about the origins and location of this study. It exists, rather awkwardly, within that field of discourse called the sociology of the curriculum. I have always felt uneasy about that enterprise yet cannot help thinking that some of the concepts and concerns of social science in the broadest sense can contribute to our understandings in this area. The first three chapters are an attempt to determine what that contribution might be in the particular case of reacting to the so-called Wiener thesis and its educational and research implications. It is certainly regrettable, but, perhaps, not surprising, that just as we are moving in this country to a codifying by the central state of the content of the school curriculum, partly justified in the interests of the national economy, the debates within the sociology of the curriculum have, in most places, become institutionally marginalized and lost.

Notes

1   Work by Patrick Wright, including *The Conscription of History* (1983) and *On Living in an Old Country* (1985) has thrown new light on the ongoing nature of the construction of national identity. Colls R. and Dodds P. (1986) *Englishness, Politics and Culture, 1880–1920* deals with the developments of cultural identity in the first half of the period studied in this thesis.
2   The contrast between such representations and those found in Japanese textbooks after 1900, when the achievements of other industrial countries was emphasized, should not go unnoticed (Ferro, 1984, p. 202).

1 The Pursuit of Ruralism

When Martin Wiener wrote his cultural explanation of Britain's economic decline (1981) he was not the first to identify and isolate a set of cultural qualities which may be variously termed ruralist, anti-urban and anti-industrial. However, he may well have been one of the few who built an explanation of a nation's economic failure upon such a cultural phenomenon.

Many writers have attempted to confront such cultural essences and have declared them to be detrimental politically, economically and educationally, but it will be argued in this chapter that the bases for such confrontations are highly questionable. We shall attempt to show the problems using the previous literary, historical and social scientific means of isolating, describing and correcting what have been so often called rural myths and anti-industrial sentiments. These problems are even more serious when it is remembered that we wish to consider the presence or otherwise of such sentiments in textbooks for children.

As an American academic writing about another nation's weaknesses, Wiener could have referred to a whole tradition of cultural criticism in his own society which had noted and regretted an American anti-urbanism or ruralist sentiment. There, ruralism has generally been associated with a definite political movement, that of Progessivism, and the ideas have been traced in fields as different as political philosophy, town-planning and schooling. More often than not these ruralist sentiments were seen as a source of problems for the United States because they could lead to irrational political forms (Hofstadter, 1962), lack of sympathy for contemporary urban problems (White, 1965) or mistaken agricultural policies (Griswold, 1952). Foreshadowing what Wiener was to say about English culture, Hofstadter (1962) declared that the agrarian myths and images of American populism moved from having some basis in reality to becoming decidedly mythical in the face of what he called 'commercial realities' (Chapter 1). For Wiener the problem with Britain was that 'commercial realities' were *never* faced.

In the light of the subject matter of this book it may be useful to consider the way some American writers related their understandings of ruralism, agrarianism and rural myth to educational issues. Peter Schmitt's *Back to Nature* (1969), a study of the Arcadian myth in popular culture, dealt most directly with education in a chapter which began, 'One of the better ways to unravel a myth is to examine its transmission to children' (p. 77). He noted that many of the attempts to bring nature and country life into urban schools in America at the turn of the century was based on the belief that the urban world was not a truly safe place for children. That, and the popular 'recapitulation' theory of genetic psychology at the time, was seen to influence the development of educational programmes which brought nature into the schools in the form of 'object lessons' and 'nature study'. Telling quotes from G. Stanley Hall proclaim the necessity that urban children experience the primitive in outdoor pursuits and in an appreciation of nature. It was observed that if the urban child could not experience nature directly then many educators provided them with a literary substitution, and it was here that anthropomorphisms abounded. Schmitt's wide sweep of educational innovation saw many of the ideas in American urban education at the time (school gardening, studying the weather, school farms) as reflecting the Arcadian myth and with it the worries about urbanization. For cultural critics and social historians to express concern about a certain anti-urbanism did not necessarily mean that they wished instead that everyone, including children, should come to love industry and the modern urban capitalist world. Some radical histories of the development of institutions for American children have identified ruralism and anti-urbanism with a middle class wanting to exert control on the urban classes and youth. These revisionist historians, like Anthony Platt, borrowed directly from liberal humanists such as Hofstadter their analysis of the agrarian myth (viz Platt, 1969, pp. 42–43). For them many institutional innovations for the urban child at the end of the nineteenth century were aimed at bringing a form of control which existed in the villages into the towns.

Writing on the custodial role of the schools Gumbert and Spring (1974) express a central argument of the revisionists as follows;

> The custodial function of the school was a result of an anti-urban attitude and rural bias that sought to protect the child from the rapidly expanding urban culture at the beginning of the century and the growing recognition that youth was without a meaningful and functional social and economic role. (p. 116)

Thus, if one basis for the critique of ideas variously called agrarian, ruralist or anti-urban was that they did not face up to the real economic changes that had occurred, another approach suggested that they were part of an oppressive and fearful reaction to the urban masses (Lazerson, 1971, Karrier *et al*, 1973).

If we were to follow these examples and attempt to identify this ruralism as an aspect of the national culture then some parts of the school curriculum may be seen as reflecting persistent ruralist or agrarian features of that culture. The first, simplest means of understanding this would be in terms of the effects that culture — usually taken as the literary, intellectual and artistic culture — had on educational theorists, writers of textbooks and others. Their ideas, in this model, would be presumed to be institutionalized in, for example, specific parts of the curriculum: in literary studies, art, environmental studies and nature study. The curriculum would be conceived as a receptacle of the elements of national culture. If, in this approach, ruralism is found to persist in industrialized countries' educational systems, then the temptation is to see this as cultural-lag; old, out of date values surviving which are dysfunctional for modern conditions. To the extent that ruralism was seen to hold back national economic success or the will to solve national urban problems then schools should be opened up to new values and modernity, positive images of the city should be presented, and the myths of ruralism dispelled. The national consciousness would have to be directed to the present and future, not the rural past. This is the way Wiener (1981) used such a conception of English ruralism in his explanation of British economic decline (p. 80).

A second, more radical-sounding critique following the revisionist historians might suggest that the numerous examples of ruralism which could certainly be found in English school textbooks during the last eighty years can be accounted for by the fact that these books were the products of a genteel middle class, nostalgic for the village, fearful of the urban proletariat.

Many aspects of both these approaches are, however, quite unsatisfactory.

There is no need to rehearse the standard criticisms of what is, in almost all respects, a consensual, functionalist position represented in the first approach.

Even if we accept the problems with the conception of national culture offered, the particular ways of interpretation that such work offers us are also very problematic:

(a)   If something called ruralist or agrarian values can be isolated within the culture of a society or class how are we to understand the way these affect behaviour, political action or educational innovation? The relation between values and behaviour offered is unacceptably mechanical.

(b)   Indicating certain cultural tendencies in the philosophical writing of educational theorists is quite different from actually explaining the presence of particular images within schools in the forms of textbooks and other educational artefacts. These have to be analyzed and studied as representations, as part of the texts and discourse implicated in the whole production of narratives and the location of subjects.

The way ruralism has come to be defined and the role that special ideological formation is claimed to play has as many problems for the radicals as it has for the liberals. The status of ruralism as a 'myth', which is how it is often referred to in the literature, is very questionable. The revisionists claimed that middle class reformers compared city life to rural life, and attempted to recreate the former in the urban centres via schools and other institutions. But did those social relations and conditions of rural life ever exist? The revisionists cannot decide. It is difficult to tell whether the revisionists' objections to the reformers were because the latter were being *unrealistic* as rural means of social control were then out of date or because their ideas were based on 'unreal' history. This predicament is perfectly caught in Katz's remark that,

> School reformers perceived the city through an ambivalent and nostalgic lense which registered modern life as at best a problematical substitute for the pastoral setting of early New England. (Katz, 1975, p. 29)

Until quite recently in Britain there has been little comparable explicit interest in anything which may resemble what American researchers have termed variously anti-urbanism, ruralism or rural myths, or, indeed, any great interest in the representation of town and country.

This could be explained by the fact that there has never been a populist political grouping which has relied on small farmers in the UK, compared to the agrarian radical movements of the US. Probably as influential in this respect has been the absence of institutionally-based academic fields in which such issues could be raised and analyzed, at least before the late 1960s. A concern for the 'national culture' — its features, essences, health and sickness has been firmly in the hands of students of English literature, and, as Perry Anderson has suggested, they have been singularly ill-equipped to examine critically anything which might be called ruralism (Anderson, 1968).

Recently, however, there has been some work on English rural and urban images which has used similar approaches to the American. Jan Marsh documented some interesting social movements of Victorian and Edwardian England (Marsh, 1982), linked only by what she called a 'pastoral impulse' opposed to the urban-industrial world. For her, this impulse was something like a mental affliction, something irrational and impractical, to be gently teased, as in the following; 'It is curious to observe the close affinity that somehow seems to exist between the townsman-turned-farmer and the hen' (p. 119). She suspected that the persistence of 'our collective pastoralism' (p. 247) may cause or exacerbate some British problems with the inner city. Some research on rural and urban images of Victorian England has been less coy than the American revisionists about the *real* nature of the rural life. In two volumes edited by Dyos and Wolff (1973) and the two edited by Mingay (1981) we find historically researched reactions to popular and literary images of Victorian town and country. We find, too, a number of explanations and reactions, mostly concentrating on the gross stereotypical over-simplifications of city and rural life—the idealizations of rural scenes (for example, Mingay, 1981, pp. 160–75), the reduction of the urban working class to the lumpenproletariat (for example, Dyos and Wolff, 1973, pp. 559–85).

Behind most of this writing is a clear indication that for social and, more often, psychological reasons, the realities of town and country were misrepresented. The title of Dyos and Wolff's book, *The Victorian City, Images and Realities* sets up the whole problematic, where the images and the realities are unrelated, except that the latter (the product of adequate research) can correct the former. The most popular explanations of the misrepresentations evoke psychological propensities for escapism and nostalgia.

To some such social and cultural historians the constrasting of the contemporary image with the contemporary reality must be seen as part of an internal critique of some historical scholarship or a reconsideration of the evidence chosen by, perhaps, earlier historians to represent the age. It is not as though, within such books, a reality of Victorian England as such could be shown to the readers (real photographs, real details of the Victorian working class) which has not itself been through processes of representation and image production, even though it may be based on greater accuracy and sophistication. This is not to deny the utility of such historical work as represented in these four volumes, but it is to suggest the care that should be exercised in the use to which it can be put in the analysis of the social significance of school textbooks. Confronting some of the images with a disturbing, historically researched alternative can be useful in identifying the history of some particular conventions of representation, but these contrasting images have different existences in, say, a Victorian landscape painting or an Edwardian school textbook. On these grounds the contrasting of 'historical reality' with image cannot be the over-ruling method for an investigation of such texts.

Contributions of Sociology and Marxism

Attempts so far considered to identify sets of cultural attributes of the sort which have been thought to adversely affect a nation's economic performance, or have other regrettable political or educational results, appear to depend on a relatively implicit critical basis. The question remains whether one could find, within the discourses of social science, some well-founded and explicit basis for approaching such cultural essences within curriculum materials used in schools. Can a 'sociology of the curriculum', based in the traditions of social science, produce a more objective and secure analysis of the presence and functioning of the body of sentiments which have been of such interest? In fact, we have found that neither social science nor Marxism could be taken as providing any particularly sound bases for the exposition of something like anti-industrialism or anti-urbanism within school curricula. This is best illustrated by looking at the way some researchers and theorists in sociology have attempted to criticize and redress a certain ruralism and anti-industrialism within their own subject. Some of them have tried empirical dismissal. Others have turned to Marx in an attempt to theoretically subsume the very differences between urban and rural, agricultural and industrial, upon which ruralist sentiments are built.

The classical sociologists most frequently accused of ruralism have been Tonnies, Simmel, and some of the founders of the Chicago School of Urban Sociology. The way Tonnies, in *Community and Society* (1887) built a typology of social relations, the way he contrasted the Gemeinschaft relations which he located exclusively in rural scenes of homesteads, fields and pre-urban, pre-industrial domesticity, and then contrasted the urban world of trade, commerce, calculation, and self-interest can appear like a pure expression of anti-industrial sentiments. If he constructed his description of social life in the city on the basis of an explicitly positive evaluation of rural life, the two other writers most often referred to in the history of urban sociology, Simmel and Wirth, did not. In their two essays, *Metropolis and Mental Life* (1972) and *Urbanism as a Way of Life* (1964) there was no offering of a picture of rural life, although it could be *presumed* from their views of what they thought happened to people in areas of concentration, heterogeneity, confusion and differentiation.

For Simmel certain key characteristics were attributed to urban-metropolitan life, and these were chosen and signified for their effects on the individual mind. The 'intensification of nervous stimulation' (p. 196), the multiplication of exchanges through money, the strict organization of time, (the 'timetabling' of every action), the growth of size in area and numbers of persons with whom interaction occurs, and the growth of specialization of tasks were all said to have a set of effects on individuals. Unlike Tonnies, only once in the essay did Simmel openly look back to rural life for the contrast. 'Here,' he wrote, 'the rhythm of life and sensory mental imagery flows more slowly, more habitually and more evenly' (p. 197).

In Wirth's essay (1964) there was a limited awareness of the positive aspects of urban life. He saw it could bring freedom, but that was balanced by a loss of participation and spontaneity. In general the essay contained a highly critical picture. Apart from a suggestion that the analysis was based on two ideal types, the urban-industrial and the rural-folk, and some superficial comments on earlier 'folk society' (p. 70), which Wirth still thought was influential, there was no attempt to construct ideal rural life. Instead we have a portrayal of the 'urban mode of living' (p. 64) i.e. the ways of life associated with large, dense, permanent settlements of socially heterogeneous individuals. Acknowledging that problems existed on what was to count as large and dense, but dealing with it in the most unconvincing and circular way, Wirth went on to list the effects. Size brought variation, an absence of 'the bonds of kinship, of neighbourliness, and the sentiments arising out of living together for generations ...' (p. 70). In their place arose competition, formal control and segmental relations. Following Simmel, Wirth noted the effects in terms of a blasé attitude and an anonymous transitory existence.

It could be said that Wirth's essay stands, to some extent, outside the general approach of the Chicago School to so-called urbanism. The major texts by Park and Burgess, *The City*, (1925) and their introduction to the *Science of Sociology* (1921), are better guides. Park, in the former text, expressed some optimism and, like Durkheim, wrote of a growing interdependence; 'a solidarity based, not on sentiment or habit, but on community of interests' (p. 16). Yet there was still the fear, among these Chicago sociologists, of the urban present and its moral disorder, when contrasted with the rural and/or small town past. When secondary relations replaced primary (Park and Burgess, 1969 ed, p. 126–7), then they saw the likely disintegration of moral order, and in a later section of *The City* (p. 151) Burgess wrote of the development of 'promiscuity' when primary and intimate behaviour occurred on the basis of only secondary contacts. In contrast to such urban pathology was an image of rural life where restraint, inhibition and surveillance rendered any criminal tendencies harmless (p. 42), where village youth were well controlled (p. 151), even though genius might have gone unrecognised. The theorists of the Chicago School also showed a great suspicion of the city as a place for childhood and family life, much as Tonnies had. In the same way as the latter thought he saw dangers in exposing children to the influences of Gesellschaft, so they saw city life as unsuitable for children. Children in the city were a liability; their natural place was on the farm (Park and Burgess, 1925, p. 44).

It is clear, then, that within the development of classical sociology itself can be found the very dualities and sentiments of anti-urbanism. How have subsequent social scientists dealt with this feature of their own discipline?

First there have been attempts at empirical denial. This, the simplest of reactions, poses the question whether there are, or ever have been, 'rural' or 'folk' societies on the one hand, and whether there is an urban way of life or mentality on the other. Such reactions, for all their emphasis on the empirical, are not always just concerned to show that something is merely empirically not the case, or that a variety of 'forms of life' can co-exist in one location. They can also be involved in discounting the values which are attached to an empirical claim. Perhaps the best known of such reactions is to be found in the attacks by Oscar Lewis on the anthropological work of Robert Redfield. In his study, *The Folk Culture of Yucatan* (1981) Redfield had developed his ideas on the folk-urban continuum, showing how, for example, the transfer from tribe to city life was characterized by increasing division, secularization, calculation and cultural disorganization.

From this research Redfield felt able to give an idealized and in some ways factually based expression to the notion of a folk society in a paper of that name in 1947 (Redfield, 1947). In this paper, with only one reference to Tonnies, and none to Wirth, he produced an empirically based equivalent of the Gemeinschaft side of the famous duality. The most substantial attack on Redfield's work was mounted by Oscar Lewis who restudied the folk community Redfield had used originally (Lewis, 1963). As an anthropologist who clearly favoured conflict theory, and a self-declared 'eclectic materialist' (Lewis, 1970), he was keen to undermine Redfield's anthropology of cultural idealism. The result was that, in Tepoztlan, the rural-folk community, Lewis found individualism, social division, fear, envy and distrust. Subsequently Lewis went further and in his studies of urban life (1961 and 1967) and he directly confronted the Simmel-Wirth-Redfield position (Lewis, 1965, p. 494). Many other researchers have also attempted to dismiss empirically the ideas of Tonnies, Simmel and Wirth and to refuse and/or reverse the presumed middle class judgments of working class city life. The titles *The Urban Villagers* (Gans, 1962), and *Urbs in Rure* (Pahl, 1965) neatly expressed the points that forms of life which the founding fathers thought could only be found in rural settings could thrive in cities, and that the dividing line between urban and rural settlements was a problem.

From the point of view of this study, the direct empirical attack on notions of urban life and rural life in some sociological writings can only be of very limited value. Some of the protagonists do hint at underlying orientations which seem to affect how others have distinguished the two. Lewis, for example, wrote about, 'a system of value judgments (underlying Redfield's dichotomy) which contains the old Rousseauan notion of primitive peoples as noble savages, and the corollary that with civilization has come the fall of man' (Lewis, 1970, p. 50). In similar vein he says that 'some of the description of the modern urbanite reads like another version of the fall of man' (Lewis, 1965, p. 497), but the points are not developed.

There may be no empirically verifiable urban or rural way of life, and this point may be worth making in the analysis of narratives for children which seem to depend upon such distinctions, but this does not confront the place these powerful images occupy either in the discourse of sociology itself, or elsewhere. Empirical dismissal does not explain why, even within the discipline of sociology itself, urban and rural have, in a way,' stood in' for fundamentally different clusters of values.

Another, more contemporary reaction to the ideas of Tonnies, Simmel and others on urban-rural differences in culture and life is, on the surface, quite straightforward. It is simply to argue that the culture, which the founding fathers of sociology associated with urbanism, and found wanting, is, in fact, the culture of capitalism (Castells, 1977, p. 19). Any attempt to suggest that values are produced by the natural phenomena of density and heterogeneity is regarded as an intended confusion (p. 15). The fragmentation of social roles, for example, identified by Wirth and the other writers we have mentioned, is seen by Castells as 'directly determined by the status of the "free worker", which Marx showed to be necessary to assuring maximum profitability in the use of the labour force' (p. 81). To state it crudely, individualization and the development of secondary relations fulfil the needs of capitalism and its labour market and cannot be seen as merely expressions of the process of urbanization.

It is difficult to see, however, how Marxism and the Marxist view of ideology which Castells holds, can satisfactorily locate or penetrate the sociological and/or everyday dualities of urban and rural in this way. If Castells' reaction to rural-urban dichotomies was one of subsumation this should not lead us to believe that there is, in the writings of Marx or Marxism, a body of theory which could clarify, resolve or even dismiss these dichotomies. Such dualities are not considered in such a form in the 'classical' writings of Marxism. To approach anywhere near these issues one has to consider the debates surrounding the so-called 'agrarian question'; in particular the issue of the peasantry and its position in the transition from feudalism to capitalism and from capitalism to socialism. Putting aside the questionable exercise of taking Marx's work or Marxist theory as a whole then it may be possible to make certain contrasts between it and the analyses and judgments of the founding fathers of 'bourgeois sociology' on these and related areas. It could be argued that, in contrast to the latter's often negative judgments on urban dwellers' life and the concentration which took them there, in Marx we can find positive assessments of the urban proletariat and a positive *appreciation* of the process which produced it. The process of concentration provided for Marx and Engels both the degrading conditions catalogued in *The Condition of the Working Class in England* and the possibilities of transformation through the social and political integration of the agent of that transformation.

There is no doubt that one can find evidence in the writings of

Marx, Engels, Lenin and others of a certain suspicion of rural life in general and of the peasantry in particular. Generally Marx saw peasant life based on small rural property as being inevitably carried away by the development of capitalism. He deduced the stages of this from his observations of the English case where capitalism grew '... in opposition to peasant agriculture' (Marx, 1973, p. 316). In *The Communist Manifesto* (1952, pp. 51–6) and in *The Peasant Question in France and Germany* Marx and Engels made clear to any peasants who were listening that their condition was terminal. As Engels put it,

> Capitalist large scale production is absolutely sure to run over their impotent and antiquated system of small scale production as a train runs over a pushcart. (Engels, 1970, p. 472)

Marx's own studies of the civil wars in France could be taken as confirmation of his suspicions of the peasantry and rural life. The peasantry was portrayed as narrowly self-interested and small minded, perceiving their enemy to be merely the tax collector. He described their actions as, 'clumsily cunning, knavishly naive, doltishly sublime, a calculated superstition ... ' (Marx, 1934, p. 71). Very similar judgments are to be found in the *Eighteenth Brumaire* and elsewhere.[1]

For those who may turn to the writings of Marx in search of the 'true' Marxism such references and quotes would clearly sustain them in any suspicions they might have of the peasantry and its rural life. Such comments may be seen as justifying an opposition to any reliance on that rural life or the peasantry, as either a model or a force for the future. There is much, too, in Marx's and Engel's criticisms of petty-bourgeois socialism, which they thought would only reinvigorate passing patriarchal relations in agriculture (Marx and Engels, 1952, pp. 79–80), their attacks on Proudhonism (Engels, 1935, p. 29), and in Lenin's critique of Populism, to help them in these suspicions. From a certain use of Marxist texts one may gain a convincing view of the reactionary nature of any ruralist, 'peasant-based' sentiment wherein the faded virtues of small property are hopelessly held up against the march of history. It might also be supposed that there was the basis for a critique of certain 'bourgeois sociology' which looked back with regret to the enchanted world of rural community or peasant self-sufficiency and could see no way out of the subsequent life of urban calculation, and no agent whose liberating future was given by the tendencies of dispossession, emiseration, concentration and polarization. One might be tempted to believe, therefore, that there was here, in this particular view of Marxism, a specification of an ideology — RURALISM — which, because of its origins, aimed at perpetuating a particular form of property which, in *reality*, was bound to disappear.

There are, however, some very real problems with this whole approach. As has already been noted, to be able to make such contrasts between a certain tradition within sociology and Marx or Marxism on a pre-given issue, whether it is taken indirectly as the urban-rural dichotomy or directly as the problem of the peasantry, one has to be able to present both Marxism and the object of consideration as unities. Work by Hussain and Tribe has shown the difficulty of this (Hussain and Tribe, 1981; Ennew *et al*, 1977). With regard to the specific questions here: What is the Marxist conception of the rural? What is the Marxist approach to the peasantry? What is the Marxist reaction to some sociological dualities of urban and rural?, then we are faced with a variety of difficulties, not the least of which are the apparent inconsistencies in the work of Marx and Engels itself. For example, in the Preface to the Russian Edition of the *Communist Manifesto*, from which quotes have been taken to illustrate Marx's anti-peasant feelings, we find Marx and Engels writing the following in 1882:

> If the Russian Revolution becomes the signal for a proletarian revolution in the West, so that both complement each other, the present Russian common ownership of land may serve as the starting point for a communist development. (Marx and Engels, 1952, pp. 11–12)

Other writings of Marx too, such as his letter to Vera Zasulich in the previous year, show clear breaks with what one might expect, and a support for rural commune-based socialist development as opposed to relying only upon the urban workers' movement, (Marx, 1953).

On the questions of history, tendency and agency it is perhaps worth noting that there are, in fact, some significant similarities between some so called Marxist writings and bourgeois sociology as represented by Tonnies, for example. This is ironical given that those who have wanted to make much of the distinctions are those who tend to present Marxism as a whole. There is a similarity in the way certain aspects of the rural pre-capitalist past are presented. Some Marxists' use of the concept of the 'natural economy' to describe that self-sufficiency in agricultural production is very similar to the representation of the economic aspects of pre-capitalist forms by Tonnies, in the sense that the forms of property in such systems are ignored by both sides. Following from this there are some similarities in the way in which the transformation of such systems is seen as the necessary extension of market relations which inevitably break up the pre-capitalist relations of production.

Indeed the whole detail of the transformation and the related tendencies, based on certain extrapolations from what was thought to be the history of the development of capitalism in England, has become suspect. Lenin's work to some extent challenged Marx's view of proletarianization as a process of loss of property and the necessary 'freeing' of individuals for the urban labour market. It pointed to the possibility, in some circumstances, of the co-existence of semi-feudal and capitalist systems of agricultural production, and indicated the way in which certain sections of the peasantry could hold on to land yet also sell their labour (Hussain and Tribe, 1981, pp. 108–9).

And there are some interesting similarities between Tonnies and Marx on the question of the possibility and agent of future social change. In Tonnies, for example, we find some pointers to a future transformation very similar to some ideas of Marx. He writes of women thrust into factories becoming cold-hearted, but also enlightened (p. 166); a situation in which there might grow a group consciousness which could develop into a 'moral-human consciousness' (p. 166). Similarly the common people, in Tonnies' history, become the proletariat, and because of the unintended consequences of the spread of calculation and education, they, too, come to calculate and organize for their own self-interest. He thought that their pursuit of a share in the ownership of capital might lead to an end to Gesellschaft (p. 169). Similarly the development of cooperatives held out some hope of this (p. 196).[2]

If the contact with calculation and education was the possible hope for future transformation for Tonnies, so it was, in another way, for Marx and Engels. For them the urbanization of large numbers of people by the bourgeoisie was a service precisely because it rescued them from 'the idiocy of rural life'. (Marx and Engels, 1952, p. 46). It was this association between concentration and contact which certainly led Marx and Engels to believe that 'education', however conceived, and urban life went necessarily together. In his attacks on Proudhonism for wanting to give workers their own private homes Engels claimed it failed to see that the move from rural, self-sufficient 'hearth and home' was 'the very first condition for their intellectual emancipation' (Engels, 1935, p. 28). He went on;

> The English proletariat of 1872 is on an infinitely higher level than the rural weaver of 1772 with his 'hearth and home'. Will

the troglodyte with his cave, the Australian aborigine with his clay hut, and the Indian with his hearth ever accomplish a June insurrection and a Paris commune? (p. 28)

In Marx's *Eighteenth Brumaire* the key feature of the peasants' life, as far as their political consciousness was concerned, was their isolation. He explained that they 'live in similar conditions but without entering into manifold relations with one another' (Marx, 1970, p. 170).

It is these associations, which make so much of a contrast with the Romantic and Rousseauean notions of education through contact with nature and with the opposed association between contact, contagion, and 'massification' (Simmel and Wirth) yet do not distinguish Tonnies from Marx.

It could be said, then, that within the writings of Marx and early Marxists, there is some basis for claiming that there is a reversal of judgments concerning the urban and rural, in comparison with many sociological writers who held a positive image of rural life. In the case of Tonnies, however, this is no simple opposition. For a contemporary Marxist, the distinction between rural and urban may be insignificant, either because of the universal nature of capitalist relations and cultural forms in, say, the USA and UK, or because of the empiricist nature of that distinction. Yet within previous Marxist political discourse there has been a concern for both the particular conditions of the countryside and the pertinence of these for the advance of socialism, and the relations between these rural conditions and the general tendencies of dispossession, concentration, etc. The relationship between Marxist debate and our concerns here is a complex one. If, to some extent, we have found highly problematic distinctions being made between urban and rural life in certain sociology, then we have *not* found, within Marxism, a secure basis for a critique or appreciation of these distinctions, either in the form of a Marxist 'theory' of the city and country, or by Marxist science which may claim to make such distinctions insignificant. The reasons are as follows.

First there is no unified and essential Marxism which could confront such a pre-constituted area of interest.

Second, parallel areas of concern, such as 'the countryside', 'the agrarian question', or the 'peasantry', which have interested socialists and communists influenced by Marx, were areas of political and other calculation in very particular conditions. Even if we accept that some of the debate about Populism and Proudhonism came quite close to confronting some aspects of a certain 'ruralism' (its backward-looking sentiments; its possible lack of political and economic reality; its attachment to domesticity), the *conditions* in which one might consider such ruralism within this study are quite different.

Third, we can find in the writings of Marx and others something like a critique of rural life and its chief character the peasant which is *not only* tied into the politics of socialist parties at the turn of the century. This critique is a product of a belief about certain tendencies. One tendency, that of concentration, has a mix of economic, geographical and social connotations, whereby, in a Marxist theorizing influenced by Hegelianism, loss of both land and the isolation of rural life can produce possession of knowledge and solidarity. But, with the development of suburbs, state policies of decentralization and the encouragement of private home ownership and so on, then the sociogeographical connotations at least have become open to question.

The Work of Raymond Williams

Finally, consideration must be given to a writer who has thrown most light on the representation of town and country in certain literary texts and has used Marxist scholarship in his analysis both critically and substantially. Without doubt the most outstanding study of the images of town and country is *The Country and the City* by Raymond Williams (1975).

The most obvious yet significant contrast between this work and the previously considered texts is that it does not present any simple evaluation or sentiment. It does not deal with a single anti-urbanism, for example, but with the historically changing, and often contradictory images of country and city. Williams refuses to catalogue any simple retrospective or nostalgia: 'Old England, settlement, the rural virtues — all these, in fact, mean different things at different times and quite different values are being brought to question' (pp. 21–2). The text allows a sensitivity to different kinds of rural retrospect because it both seriously questions the validity of the images of the rural past and sees 'real' values represented, whereas, in most of the studies so far considered, it is one or the other. In the American work there was either the acceptance of the memories of rural New England as both encapsulating values and reflecting real conditions which changed, or the complete rejection of both the validity and the values. Williams is certainly not an anti-ruralist, in the simple sense of dismissing all rural retrospects as melancholic sentimentality, but he *is* uncompromising in contrasting the myth with the reality. For him, retrospects can be more or less perceptive, and based on some real observations. If it were accepted that rural retrospects are constructed at different times in the development of agrarian capitalism, and from different places within that evolving class structure, then it must also be admitted that what has so often been called the rural myth of a previous paradise is only one form of representing the rural. Many other representations of the rural, as Williams shows in his analysis of Pastoral (p. 30), just refer to country life in general, and not to any past Golden Age, real or imagined. Williams shows that the myth of a happier natural past, whilst often tied to the middle orders in rural history—who looked back to a time of small scale independent farmers and feared the future (p. 38) — has also had a different content when held by other groups. To the landless the Golden Age was one of primitive communism, when no landlords existed. To the lordly it was a time when true lords lived among their people, paternally all-powerful and able to see what was in the common interest. Thus we are shown different types of retrospect from different places in the class structure as well as the idea of rural innocence in general, without a historical dimension. Williams' point is that for the latter to hold the agricultural labourer must be *hidden*, and the images must be of rural landscapes in opposition to the towns. As the ideology of improvement took hold in England, and with it the conflict of values, so developed the conventional structure of retrospect and ideas of a loss (p. 78). Under these conditions 'nature' came to be seen as *substitute order*, not part of the natural conditions of a settled life. If the text shows that there is no simple urban-rural contrast it also explicates a whole set of attitudes and visions of the town, related to differences between the growth of London and the Northern industrial towns, and the distinctions between London's own East and West End. Williams finds there are both dark and light images of the city in English literary culture (chapter 19).

The thesis of *The Country and the City* can incorporate, therefore, changes in the representations of the town and country with changes in the positions of different classes within the development of capitalism, but how does it go beyond the previously considered explanations couched in terms of, for example, fearful nostalgia or Schmitt's idea of a psychological need for nature? Because Williams sees capitalism as still in evolution, and because he rejects a view of texts as either simple records of held values or records of ways of life (Williams, 1979, p. 304), and instead sees them as representations and misrepresentations of history, any ideas of them as simple cultural-lag or nostalgia can also be rejected.

If tenant farmers have had variable fortunes, then agricultural workers were and *are* continually exploited. It is here where the basis of Williams' sense of persistence and continuity could be said to lie. And if some should think that an appreciation of this exploitation must be diminished in the light of the comparatively few agricultural workers left in Britain, and their radically changed working conditions, Williams brings in the rural workers of the Third World. For him the idea of a lost idyllic rural world is absurd, for not only was it far from idyllic for the rural workers alive then, but its extreme exploitation is far from lost for those working now within that part of an internationalized capitalist market.

Thus the essential basis for continuity within this study of the literary images of town and country is the continual reappearance of the workers throughout history, as both real people speaking for themselves, through, for example, the pages of Mayhew's *London Labour and the Labour Poor* (Williams, 1975, pp. 262–3) and the writing of Fred Kitchen (p. 314–5), or by the texts' own references to the class made indistinct and often invisible by the poets. By comparison the working class was ignored by the American writers, whether liberal or radical.

Williams also sees and feels a certain continuity of rural images within English literature and literary criticism, and a persistent retrospective radicalism in these fields. 'In Britain,' he writes, 'there is a precarious but persistent rural–intellectual radicalism' (*ibid*, p. 49). It is a critique and structure of thought he rejects, on the grounds that it is moralistic in its distant condemnation. The criticisms of industrial capitalism by Lawrence are seen as symptomatic of a rural retrospect which also attacks democracy, education and labour, and Williams' relation to this critique is clear: 'But as I have watched it settle into what is now a convention — in literary education especially — I have felt it as an outrage . . .' (*ibid*, p. 325).

It is also through this channel of the institutionalized English educational tradition that ruralism is brought up to date. There is no simple identification of a sentimentalizing ruralism of the middle class (although this is also acknowledged), nor is the rural retrospect understood as placating criticism of the present order. Rather there are suggestions that such a literary ruralism continues to have effects on the consciousness of the educated middle class in England, and that these effects are regrettable: the individualizing of social criticism; the distancing of the cultured from the working class. This text, then, is not just a pursuit of an 'ism' or set of attitudes to the town. It does not merely show the presence of some sort of ruralism in a variety of literary texts, for this is a far too static project for Williams with his sense of history. It is, instead, an analysis of the reactions to and images of the changes in country and town; an analysis which shows certain forms and their evolution, a great variety of reactions by human subjects against a background of partially understood or mis-understood processes.

Like much of the American literature the reactions and images are located in personal histories, the class backgrounds of the authors, but they are also located in specific stages of socioeconomic trans-formation. The contexts are theorized, however, as stages in the development of a national capitalist economy, and not as stages of urbanization, industrialization or bureaucratization. This allows Wil-liams to consider labour, social relations and changes in the relative positions of different rural classes. Unlike the revisionists, for exam-ple, there is no mere attribution of error by hinting at the subject's social origins and thereby suggesting inevitable bias. Instead there is an explicit challenge to the subject's representation of *real* history. If Langhorne blamed the absent landlords for the rural decay in the 1770s Williams' unambivalent response is as follows;

> The real process of transforming rural England was firmly in the hands of the all too present and commercially active land-lords. And the real origin of change was the developing system of agrarian capitalism, which, as has been characteristic of capitalism throughout its history, succeeded in transforming its environment in a dramatically productive way, by making both men and nature instrumental to a dominating purpose. (1975, p. 104)

In contrast with much of the American literature one could say that *The Country and the City* deals with a complex structure of beliefs and images against a background of a critical, real and continuing history of rural labour and literary conventions.

How, then, does Williams deal with the concept of 'myth', so often linked to the rural and contrasted with 'history'? We have already found that he distinguishes between images of the rural which have a historical element and those which are born of static contrasts between town and country life. His concept of a 'structure of feeling' serves to denote both (Williams, 1977, chapter 2). It will be remem-bered that the role the concept of myth has played in the literature previously considered was that it often combined an implicit critique and a desire not to dismiss. In this way agrarian or rural myths have been seen as mistaken or impractical in the face of 'commercial realities' yet enshrining some worthwhile values. But because Williams' judgments on the validity of the images are in terms of a holistic appreciation of the *system* and not as pragmatic, partial understandings which may have temporarily satisfied the tenant farmer or the land-lord, then the myths cannot be seen as enshrining any laudable values in the abstract. The rural myths are, for him, too much concerned with the naturalizing of social conditions by celebrating ideas of rural society (Williams, 1975, p. 41) and hiding rural labour. The only valid aspect of such a myth derives from the fact that it evolved from some real observations, but was distilled into some very general history which, in turn became a myth (*ibid*, p. 104). Such myths continued in the past because the poets were linked and dependent on rural landowners (*ibid*, p. 105) and the poor were voiceless. They continue in the present, according to Williams, because a certain literary tradition still mythologizes the origins of England's problems.

> ... there is a sense in which the idea of the enclosures, local-ised to just that period in which the Industrial Revolution was beginning, can shift our attention from the real history and become an element of that very powerful myth of modern England in which the transition from a rural to an industrial society is seen as a kind of fall, the true cause and origin of our social suffering and disorder. It is difficult to overestimate the importance of this myth in modern social thought. (*ibid*, p. 121)

Such myths cannot be accepted as enshrining worthwhile values for they too misrepresent the contexts in which the values were said to exist — rural kindness was, in fact, paternal charity, rural local com-munity a product of Tudor poor law (*ibid*, pp. 105–7). Myth is continually contrasted with a 'real sense of context' (*ibid*, p. 315) and seen as composed of false history.

Williams, then, is uncompromising in his posing of the real against the false or imagined, and that reality is of labour and the development of capitalism. It is not surprising that he has expressed reservations about the critique of realism mounted by theorists who write in *Screen* and elsewhere believing that they confuse realism with the more legitimate target of naturalism (Williams, 1977).

Some of the problems in this aspect of Williams' work tend to be more explicit in his followers. For example, *English Literature in His-tory 1780–1830—Pastoral and Politics* by Roger Sales (Sales, 1983) and published in a series edited by Williams, presents us with an over-direct view of the way pastoralism functioned as a political creed

(p. 28). He thinks it 'offers a political interpretation of both past and present. It is a propagandist reconstruction of history' (p. 17). And there is also an over-simplified and reduced 'reality' which pastoralism was said to hide — a rural economic system (unexplicated) and the cruelty which followed the Swing Riots.

Other followers of Williams, however, do seem to go further in the problematizing of realism. In John Barrell's study of the representation of the rural poor in English landscape paintings there are clear signs of a simple contrasting of ideology with reality (Barrell, 1980).[3] Using E.P. Thompson's history of the eighteenth century as 'the actuality of eighteenth century life' he compares the 'image of rural life' (p. 1), its ideology, with what existence was really like for the poor. Parallel points are made to those of Sales but certainly the processes of representation and mediation are taken more seriously. He is interested in the following questions: How is it that the art of rural life gives one a view of a stable, unified society? How did Gainsborough, Marland and Constable get away from the Arcadian visions of, say, Claude, yet still present the life of the rural poor as somehow enviable? His study shows, in a quite intriguing way, how everyday issues like labour were allowed into the scenes, *in the interests of realism*, yet made acceptable to the artists' patrons.

Now although he depends implicitly upon Marx and Marxist scholarship for his orientation to exploitation and for his appreciation of the reality of the development of agrarian capitalism, Williams is not uncritical of some Marxist conceptions of the rural. He has reacted against both the parody of country bumpkins and the Marxist idea of 'rural idiocy' (Williams, 1975, p. 50; and Williams, 1979, p. 319). Marx and Engels who used this phrase in the *Communist Manifesto* and others who have repeated it,

> should have described these (rural ignorance and illiteracy) as they were, the products of social deprivation and exploitation, whereas they picked up the term idiocy as a conventional form of court dismissal of the country. (Williams, 1979, p. 319)

He suspects that both the notions of rural idiocy and the Labourist criticism of British capitalism as old and tired and better run by socialists derive from a 'celebration of mastery of nature' (Williams, 1975, p. 50). Indeed he finds an ambiguity in the heart of Marx and Engel's view of the city. Whilst he goes too far to associate Stalin's notion of a 'victory' over the peasantry with these ideas he is clear in his critique of the faith in what has been called previously the tendency of concentration:

> ... to see exposure (in urban concentration) creating revolution was one thing; to see more of the same producing more of something quite different was at best an apocalyptic hope. (Williams, 1979, p. 365)

When he presents us with the positive side of the city it is not because it is the birthplace of the urban proletariat but because in it originated the *institutional* development which holds out hope for the future:

> Out of the very chaos and misery of the new metropolis, and spreading from it to rejuvenate a national feeling, the civilizing force of a new vision of society had been created in struggle, had gathered up the suffering and hopes of generations of the oppressed and exploited, and in this unexpected and challenging form was the city's human reply to the long inhumanity of city and country alike. (Williams, 1975, p. 278)

On the question of the urban proletariat compared to the rural workers he is keen to show the latter fighting back against their conditions and not alone in sometimes being incorporated (*ibid*, p. 231). His approach to the city and the urban proletariat is most explicit in *Politics and Letters*. Pressed by an interviewer who seems desperate to preserve the urban working class as an integrated agent (viz p. 321), Williams, instead of confronting these notions of politics, responds with a criticism of the urban workers' tendency to disregard the conditions for the production of raw materials and food — an 'urban idiocy' (*ibid*, p. 322) as he calls it. He rightly acknowledges that reactionary policies have had support in the country because of this, but takes a rather simple uncritical view of agriculture as an undifferentiated economic sector and of its general necessity for national well-being.

Williams' own attitude to the country is very difficult to appreciate. It is one of affection and one of respect for the site of labour and suffering. Even though the moral protests of the upper peasantry are unreal for him they are still moving. It is as though he believes that a forgetfulness of the country, 'the song of the land, the song of rural labour' (*ibid*, p. 325) will make the urban socialist movement the poorer because it will have lost at least some of its roots. Much of his cultural criticism is aimed at what one might call the misuse of the countryside in English literary culture, eventually producing in contemporary conditions the images and consciousnesses of moral individuals whose moral sustenance is somehow derived from the past. Such a consciousness cannot really relate to modern urban life except as a lone, cultured moral individualism. For Williams, who has seen invitations to that consciousness and identity offered to so many students by his colleagues in the Cambridge English Faculty and elsewhere, this is important, but it is only part of the story. This book, however, is concerned with the images of town and country life found elsewhere in the culture and made available in a quite different part of the educational system. For this project the approach of Williams brings with it certain difficulties.

The Country and the City does not deal directly with the educational aspects of the things he discusses there. There are some suggestions that the modern form of rural retrospect was made and used against democracy, the labour movement, and education, and he does show that literary education and some of its critique of industrial capitalism turns, in effect, against *democratic* education (*ibid*, p. 325). But these are matters very much within the literary tradition.

To find more explicit reference to education one has to turn to his earlier texts but one is faced with the problem that these had a quite different theoretical orientation from that develeoped in *The Country and the City* and other work (for example, Williams, 1973, 1977a, 1977b and 1981).

It would be comparatively easy to show the problems with any application of the ideas from Williams' earlier texts, for there can be found in them what Eagleton has called an 'uncertain nostalgia for the organic' (Eagleton, 1978, p. 40). But I accept that *The Country and the City*, in its Marxist attack on rural illusion, breaks to some extent with the old dualities. Eagleton puts it this way:

> . . . if there is one point at which Williams is most decisive in this rejection of the 'organic' image, it is in its application to *rural* society — the patronising Scrutiny mythology of the lost organic England . . . Williams rightly insists, rural society is rural capitalism, permeated at every level by the forces and relations of capitalist production; it provides no alternative to the dominant social mode. But for Williams to 'defend' the reality of his own childhood conditions by emphasising their integration with industrial capitalism is for him a significantly uncharacteristic move. For it forces him to break with the reductive binary opposition he otherwise employs: regional culture/dominant culture, working class/middle class, solidarity/individualism and so on. The reason for that break with the binary model is, indeed, part of the very reason which motivates it in the first place: it is to insist on the real

existence of rural society, as 'community' is set against 'individualism', to underline the already existent reality of an
alternative culture. But because the bourgeois ideology of pastoral absorbs the rural by *alienating* it, positing it as an 'unreal'
enclave, Williams in turn opposes bourgeois ideology by in-
sisting on the contradictory *unity* of the agrarian and industrial.
(*ibid*, pp. 40–41)

It appears that the very ways in which Williams undermines
certain ruralism and rural images in the past, and the basis of his
historical understanding of continuity, make for some difficulties if
the full logic of his position was accepted and applied to the analysis
of representations of town and country in elementary and primary
education. To express it very directly and crudely, there is, in his
presentation of undifferentiated rural labour as both the foundation for
a vital critique of past literary imagery and as a means of providing
historical continuity, a certain economic naivete and, possibly, an
ephemeral anti-industrialism. His new rapprochement with Marxism
is no guarantee of virtue.

In his later work there can be detected some ambivalences on the
theoretical and evaluative significance of the following dualities:

rural — industrial
cultural — economic.

Within these dualities, these remaining dualities — *pace* Eagleton —
one may find a residual, and in some limited respects, *'ruralist'* reserve
about industrialization. This is not through any idealizing of the past
rural life or through any concepts of the Fall but through the very
way he refuses this tradition — through his appreciation of rural
labour. The point is that the rural labour to which he refers appears
undivided in a technical sense, and it is thus used as *a sign of labour in
general* against which are posed BOTH the rural idyll (which hides all
real and exploited labour) *and* industrial capitalism (in which labour is
obviously divided).

It is not that, in Williams' critical analysis of the literary images of
the country, there is an omission of economic developments, but that
the economy *generally* is not given sufficient 'respect' and industrialization (capitalist or otherwise) is not seen sufficiently in terms of
the development of the division of that labour. In that limited sense
Williams may still be caught in contrasting present industrial capitalism with an image of past agrarian capitalism where labour was, by
comparison, technically unified. Evidence of his reserve about giving

sufficient weight to a national economy can be found in some of his later work. In *Politics and Letters* some of his reactions are interesting in this regard:

> If you want to be told that our whole existence is governed by the economy go to the city pages of the bourgeois press — that is really how they see life. (p. 141);

an example of subverting the significance of the economy by association. In that text he refers more than once to the significance in late capitalist society of economic activities which have nothing to do with physical subsistence, for example:

> What one then has to say is that these forms of production are really very basic indeed; they are the production of food, the production of shelter, and the production of the means of producing food and shelter — an extended range which is still related to the absolutely necessary conditions of sustaining life. The enormous theoretical shift introduced by classical Marxism — in saying these are the primary productive activities — was of the most fundamental importance. Very often today, however, there is a slide from this pattern of activities to the structure of a late capitalist economy, as if everything which occurred in contemporary industry or agriculture were forms of production self-evidently related to primary need, as opposed for example to writing novels or painting pictures. I think in moments of polemic I've tended simply to reverse the emphasis, which is wrong. But what I was reacting against was the characteristic use of phrases like 'the linchpin of the British economy is the car industry'. There is no sense in which the car industry is primary production for the maintenance of human life in the same sense as the production of food or shelter or building materials. It is not even the primary answer to the need for mobility, since there are other forms of transport that are less socially differentiated. (Williams, 1979, p. 353)

But there is a sense in which the production of certain commodities in the UK for sale on international markets is vital for the ability to buy the materials for subsistence, for the production of food, etc. There is an almost absurd looking back, not unlike a rural idyll, to a period before certain commodities were produced for profit (*ibid*, p. 355) yet which now make people's lives more pleasant. His commonsense distinction between agriculture and industry is also significant in the above passage, making for difficulties in analyzing the relations between sectors of industry among which agriculture should be included. In a way such a distinction helps to maintain the mystique surrounding agriculture. (It should be noted, however, that in a recent essay Williams has spelled out a more explicit and defensible position with regard to agriculture and the countryside, showing how specific aspects of finance capital (high interest debt and credit) have dominated farming. He suggests how the separation of agriculture and the identification of the countryside with it may have blinded us to progressive ways of halting rural decline.) (Williams, 1984, p. 213)

It is possible that Williams' position derives in part from two recurrent issues in his thinking; his anti-Stalinism on the one hand and his attempts to argue against idealist views of culture on the other. We have already noted how he associates the drive for mastery over nature with Stalin's attack on the peasantry and with some Marxist anti-ruralism. His particular reaction to Stalinism is clear in *Politics and Letters*; 'Soviet society was presented as socialist, merely because it was becoming urbanized and industrialized in the 30s' (p. 313). Yes, that was quite mistaken, but one cannot help suspecting that Williams' anti-Stalinism moves to a critique of industrialization per se and to a general lack of concern for the economic base of a particular nation state. As far as arguing against idealism is concerned then a similar effect can be found. In his attempts to argue against idealist views of culture as values and thought he appears also to fail to distinguish sufficiently between production and industry, welfare and entertainment. Such distinctions are vital in any planning or national policy formation, and would need to be understood by any economically educated electorate. But when Williams is describing the material nature of the social and political order maintaining the capitalist market he argues that:

> These are never superstructural activities. They are the necessary material production within which an apparently self-subsistent mode of production can alone be carried on. The complexity of this process is especially remarkable in advanced capitalist societies, where it is wholly beside the point to isolate 'production' and 'industry' from the comparably material production of 'defence' 'law and order', 'welfare', 'entertainment', and 'public opinion'. In failing to grasp the material character of the production of a social and political order, this specialised (and bourgeois) materialism failed also, but even more conspicuously, to understand the material character of

the production of a cultural order. The concept of the 'super-structure' was then not a reduction but an evasion. (Williams, 1977, p. 93)

One finds oneself in a difficult position here if one is concerned about Britain's industrial decline, yet not in sympathy with the idealist, cultural explanations offered by writers like Wiener. Sharing Williams' vision may tempt one to 'materialize away' the problems of sustaining the arts and so on in a national economy which has difficulty in keeping its manufacturing base and, with it, a satisfactory level of employment.

The implications of these criticisms for the use of Williams' approach in the study of rural and urban images in education may not be immediately obvious but are, in the end, significant. In the analysis of some of the materials used in schools — school textbooks, reading books, curriculum developments — then it may well be that different forms of rural retrospect are distinguishable. Questionable images of the rural past may be found and compared with the realities of seventeenth or eighteenth century rural life, for example. Agricultural labour and agricultural labourers may well be missing or idealized in the predominant presentations of the countryside of both Britain and other countries. As we shall show 'the farmer' almost completely replaces 'the farm worker' in much children's literature. Williams' suggestions about rural stereotypes (Williams, 1975, p. 309) may be useful in the analysis of educational artefacts. Are country people and the English countryman seen as similar in all parts of Britain? Can these educational images be seen as part of an 'abstracting literary anthropology'? A whole convention of contrasts between town and country can be found in geography and history and in children's reading books, from questionable histories of the nineteenth century to stories about 'town and country mice'. Received Victorian images of London go unanalyzed and unchallenged. Williams' study may also alert us to the way in which 'nature' has been brought into the curriculum in the form of 'nature study' and 'environmental studies' and out of his work we may well pose key questions *about* the extent to which such curricular content 'naturalizes' images of past and present social orders. Also important is Williams' argument that it is not just what is being said *about* town and country but what *else* is being said; what is implied by and associated with country life, for example.

But when it comes to the combination of an explanation, a critique, and an alternative then the above limitations in what

Williams has to offer must be acknowledged. For all its perceptiveness Williams' work in this area has been directed predominantly at English literary culture and its conventions and not at state educational pedagogy and its more general ideological origins and effects. Where, in *The Country and the City*, he was dealing with literary conventions and the conditions for their production, we have to consider the 'conventions' of pedagogy and the conditions for their existence.[4]

Given the differences between a social-literary critique of the English *literary* tradition and a sociological and educational explanation and critique of *educational* artefacts, yet accepting that Williams has much to say on representations of town and country, one may be tempted to use the earlier suggestions of his about the forms of educational ideologies to locate those representations in a conflict of educational contents. Indeed his original map of nineteenth century arguments about universal state education (Williams, 1961, p. 162) which distinguished the industrial trainers, the old humanists and the public educators has had a continuing use within the sociology of education (viz Whitty 1983, p. 181; and Dale, 1983, p. 237).

According to this map of educational ideologies the specific rural images maintained in English education could be seen as part of that old humanist tradition, adopted and adapted perhaps by the new petty bourgeoisie and used to distinguish education and culture from the vulgarity of the urban masses and industry. But it is significant that Williams criticized this continuing influence as damaging to education and culture but did not mention any damage to the industrial economy:

> The continued relegation of trade and industry to lower social classes and the desire of successful industrialists that their sons should move into the now largely irrelevant class of gentry, were alike extremely damaging to English education and English life. (Williams, 1961, p. 164)

The hints in *The Country and the City* that modern forms of rural retrospect have been made and used against education and democracy reflect these earlier ideas (Williams, 1975, p. 325). The English literary tradition, in which rural retrospect has played such a part, has produced a critique of industrial capitalism yet also a cultural elitism. But we are only offered a single means of approaching rural imagery here i.e. as part of the anti-vocational, anti-democratic elitist tendencies in literary education — an education which develops a consciousness which sees the urban population as a mass and industry as foreign and distasteful. It may be that some rural and urban imagery in education works much less directly and has to be analyzed somewhat differently with regard to its occurrence in texts representing different disciplines important for social, political and economic education. Furthermore, the distinguishing between the ideological positions 'industrial trainer' and 'old humanist' has not led to much in the way of the production of alternative educational contents which are not simply *reversals* in form of 'urbanist', proletarian and popular. Our analysis of the representations of town and country in geography and history books cannot only be couched in terms of their lack of historical reality and/or because of their attachment to the literary tradition. Whilst acknowledging these aspects we need also to look at their wider, less direct and more general ideological presence so that we are not forced to oppose such images with either a non- or anti-industrial programme or an anti-democratic, vocational industrialism. As far as alternative curricula are concerned then the implications of both the useful perceptions of Williams' thesis, and its problems, need to be considered, especially in the light of the present debate on industrial education. Alternative proposals which avoid the idealist arrogance of the literary tradition, the undemocratic and anti-educational implications of industrial training and the implicit anti-industrialism of some of the radicals are necessary. It is perhaps ironic that, before his full embrace of Marxism, Williams' own curricular proposals in *The Long Revolution* included 'social studies' in which he thought the 'organisation of industry' (Williams, 1961, p. 172) should be considered along with 'descriptive economics, geography including actual industry and trade' (*ibid*, p. 175).

Summary

Across a range of research, theoretical discussion, and debate we have found an emergent and continuous reference to what may be variously described as 'ruralism', 'rural myth' or 'anti-urbanism'. In social science and some Marxist writing this body of sentiments and images has been identified in various ways. Some have seen it as a legitimating ideology for contemporary conditions, or as part of an unscientific account of human history, or associated with previous, agrarian-based political groupings. Others like Lewis have considered that a certain anti-urbanism has been influential in some misunderstandings about the nature of both rural 'folk' societies and urban social life itself. In social histories and cultural studies, for concerned, consensus-orientated writers anti-urbanism was a problematic feature of the United States and the English national cultures making it difficult for those nations either to deal with their urban problems or advance economically.

In most cases we have noted that the ways of confronting such 'myths' have been by way of empirical evidence of rural or urban realities as in the Dyos and Wolff and Mingay volumes or at least by historically informed declarations as in Williams. But it is clear that there are problems in any attempt to apply these approaches as described above in a sociological analysis of school textbooks. The major difficulty is that much of the work on the images of town and country, the so-called ideology of ruralism, and anti-urban sentiments, conceptualizes a whole variety of texts and institutions as but *expressions* or *instances* of that ideology. The analysis of a particular kind of text — the school textbook — would thus be reduced to showing, in this case, whether it perpetuated these sentiments and ideology or not. As will be shown in the following chapter, this implies a very restricted mode of socialization and cultural transmission.

Where writers like Williams have concentrated on literary examples then the literary judgments in which their analysis is involved also seems inappropriate when one studies the school textbook. These can never be seen as part of the literary tradition. The force of aesthetic and literary criticism seems singularly misplaced. But given that geography and history school texts have been seen as representing the human sciences, does it make any more sense to use the theory and research of contemporary human sciences to give us a critical entry into the texts? In view of what has been referred to above we think this is not possible in any direct way either. Debate and discussion in sociology, at least, has not provided any theorized truth against which to judge the possible falsities of children's books. Not only that, but the correction of one discourse by another is bound to misconceive or overlook the differences between them. All these approaches seem to distract from the particularity of school texts, and so it is on the basis of establishing that particularity that we must proceed in the next chapter to develop a more appropriate theory and method.

But there are difficulties in a too iconoclastic posture with regard to previous studies. Wholesale rejection of both previous theoretical and empirical work, perhaps in the interests of establishing the autonomy of political or educational discourse and calculation, can be as problematic as the empiricism and theoretical subsumation which we have outlined above. It must be acknowledged that some points which previous writers have made are very pertinent to this study.

First, some writers have shown in a variety of ways how certain representations of urban-rural differences can replace or draw attention away from other differences between people and their conditions of life.

Second, painstaking empirical work on the *variety* of attitudes to and images of town and country does alert one to the problems of conceptualizing imagery in terms of any simple, evaluative dualisms. Williams' sophisticated exposition of this variety, and his interest in both the forms and the relations between the images, has been vital for our work.

Thirdly, some of the discussions we have outlined do touch on educational matters, if very tangentially, and suggest interesting points of contact. For example, disproving empirically some of the anti-urban positions in anthropology may itself have had some effects on educational theory and suggest connections between a conception of childhood and an anti-urban or pro-nature philosophy. Set against that Rousseauan position has been the belief that vigorous, close urban life is the condition for true emancipatory education. But the exact relations between texts *for* children and the representations of the town and the country have never been made explicit, except by claiming, as Schmitt did (1969), that if there are rural myths in the national culture then they will be most explicit when transmitted to children. We reject the research enterprise suggested by such a notion, for whilst we have been able to isolate and distinguish, just like others, an anti-urbanism in at least most of the history textbooks, this approach only allows a method of superficial content analysis and a theory of internalization through repetition (Sumner, 1979, pp. 68–9).

Notes

1 Michael Duggett locates many of these references in Marx on peasants, in *Journal of Peasant Studies*, vol. 2, 2, (1975).
2 Mellor (1977) puts differences in 'methodology' as vital in distinguishing Marx from Tonnies (p. 174), claiming that Tonnies was an empiricist, and it was *that* which made him a pessimist.
3 Barrell has also developed some ideas on the *combined* effects of technology and notions of 'the dignity of labour' on rural images produced by old photographs of farm workers and village life. In *The Golden Age of Labour* he notes how they 'always suggest the importance of work in this "bygone" way of life, but always in such a way as to conceal its difficulty' (in Mabey, 1984, p. 178).
4 What Williams' text *The Country and the City* shows most clearly is the

unacceptable nature of any direct, unmediated and simplistic explanation of the relation between cultural products, in his case, poetry and novels, and historical reality. Literary conventions, like pastoral and neo-pastoral, were the means of literary production and the developments of agrarian capitalism were the conditions. There are, if not conventions, then certainly pedagogic forms which need independent consideration, and there are the social conditions making them possible and acting upon them. For example, the 'narrative form' could be seen as a pedagogic convention which can have mystifying effects when used in the human sciences in certain ways.

2   *The Text and the Child*

It is noticeable that other approaches to textbooks have never established the particular nature of such books except with regard to their use by children. An attempt will be made to outline the particularity of these books in this chapter insofar as it has a bearing upon the theory and methodology adopted in the analysis. In discussing the problems of theory and method in terms of appropriateness to the object of study it is being assumed that there is not available a universal method of 'reading' all texts, or a universal standpoint for all contexts from which all texts can be read. It appears to be the case that work on textbooks and other educational artefacts raises some important issues which do not occur for students of literature or even of the mass media.

The dangers of eclecticism in this approach are all too clear, but no single contemporary paradigm seems to produce the necessary ways into the problems set by the materials and the educational concerns. Structuralist and post-structuralist readings alone prove highly problematic when applied to non-fiction for children used within the institutions of state education, and yet the alternatives, be they literary, materialist-Marxist or sociological have shown themselves to be equally so.

In very general terms Richard Johnson has attempted to indicate a position which may be termed similarly eclectic in relation to education and pedagogy, and which calls for a necessary combination of elements from different intellectual and political traditions (Johnson, 1980). I have expressed elsewhere my sympathy for his criticisms of what he has termed the 'intellectual lumberjacking' which so characterized the debate between theorists over the last twenty years (Ahier, 1983, p. 4) but equally my reservations about his special combination of positions and its educational and political effects. In his article

Cultural Studies and Educational Practice he argues that it is impossible to see any pedagogic practice which is or could be based on deconstruction alone. He is, I believe, right in this respect, and so, by implication, any critical analysis of a set of pedagogic artefacts, if it seeks to inform practice, cannot proceed solely by any complete form of deconstruction. But Johnson's resolution of the problem, and his emphasis on a pedagogy which favours the experiential and thus, for example, the activities of personal and local history and cultural studies, is not acceptable, as will be made clear. In general, concepts of experience and consciousness have been found to be too dissolving of the distinctions between, for example, pedagogic and ideological practices and institutions, and economic ones. That does not mean that the distinction between 'the economic' and 'the pedagogic' is in any way comprehensible on the basis of materialist declarations derived from simple base-superstructure models or any presuppositions about the immaterial nature of school knowledge.

As a means of proceeding, the simplest everyday description of the type of book we are to study, although it may be made problematic in our own characterization, does provide headings under which to discuss problems in contemporary theory and method when applied to the analysis of past textbooks. The most obvious features of these books are as follows:

1 They were (with just one or two very early exceptions) for use in the schools of the state.
2 They were specific only according to the chronological age of the reader.
3 They were divided according to the academic discipline or standard curriculum subject they claimed to represent.
4 They were works of non-fiction.

Books for State-institutional Use

An inescapable feature of these textbooks which must be explicated is their existence within material practices, within the material existence of the classroom, the organization of human bodies, (according to age), quite as substantial as any factory or workshop. As in all other institutions, power relations within the school subject the body, and, to use Foucault's words for describing another context, 'invest it, mark it, train it, torture it, force it to carry out tasks, to perform ceremonies, to emit signs' (Foucault, 1977, p. 25). The textbooks analyzed in this thesis have been used and consumed in historically specific classroom regimes and it is difficult to imagine one without the other, the book without the pedagogue and children. Indeed many of the texts themselves have frequent references within them to the very classroom itself, and the 'characters' are often teachers and children. They address the reader as pupil quite explicitly, and the position of the author is 'teacher'. For example, the unnamed author of *Longmans Ship Series of Pictorial Geography Readers* spoke to the children thus:

> Now I can hear you asking me quite a number of questions
> ... Well, I will try to answer your questions, but I must take
> them one at a time. (Longmans, 1900, Book 4, p. 13)

The texts frequently require the reader to do things within the classroom; to draw a picture, make a model, or write down answers to questions. At times, and especially in the later, more 'progressive' of the texts, these books came to look like instruction manuals. Because of this extreme coexistence of text and context two tendencies in contemporary theoretical debate are unhelpful in their analysis. The first, associated with what I will call epistemological Marxism, has the effect of concentrating on the hidden curriculum of the school, and on the everyday routines of schooling, *in contrast to* and *in distinction from* the actual content of the curriculum. Rachel Sharp, for example, heightened such distinctions in the way she argued that the 'pervasive representations of man and society are not merely abstractly stored in the head but are materialized in social practices and rituals which have *explanatory priority*' (my emphasis) (Sharp, 1980, p. 109). Used as an original position from which to criticize ethnomethodology and social phenomenology in *Education and Social Control* (Sharp and Green, 1975) it seems now a problematic prioritizing in the light of recent developments in the analysis of practice and discourse, especially in view of the uncritical use of Coward and Ellis's *Language and Materialism* (1977) in her later book. Activities and practices of the classroom may seem so much more material, and by privileging them one may feel one has escaped from idealism, but the texts being considered here, given their use and orientation, can never be satisfactorily approached as 'mere' content or ideas.

Equally, however, tendencies within original structuralism which were concerned with the interiority and internal, textual nature of cultural products could be inappropriate in the analysis of such products. Some of the approaches to film and the novel associated with this position have to be regarded with reservation in view of the very different forms of consumption. Textbooks of the predominant type analyzed here were consumed publicly in the context of a public classroom, whereas the cinema, for example, especially since World War 2, has been a place of darkness, separation and individualized consumption (Ellis, 1982, pp. 27–30). To some extent there has been a similar change in primary school classroom regimes over the last twenty years, but the books considered in the period of study are chiefly readers, that is, textbooks, often in series of four, which were used in conventional knowledge- and teacher-centred pedagogic regimes. This was the predominant form of the non-fiction school book, at least for children up to 14 years of age, until, that is, practices of individualized learning, project work etc. had the effect of confining these books to the schools' store cupboards. Such books, then, must be clearly distinguished from both information books used in schools in other pedagogical regimes, and from children's books intended for consumption in domestic situations.

Given that the books studied here were in use during the earlier decades of this century then an examination of their use in the classroom is impossible, and work has yet to be done on the complex processes of negotiation and mediation of texts currently in use in schools and colleges. Nonetheless an attempt has been made to approach the books as texts-in-use as opposed to texts-as-expressions. The effect of this is that one cannot but acknowledge the presence of what might be called 'internal' ideologies and/or principles of calculation concerning the nature of childhood and, especially, the process of learning which determines what is to be taught, how, in what order and so on. Thus any attempt to *context* these school books beyond locating them in the regimes of schooling is highly problematic and has to be handled with caution, for it is here where sociology and some Marxisms can so easily lose the specificity of the texts, their production and use. The chief purpose of emphasizing the existence of these books in material practices is to avoid any reduction of them to some national, all-embracing culture, or to another material base elsewhere. Various forms of sociology and Marxist derived social science which could be used to context these books in such ways are considered here unsatisfactory, both in themselves and in their applications. The view which may consider school textbooks as expressions of the values of their national cultures was dealt with in some detail in Chapter 1 when we looked at the belief that ruralism was but one feature of such a culture. It is sufficient to say that such an approach has been used to compare the content of children's books internationally (McClelland, 1961) and can be the most innocent of ways of contexting school texts. Insofar as it presumes a unified cultural essence or set of core values, and a functioning of the state schools with regard to the expression and perpetuation of such values, then it has generally been dismissed by sociologists of the curriculum as naive, consensual and tied to the preoccupations of structural functionalism. The point here is that some of the theoretical positions which were thought to overcome such problems, and which could be used to context school books, also have major difficulties with regard to coherence and application. Two approaches, both claiming Marxist origins, are worth considering insofar as they indicate the difficulties. The first would require a contexting of these books by a social class location of their authors. The second would proceed by identifying the reproductive functions of the apparatus in which the texts were used.

School books could be seen as the products of members of a social class, whose writing represented the consciousness or ideology of that class. This approach could be informed by some notions of a 'selective tradition' (Williams) whereby what was taken as legitimate school knowledge was that which was recorded and organized by such representatives of the class as writers of textbooks. At its simplest this position would present the texts as products of an individual but class-derived bias, and proceed by piecemeal commentary on the books by drawing attention to individual and discrete representations of, for example, middle class values and preconceptions. Some of the commentaries on children's books and readers have proceeded in this way.

A grander and more penetrating approach to contexting via authors' origins may look at the whole structures of the texts and relate them back to wider philosophical structures and then, ultimately, to the whole social structure within which the authors could be located. Lucien Goldmann's genetic structuralism proceeded in this way. In *The Hidden God*, his study of the tragic vision in Racine and Pascal's PensÃ©s, he outlined his method as follows;

> In the first (stage) the text will be seen as the expression of a world vision; in the second this world vision will be more closely analysed as constituting a whole made up of the intellectual and social life of the group; and in the third the thoughts and feelings of the members of the group will be seen as an expression of their economic and social life. (Goldmann, 1964, p. 99)

Such an approach to texts is not to see them as products of individual psychological bias but is a study, ultimately, of the world view of a class, of which the particular texts are a more or less adequate expression.

Given that Goldmann's dialectical sledgehammer was aimed at the greater works of philosophy and literature (being considered by him the fullest pure expressions of class consciousness), and hardly adaptable to the cracking of the small nuts of school textbooks, it could still be said that the latter were indeed the products of a class, perhaps, in this case, the old petty bourgeoisie (Poulantzas, 1975, Part 3) in decline, complete with expressions of its own 'tragic vision'. Thus one might explain their tragic history of the passing of rural England and the independent yeomen, and now preserved only for the children. The whole, historical narrative could be seen as the expression of a class, feeling itself being dispossessed, but whose only hope was a fair-minded English people, made respectable by schooling, who may keep things from getting worse out of respect for the past. Given Goldmann's concern for the totality of world views, culminating historically in the world view of the proletariat, it may be that the 'visions' of textbook writers were, in their partiality and distortion, but lesser ideological expressions.[1]

Another way of contexting these school books within a broadly Marxist tradition may be to stress the apparent or relative autonomy of the schools themselves as part of the apparatus of the state and requiring, for their very functioning, such autonomy (*ibid*, Section 4). This would appear to have both the benefit of acknowledging the specific tasks of these texts-in-use and yet also relating their use, if indirectly, to the social formation as a whole. In this theory, what textbook writers produce is not so much comprehensible in relation to their class as in relation to their class function within the apparatuses of the state, i.e. the reproduction of the social relations of production, or the legitimation of capitalist relations. The concepts of reproduction and correspondence associated with the work of Althusser, Bourdieu and Bowles and Gintis (Althusser, 1971; Bourdieu and Passeron, 1977; Bowles and Gintis, 1976) could be used to show how the texts of school history, for example, offered children a conflict-free view of their society, taught the values of hard work and an appreciation of the freedom of wage labour.

Another way of institutionally contexting the texts would be to study the production and distribution of such books insofar as those things determined their form and content, on the grounds that only the non-critical, uncontentious understandings of, say, north-south international trade were thought sufficiently acceptable by publishers and their teacher-purchasers for profit to be made. Although referring to a quite different system of textbook production and distribution to that which operated in the United Kingdom, Fitzgerald used this type of contexting to good effect in *America Revised: History Schoolbooks in the Twentieth Century* (1980).

In spite of their variety and differing intellectual origins these means of contexting have been found to have both some problems in general, and in particular, proving impossible to use here without restrictions, and for very limited purposes. Where, in the case of textbooks, the details of the authors and their biographies seem inappropriate given the strict conventions of representation which dominate such texts any simple reduction of such texts to the artefacts of a state apparatus with a single reproductive function would make it impossible to even hint at HOW the texts work. In general it could be said that, as in most attempts at a sociology of knowledge, contexting in the ways outlined above moves too directly to *what* the texts mean as opposed to *how* their different meanings are produced. This must be the resulting effect of either taking texts as reflections or expressions of a reality elsewhere (for example, of the economic class position of the author) or as part of an enterprise which has its functions determined by the essence of a whole of which it is part (for example, the national culture or some economically determined binary opposition). The concomitant of these problems is that the ways in which the texts work are often reducible to the sociological models of socialization and value-internalization. In the structural functionalist model of a national culture textbooks are the expressions of that culture and the nation's children are socialized into these cultural values. In this study we have, in a way, reversed this procedure and tried to outline the sometimes desperate attempts by the texts to produce images of that national totality which such a model presumes. On the other hand any Marxist model, which sees the textbooks as expressions of the culture or values of a class which has dominance over the educational system, has similar difficulties. These issues will be dealt with more fully in the following section when the problem of the readership of the books is analyzed. It is sufficient at this point to indicate that some ways of contexting the text and the author necessarily involve a restricted understanding of the child-reader as the unproblematic receiver of given messages which are themselves reducible to their origins elsewhere. The author, on the other hand, has the role of conscious or unconscious manipulator.

Other difficult problems arise if we approach the authorship of textbooks as part of the search for the origins of meanings in the social locations of those authors. Where should we choose to locate any particular author? In their representation of the geography of Britain, for example, is it significant that the vast majority came from the south of England? And how important is it that many of the writers of textbooks for the younger children were women? Put in terms of the concept of ideology then Sumner has correctly pointed to the problem of class reductionism which 'limits the social relevance of ideology to its class forms and its place in the class struggle' (Sumner, 1979, p. 45), and, in the case of the object of this study, the tendency of Marxist analysis hitherto to ignore or reduce nationalist ideology is particularly restricting. Sumner proposes a quite sophisticated consideration of the ways different ideologies from different practices mix, 'become compounded, serialized or clustered' (p. 52). However, in spite of emphasizing the existence of ideologies in structured material processes (p. 22) he still has a relatively limited conception of *how* the ideologies work; how, on the one hand, nationalism might exist within the school texts to produce the apparent reality of national unity, and also how the texts might function to secure an appropriate place for the pupil reader. It is noteworthy that Sumner's analysis of structuralist work on ideology excluded a consideration of Althusser's albeit primitive use of Lacan's ideas in the paper on ideological state apparatuses. And in the end, Sumner's variety of ideologies are 'fundamentally grouped around the class axis' (p. 53).

All the above problems with what we have called contexting, along with many of the presuppositions behind it, especially related to the reflectionist theory of ideology and the essentially empiricist notion of the author (and also the child-reader) as subjects influenced by a given external reality, have forced some theorists to dismiss the whole basis upon which a sociological study of school knowledge might proceed. Writers associated with the journals *Screen* and *Ideology and Consciousness*, for example, have declared that 'the author' is actually produced within the text itself, as narrator, and they have used the concept of 'discourse' to focus attention on the *position of the speaker within the utterance*, as opposed to any, what might be termed, external contexting. At the high-point of formalist structuralism (later the subject of self-criticism) MacCabe wrote uncompromisingly about the production of the subject by the text (MacCabe, 1974). Author is, therefore, a place, and thus, any consideration of his/her biography loses all significance. Other related considerations have led Wexler to producing a wholesale attack on any attempts to analyze school knowledge in terms of representation, reflection or reproduction. From a mixture of considerations, some apparently humanistic, as in his view that in some sociology of the curriculum 'conscious rational human activity is dissolved between the poles of manipulative human relations and iron-like systems laws', (Wexler, 1982, p. 276), he states that:

> a critique of ideology requires a mode of analysis which makes the tenuousness of the object apparent, not by contextualizing it, but by deconstructing it. To deconstruct the object, whether it is school knowledge, film or social organization, means to show how it is itself an outcome of its own composition, a result of its own internal production, and not an entity among other self-generating entities. Objects, knowledge, and relations are not simply representations of something else, but stabilized moments of the internal processes out of which they are made, and which is the task of ideology to naturalize by freezing the present into a convenient snapshot. (*ibid*, pp. 279–80)

It would appear that the crucial questions here are as follows; is the whole project of contexting school knowledge, which began with the use of the approaches of the sociology of knowledge, indefensible because it fails to 'break the spell of realism' (*ibid*, p. 282) which is the reifying quality of that which is analyzed, and fails to 'disturb the narrative' (*ibid*, p. 283) by merely replacing one story with another? The position adopted in this research is that some limited forms of contexting are necessary. Indeed Wexler himself admits the need for an analysis of the sociohistorical process through which school knowledge is produced (*ibid*, p. 283) and that itself could be seen as contexting. The difficulties are considerable, as is evidenced by Sarup's attempts to balance the progressive aspects of taking the activity of deconstruction into the curriculum with Marxist-inspired materialist requirements to socially locate school knowledge (Sarup, 1984).

The irony is that the texts analyzed here *themselves* attempt to context the child-reader in a social unity. The history books try to context and locate the child in a nation's time and chronology, and the geography books place him or her in a national territory or space. At least part of the critical entry into that historical and geographical unity must be to problematize it without necessarily replacing it with a similar, if negative, holistic construct.

Some standard forms of contexting are of limited use anyway because of the nature of that which is being studied. Explaining the changes in these books on the basis of any rigid periodization of British social history is inappropriate because of the ways in which the same texts were reprinted over as long a period as thirty years and because of the existence of sustained pedagogical and technical conventions over equally long periods. Textbook writers seemed to derive as much from one another as from any external factors. But there are some sociohistorical developments which it would be churlish not to include, insofar as one is giving any account of the changing context of the books, such as the development of the social democratic faith in, and the growth of, the instruments of social planning, and the changing position of the United Kingdom in relation to its Empire. We cannot ignore the way schooling and its knowledge was influenced by imperial claims about the quality of the imperial race in comparison with other races, yet this does not mean that these books are fully comprehensible as expressions of the imperialist or social democratic political ideologies. Nationalism and imperialism cannot be understood as relatively free-floating 'isms', and it would be a superficial analysis which would merely search the textbooks of a declining imperial power for instances of such ideological units. The institutions of state education and their curricula do not just express, in a neutral language, some pre-existing values which originate elsewhere. Past textbooks, their emphases, omissions, and structures, must be minimally contexted by a social history, because a purely internal and formal interest in the ways they located and constructed the subject, determined reality, and the position of 'author' and 'reader', can never be sufficient, for always one needs a minimum history which might enable us to see which locations were made available and the likelihood of their occupation.

The questions which are unlikely to be resolved here are (a) whether it is possible to combine a respect for what Coward has called 'the determining action of the means of representation' (Coward, 1977, p. 92) without falling back on inherently unstable concepts such as that of 'relative autonomy'; (b) whether one can reconceptualize the conditions for the existence of particular texts-in-use without losing any ability to criticize the representations contained within those texts; and (c) whether one can work with a notion of sociohistorical context which is not devoted to merely providing a 'real' material background for individual subjects to interpret freely.

Books Specific to the Age of the Child-reader

We have attempted to show in the previous section some of the difficulties of analyzing textbooks as products of authors with particular social origins and have attempted to argue the need to see the books as texts-in-use. An equal and interconnected difficulty arises in the conception of the child-reader in such an approach, and in common sense. Even if we want to keep to some contexting of author and reader one cannot ignore the fact that the most striking feature of these books is the way the author within the text addresses the imaginary reader, with one depending on the other.

The range of methods which rely upon either conceptions of unified class or national cultures, or on any expressive relation between school curricula and the social structure, have been found to be inappropriate as they fail to deal with either the problematic nature of 'writing for children' or the internal, autonomous effects that activity has upon what is produced. They tend to minimize the importance of the fact that these books and knowledges were intended for children, and their production was informed by discourses concerned with the nature of childhood, child behaviour, interests and motivation.

One aspect of the texts is that the imaginary children who were addressed by them were quite undifferentiated except on grounds of age and, very occasionally, sex and geographical location. In the case of the latter, W.J. Claxton's *The Homeland Histories* (1949) was the only series of history or geography textbooks which we found aimed specifically at 'country children' and was produced in reaction to pressure from rural teachers and from the Rural Schools Advisory Committee on Education in the 1930s. In the same way as the popular press and government publications on schooling address their parent-readers as a unified category (Johnson, 1981, p. 22), so the addressees in these books were the unified children of the nation. These children were, for the most part, a tabula rasa, and innocent. This conspiracy has been maintained in the reviews and criticisms of textbooks in the educational press. Just like traditional literary criticism which, as MacCabe (1976) described it, 'holds text and author/reader separate with the author able to inject meaning which is then passed on to the reader' (p. 25), their major points have been generally concerned only with suitability for the stated age range, clarity and realism.

But seeing the effects of concepts of childhood, or what might be called pedagogic ideologies, on the nature of the texts can only be an initial step, first because, alone, it returns us to a purely idealist procedure of tracing the influences of ideas, and second because it ignores what the text does for the adult and teacher. Walkerdine (1984a) has shown how it might be thought that, in the apparatuses and practices of pedagogy, *both* teacher and child are produced and the object of these material practices (the developing child) places both of these. We need to remember continually that these textbooks were part of material practices in this respect, and the 'images of childhood' did not come first and then somehow proceeded to inform the practices and their texts.

On the question of what the texts might do for adults, when reading them it is difficult to avoid the conclusion that, written in the way they were, they secured, *for adults*, an ordered world and a repository of innocence. Rose expresses this point succinctly in her study of Peter Pan, the book that was for *all* children:

> ... the very idea of speaking to all children serves to close off a set of cultural divisions in which not only children but we ourselves are necessarily caught. (Rose, 1984, p. 7)

Her book constantly hints at how writing for children helps us, the adults, by taking away the threats of a child's perverse sexuality, restoring or retaining the belief that there is a primitive world, and that we have a safe relationship to it. In the textbooks of this study certainly the adult is constituted as a knower who 'tells'. The didactic voice is loud and clear, lasting much longer, it would seem than in children's fiction (*ibid*, chapter 2). Therefore the reader is in a very definite relationship to that speaking subject, as defined by their mutual positions in the text, consistent with the pedagogic regime in which these texts have been used.

These texts inscribe an objective position of reading which is developmental and some of the ways of conceiving the subject in Coward and Ellis (1977) could be applied, for example, to the way the national narrative of the nation's history proceeds. It gives the reading subject an 'unfolding of the truth' (*ibid*, p. 50), and that subject, as far as the immediate and imminent aspects of the text is concerned, is in a position of:

> observation, understanding, synthesis. The subject of narration is a homogenous subject, fixed in a relation of watching. (*ibid*)

In another language (a moralizing pedagogy) and at another time (1932) two textbook writers explained their approach in the preface to a history textbook:

all children love stories. The story may contain things unexpected, causing surprise; but it happens as the child would wish it to happen; it ends — not always happily, but worthily, and because it ends worthily, not making human nature ugly or small, the story has been worth telling. (Houseman and Marten 1932, Book I, p. iii)

Important too for this thesis is the way the child-reader is addressed with intimacy, as though known, because all children are within the family of the nation's schools; all are part of the 'imagined community' (Anderson, 1983). And an important aspect of this location of the reader, the one with which this thesis is centrally concerned, is the textual way that reader is located within, and/or against a background, within national boundaries, simply differentiated between town and country.

So far in this section it could be said that, by pointing out the autonomy of the practices of schooling, by emphasizing the way 'the child' is produced within those practices and their artefacts, as opposed to being 'conceived' elsewhere, we have come to that difficult conclusion that the text produces the reader, 'with all its implications of subjugation, unilateral determination, not to say terrorism' (Willemen, 1978, p. 45). If incorporated within a state-functionalist, reproduction thesis, as in the original use of Lacan's ideas by Althusser in his paper on the ideological state apparatuses (Althusser, 1971) which was so influential initially on British structuralist and post-structuralist work on ideology and discourse analysis, then the emphasis on the production of the subject gives rise to a series of difficulties.

It is necessary to reiterate three points which Althusser suggested in his formulation. First and foremost he wanted to locate the subject within material practices and outside of any conception of a person with beliefs and ideas who then acts them out. He explained the point thus:

... where only a single subject (such and such an individual) is concerned, the existence of the ideas of his belief is material in that *his* ideas are his material actions, inserted into material practices governed by material rituals which are themselves defined by the material ideological apparatus from which derive the ideas of that subject ...

Disappeared: the term ideas.

Survive: the terms subject, consciousness, belief, actions.

> Appear: the terms practices, rituals, ideological apparatus. (*ibid*, pp. 158–9)

Second he suggested that the subject is produced through a process he called interpellation:

> Ideology 'acts' or 'functions' in such a way that it 'recruits' subjects among the individuals (it recruits them all), or 'tranforms' the individuals into subjects (it transforms them all) by that very precise operation which I have called *interpellation* or hailing, and which can be imagined along the lines of the most commonplace, everyday police (or other) hailing: 'Hey, you there!' (*ibid*, p.163).

He used the example of addressing his own readers to show how, you and I are always already

> subjects, and as such constantly practise the rituals of ideological recognition... The writing I am currently executing and reading and you are currently performing are also in this respect rituals of ideological recognition, including the 'obviousness' with which the 'trick' or 'error' of my reflections may impose itself on you (*ibid*, pp. 161–2).

To transpose to the concerns of this volume — children are recruited as subjects in the rituals of textbook reading.

Third, arguing from a religious example, Althusser suggested that this interpellation of individuals as subjects, 'presupposes the 'existence' of a unique and centred other subject, in whose name the religious ideology interpellates all individuals as subjects' (*ibid*, p. 167). What he calls the mirror structure of ideology thus makes the existence of God, (or the nation-state in a secular age) and the individual as subject, interdependent.

Numerous criticisms of Althusser's formulation and possible solutions to the problems have been explicated since the publication of the ISA's paper, and some reference to these is necessary here before showing what bearing these theoretical debates have on the question of textbook readership.

The most often expressed reservation concerns the implicit loss of the subject as agent within Althusser's formulation, and with it, the loss of the possibilities of change or resistance, as well as the apparent collapse of material reality itself, in the form of the context for that agent. Such points are clearly explicated in a recent study by Thompson (1984) which seeks to use a notion of contexts of rational discourse derived from Habermas as a means out of relativism. Althusser, Pecheux and others are criticized for their 'dissolution of the agent' (*ibid*, p. 251):

> ... if the subject were simply an individual interpellated by a pre-existing ideological formation, then no room would be left for the emergence of resistance and revolt, for the revolutionary *creativity* which is an irrepressible feature of the historical process. Moreover, what would be the point of attempting to link an analysis of ideology to the presuppositions of historical materialism, if it were not assumed that the results of such an analysis could be appropriated by agents capable of acting, knowledgeably and creatively in the social world. (*ibid*, p. 252)

Similar points were made by Erben and Gleeson (1977) who thought Althusser's reproduction thesis produced a 'passive model of socialization' (p. 74).

Another critique and way out which has been more influential in the sociology of education is that associated with the Centre for Contemporary Cultural Studies and, in particular, with the work of Paul Willis. Richard Johnson, for example, in *Three Problematics: Elements of a Theory of Working Class Culture* (Johnson, 1979) inserts the notion of 'self-creation' (p. 234) to overcome the apparent complete determination of pupils within Althusser's ideological state apparatuses and to argue instead that children are already 'pre-constituted' and do not come as naked subjects. Willis, in his study of the schooling of working class boys (Willis, 1977) used the concept of resistance to deal with similar problems. Here both the traditional socialization model of sociology is rejected, on the grounds that it saw culture as a set of structures simply transferred, as well as Marxist views of the transmission of the dominant culture (p. 4). Both are attacked for their peaceful, consensual model of structural reproduction (p. 175 and related footnote). The practice of reproduction is made problematic and the ethnographic work of the study seeks to present an active cultural life in place of simple one-way transmission. It is thus that the 'penetrations' by working class boys of the key elements of the capitalist system of production are made; its individualism, its abstraction of labour, and its progressive de-skilling. Such penetrations, whilst they contradictorily, and in a distorted way, secure the right cynical, instrumentalist and fatalistic states of mind in this part of the future work force, do provide some ways out for Willis and other radicals. He writes

> If there are moments when cultural forms make real penetra-
> tions of the world then no matter what distortions follow,
> there is always the possibility of strengthening and working
> from this base. If there has been a radical genesis of conserva-
> tive outcomes then at least there exists a *capacity* for opposi-
> tion. We have the logical possibility of radicalness. (*ibid*,
> pp. 174–5)

It was this possibility which was taken as the escape from Althusser
and structural determination (chapter 5, note 3).

Even among those theorists originally most influenced by Althusser there has been considerable discussion about both interpellation
in general and the implied approach to texts and the subject. Paul
Willemen (1978), for example, attempted to express the problem
of the pre-determination of the individual subject as follows:

> Individuals do have different relations to sets of discourses in
> that their position in the social formation, their positioning in
> the real will determine which sets of discourses a given subject
> is likely to encounter and in which ways it will do so. In other
> words this position will determine which discursive forma-
> tions are likely to combine and produce given individuals as
> subjects in ideology. For example, the function of the educa-
> tional apparatus and its manifold institutions is not merely to
> train certain people for, or keep others from, specific jobs. It
> also has a more elaborate function; the control of the dis-
> courses through which subjects are to be constituted. This
> control is never total: unpredicted discourses always threaten
> that control and are therefore censored with various degrees of
> severity. (*ibid*, pp. 66–7)

He added, however, that,

> it is equally necessary to recognise that the real is never in its
> place to borrow a phrase from Lacan, in that it is always and
> only grasped as reality, that is to say, through discourse. (*ibid*,
> p. 67)

This approach, in turn, has given rise to debate within the pages
of *Screen* about whether, for example, this was a return to the base-
superstructure model (Connell, 1978; Branigan, 1978).

Finally there would appear to be what Henriques *et al* (1984) have
called a 'logical problem' in Althusser's thesis (p. 97), in that the
subject must already pre-exist to be able to recognize him/herself in

the procedure of interpellation. This argument was originally developed by P.Q. Hirst in *On Law and Ideology* (Hirst, 1979) where he argued that, 'something which is not a subject must already have the faculties necessary to support the *recognition* which will constitute it as a subject' (p. 65). Hirst notes that this presumes some notion of the child having attributes of knowing subjects independent of their social existence, and that Althusser just 'reproduces certain of the terms of religious and political theory' (p. 67) which he had used as illustration.

It is difficult at this stage to see how these issues can be finally decided upon, whether to the satisfaction of the epistemological Marxists who despair over what they see as a whole 'agnosticism towards the real' (McDonnell and Robins, 1980, p. 176) which they find in the debates within *Screen* and the post-Althussarian positions, or by those who seek to use the work of Foucault and Lacan to overcome the individual-social dualism (Henriques *et al*, 1984).

What remains clear for this thesis is that two ultimately separable and highly problematic unities which were presupposed in Althusser's formulation — that of the subject and the social — were a necessary part of his and other reproduction theses, and these unities, along with any belief in the dominant, uncontradictory nature of the texts in which the reading subjects may 'find themselves' must be rejected.

The concept of resistance, as used by Willis at least, (the dull, subterranean pull against the inevitable) has proved inappropriate in this thesis partly because of the age-range of the child-subjects covered by most of the texts. In practical terms too these were texts in use up to eighty years ago so it was impossible to deal with the pupil's classroom reception of them.

But there are other more significant reasons for rejecting this particular resistance thesis. For Willis it did seem to provide a kind of autonomy for schools as sites. But these counter-institutional processes, which ultimately bring about the preparation of the workforce, are anyway in the end only 'regional instances' (p. 60) of the essential class struggle:

> The state school in advanced capitalism and the most obvious manifestations of oppositional working class culture within it provides us with a central case of mediated class conflict and of class reproduction in the capitalist order. (p. 60)[2]

If the position is positive in its acknowledgement of the *pre-existence* of the pupils in schools it tends to reduce those pre-existences to but one — the material life of a class (or rather of a set of occupations of the pupils' fathers) which has class-cultural effects. With reference to other work originating from the Centre for Contemporary Cultural Studies Rosalind Coward makes explicit what lies behind the notion of youth sub-culture in Clarke *et al*'s *Sub-cultures, Cultures and Class* (Working Papers in Cultural Studies, 7/8) — a view which has some similarities with the thesis of Willis:

> The cultural formation described as youth sub-cultures is located in a general theory of cultures as the product of responses to determinate material conditions. (Coward, 1977, p. 79)

and, in an analysis based on social class, then,

> different 'cultures' are asserted to exist belonging to particular classes or groups, and this difference is attributed to the fundamental social division in capitalist social relations; the difference between labour and capital. (*ibid*, p. 80)

Resistance occurs in this thesis because of the fundamentally different material origins of bourgeois and working class culture.

As far as the reception of the textbooks studied here is concerned, many other locations, contexts, practices and/or discourses would seem relevant. Willis contexts his 'lads' and their school by reference mainly to the labour process, the occupational structure and size of enterprises in 'Hammertown' (Willis, 1977, p. 6). Given the time many of the textbooks analyzed here were in use then even the minimal historical contexting requires reference to immigration and race, changes in demography and settlement, the development of social democratic policy and planning, and issues of gender, all quite irreducible to class culture and economic-institutional change. (Althusser himself banished the need to consider the discourses or regimes of other places, such as the home, church or even sports club (Althusser, 1971, p. 158) by collapsing all of them into the category of ideological state apparatuses tied into the reproduction of the social relations of production.)

If an individual child-reader does not originate from any unity, and is not destined to subsequently enter one, then from our reading of them the very texts themselves are also contradictory, and make available different subject positions. The two questions which the school geographies and school histories attempted to answer, 'Where are we?' (geography) and 'How did we get here?' (history) may be what give the texts movement, but they also provide contradictory locations and identities. The geography books emphasize how 'we' (as civilized people) are distinct from other peoples who live too close to nature. Yet the same books seek also to promote the child as 'natural' and childhood as best lived close to nature (p. 130). History books attempted to establish for the reader the primitive bonds of the Anglo-Saxon race (p. 187) yet the geography books belittled other, similar lives as foreign and primitive.

It could be said that given the essentially contradictory nature of the economic system then the texts merely reflected that, and any attempt to address the national child would therefore be bound to fail, coming, as children do, from different economic classes. But, as I think the study makes clear, this does little justice to the internal nature of the texts and their institutional use. For example, an established internal pedagogic (and philosophical) principle that children learn from nature was absurdly re-presented in textbooks by representations of children carrying out their 'learning activities' in fields, woods and suburban gardens, thus making the ideal child-learners those who *were* so located. Unless one could maintain that the working class was a geographically and locationally specific class (a particularly absurd claim for much of the period under discussion) then the contradiction between addressing *all* children yet showing only *some* cannot be reduced to either class contradictions or a simple middle class bias.

But if the texts were inescapably contradictory, and if they made available different subject positions, they were always trying to stabilize and pull together the position of the reader as child of the nation, and addresser as teacher. The frequent use of 'we', 'our' and 'us', 'you' and 'your' in many of the titles through the period suggests how this was attempted, for example:

Our Yesterdays by Margaret M. Elliot (1937)

You and the Commonwealth by R.P. Brady (1951)

Your World Past and Present by Patrick Larkin (1953)

All *Our* Past by Andrew Scotland (1953)

The World Around *Us* by Zoe Thralls (1956)

Our Heritage, *Our* People and *Our* Democracy by R.W. Purton (in the series New View Histories, 1958)

An interesting example too was the way a historical series entitled *The Pageant of the English People* by H.E. Priestley was dedicated to, 'The Boys and Girls of *Our* country Who Still Have *Their* Part to Play' (1949).

In view of the above theoretical considerations — the need to keep to a minimum of contexting of the child-reader, but not to reduce that to social class, and the need to maintain the significance of the internal procedures of the texts — we have used the concept of 'invitation' to describe the relation of these texts to the reader. Of course this metaphor is not theoretically innocent. It was used, for example, by Tom Nairn when referring to the development of nationalism as in the following quote:

> The new middle class intelligentsia of nationalism had to invite the masses into history; and the invitation card had to be written in a language they understood. (Nairn, 1977, p. 340)

It is hoped, however, that the assumptions about the unified class subjects as givers and receivers in this use have not been imported into our study. Instead we have used the concept as it appeared to allow consideration of both *how* subjects are produced and what it is they are being located in, the minimum of historical locating of both author and reader as well as the space for making problematic concepts such as 'our nation' and 'our people'. It is less militaristic and final than Althusser's metaphor of 'recruitment', (Althusser, 1971, p. 163) permitting refusal, partial, begrudging acceptance, and indecision (turning up, but not enjoying the party!).

'Invitation' also appears to encapsulate that projection of future pleasure, only to be enjoyed by those who join 'us', and demands that we examine the images and representations of 'us'; our togetherness as a self-sustaining, cosy people who are, 'at home'. For its use it does not rely on any internalization thesis for no given values are referred to explicitly. Thus refusal or partial acceptance is not the same as the resistance of Willis' 'lads' and could be the result of factors which are the most specific and internal to the very chronologically organized regime in which the texts were used. For example, the changing history of childhood in school and domestic regimes can make the very texts which sought to produce English children seem *childish* to their intended readers.

Representations of Academic Disciplines and Works of Non-fiction

It is helpful to put together these two aspects of our definition of textbooks as it will enable consideration to be given to some questions which have been at the centre of the philosophical and theoretical debate on the sociology of the curriculum and to put these questions in a particular context. History texts and geography texts from the 1900s to the 1960s have been produced as books for use in the traditionally subject-divided elementary and primary English school curriculum, but they could never be regarded as historical or geographical works. The writers were very rarely academic historians or geographers. More often they were educators, heads of departments in secondary schools, headmasters and mistresses of primary schools. Some earlier writers had personal connections with the world of the universities. For example, F.D. Herbertson who produced the school text *The British Empire* (in the series, *Descriptive Geographies of the World*, 1906) was for a time an assistant mistress at Cheltenham Ladies College, but was also the wife of the famous A.J. Herbertson, Professor of Geography at Oxford. Some were lecturers in training colleges who, for their assumed expertise in pedagogy and ability to produce texts acceptable to the publishers, wrote and/or edited books in both subjects. For example, Eric J. Barker, a lecturer at Trent Park Training College, wrote, with C.C. Hammer, the series called the *Queensway Junior History* (1962) *and* the *Queensway Junior Geography* (1959). E.J.S. Lay, a powerful figure in the world of school textbooks, also wrote and edited across the disciplines for the Macmillan publishing house. He edited Macmillan's *History Picture Books* (1958) and wrote the influential series *The Empire Geographies* (1937) later to be retitled *The Commonwealth Geographies*. These books, as our analysis of them will attempt to show, were dominated by conventions, the same illustrations and examples were often used by different authors widely separated by time. The discourses of the academic disciplines were elsewhere. On the other hand one cannot ignore the way sophisticated theory was hidden and implicit in the way material was organized for children. The simplicity of the 'windows on the world' provided by the children's regional geographies was informed, however indirectly, by the theories of the regions of the world argued about and developed in universities and learned societies of the time (p. 154). And so, at best, one must acknowledge the conflicting claims of scholarship and pedagogy (Nowell-Smith, 1976, p. 27).

One superficial reading of these books would easily show how inadequate these school texts were, and there is something of a scandal in the way teachers and texts represented these disciplines in ways which excluded pupils from their uncertainties. What is argued in this section is that, whilst corrections of inaccuracies and misunderstandings (possibly based on historical and geographical research) is necessary, it can only be part of a wider structural analysis along with a consideration of the ways in which the texts produced a sense of reality, regardless of the apparent unrealistic idealizations within them.

There have been problems, however, in defining how a *sociology* of the curriculum can intervene in these issues. Originally such an approach drew upon the sociology of knowledge tradition and/or social phenomenology, as, for example, in Michael Young's work in *Knowledge and Control* (Young, 1971), with all their implications of relativism and the social construction of reality. An integral part of a claim like Gorbutt's (1972) that all knowledge was 'thoroughly relativized' (p. 6) was that sociology (or at least its central messages) should be included within the curriculum itself, if only to destroy the apparent certainties elsewhere. This could be done, for example, by locating what school history said as specific to a society or class. Such claims could be seen as part of the project of bringing society and an appreciation of the social into an individualized curriculum, where English literature was the study by individuals of the products and feelings of other individuals, and history was the study of great men (sic). There are two difficulties in this whole enterprise which are relevant here. First it was subject to all the pitfalls of relativism, especially with regard to its own knowledge (Ahier, 1977, p. 71), and therefore could not speak of or use even the obvious errors of fact *within* the disciplines of a conventional curriculum. Secondly it was tied very much to the predicament of either seeing reality as socially constructed by interacting individuals (and, hence, returning in the end to the very individualism which was one of the points of criticism of that traditional curriculum) or conceptualizing a 'centred' social totality which somehow *required* such knowledge or understanding in schools. Criticism and change of school knowledge might therefore be seen as comparatively ineffective. Neither from within the traditional school disciplines themselves, or from the sociology of the curriculum beyond, could certain important questions about the *representations* of reality be posed. Alvarado and Ferguson point to these issues in the following quotation from their paper, *The Curriculum, Media Studies and Discursivity* (Alvarado and Ferguson, 1983). After distinguishing between the construction and representation of reality they state that:

> ... one should reveal that it is not the 'real world' that is being taught about in history lessons but rather a discourse (or, if you are lucky, discourses) about the world — a *representation* of the world that is 'historical' — that which belongs to discourses which can be institutionally specified and analyzed.

And the same could be argued for *all* other subject areas/ academic disciplines: they all offer representations of the world, discourses (usually educational) about the world and never (because it is impossible) the world itself. However, this is denied by the curriculum as it is currently conceived and constituted, for it is based on an essentially 'realist', i.e. empiricist, pragmatic and utilitarian, conception of both knowledge and the world. (*ibid*, p. 25)

Notwithstanding their strange differentiation between the world of the school and the 'real' world of work beyond (p. 32) their criticisms of the initial sociology of the curriculum, and the projects outlined by Alvarado and Ferguson are, indeed, persuasive. The use of some aspects of the work on cinema to which their approach is related has provided some ways forward for this thesis, but with certain reservations, partly because the target for the theorists of *Screen* was the realist text of fiction. This is not to say that work of non-fiction intended for educational purposes cannot be adequately dealt with by such analysis. Grahame Thompson clearly demonstrated, in his work on Open University programmes that, in his words, 'it has become possible ... at least to borrow certain of the theoretical results of the analysis of realism undertaken in relation to fictional texts for the analysis of non-fictional forms' (Thompson, 1979, p. 168).

But, from our point of view, there have been, in some of the writing on cinema, noticeable, and regrettable, similarities with the rejected social phenomenological traditions in the sociology of the curriculum, as, for example, when Ellis (1982) writes of the meanings which television and cinema create as, 'common sense, as the taken — for-granted, a kind of natural horizon to life, beyond which anything is unthinkable' (p. 14). This similarity has not escaped other commentators. In a footnote on the formalists like Shklovsky, Sarup rather naively suggests that 'Some research needs to be done on the similarities and differences between the following concepts; defamiliarization (Shklovsky), making strange (Schutz), making problematic (Garfinkel), theorizing or reformulating the self (Blum and McHugh) and dereification' (Sarup, 1984, p. 173, note 9).

The problems which these apparent similarities point to have been seized upon by epistemological Marxists who have conducted a critical campaign, first, against Althusser, and subsequently against his intellectual descendants in *Screen* and elsewhere. From what has been argued already some of their criticisms concerning the post-Althussarians' loss of concern for the totality, and their inability to conceptualize a whole structure in which the class subject can be located, must be rejected (viz McDonnell and Robins, 1980). But other writers, like Perry Anderson, make some charges which, even if they ultimately rely on a highly problematic epistemology of correspondence, as in his attack on Derrida and Foucault (Anderson, 1983, p. 46), do at least illustrate the difficulties in cutting away what has been thought to be the relatively secure grounds of Marxist materialism from which the criticisms of social phenomenology were mounted. However, Anderson's criticisms of the work of Levi Strauss, Lacan, Foucault and Derrida in terms of its 'exorbitation of language' (*ibid*, p. 40) and resultant 'attenuation of the truth' (*ibid*, p. 45), like other epistemological Marxists attacks, do not satisfactorily avoid the shortcomings of Marxist theories of ideology, which have either relied on simple distinctions between truth and falsity or on proclaiming one part of the world more real than another. Such notions close off many of the important areas concerned with the production of the subject, and the role of language in that respect, which have been found useful in the investigation of how these texts might work. It has, for example, been felt necessary to see the language of the texts as more integral to the production of subjects than some Marxist views of the practical-concealing functions of language would allow. Where Larrain makes some useful points about the necessity of relating the textual to the extra-textual (Larrain, 1979, p. 140), so often the critical Marxist analysis of ideology proceeds by simply showing how texts function ideologically by hiding and concealing contradictions (in the case of Larrain) or making universal and unhistorical one partial view of the world (Parekh, 1982). It is possibly true that one can show that the texts studied do conceal or transpose contradictions, but their language does not hide a reality in that sense, but produces subjectivities and places for them. A critical confrontation of these texts cannot only rely on the production, alongside, of other narratives which rely on some epistemologically based claim to represent reality. Making some advance on earlier positions MacCabe has written that 'realism is no longer a question of an exterior reality nor of the relation of reader to text, but one of the ways in which these two interact' (MacCabe, 1976, p. 25).

On the question of the reality of the texts and their representation of town and country which we have studied, then, given the tendency of so many literary and cultural critics to draw attention to the *unreal* images of the country in, for example, English literature it may be necessary to clarify the strategy in this volume. Exposing the ways in which the books have idealized the lives of people in past rural locations, by showing how they omitted whole areas of those lives, and whole sectors of those populations, has been necessary, but not because it is believed that one could ever present to children the *reality* of rural life, like some object lesson from a previous pedagogic regime. Claims may be made of some books that they tell children 'what life was really like', but this project appears quite as absurd, whether it dwells on lives of rural destitution or pastoral pleasure, or even some mixture of the two. If one works from a view of these texts as ideological, in the limited sense of hiding contradictions or conflicts through an idealization of conditions, one is tempted into advocating oppositional, realist texts which reverse the images, include the hitherto excluded rural labour, and present a world of calculation as opposed to that of moral, mutual aid. Such strategies, which can end in the production of radical, realist texts, do seem to depend upon a view of the offending texts as working by manipulation and by quantitative bias. The results, whether they be produced by alternative film-makers who seek to promote 'the voice of the people', (Johnston and Willemen, 1975) or community educators who produce localized working class curriculum materials, are also held within the limits of that problematic.

Our interest in idealization of rural conditions arises from the fact that it is a form of representation of the country relevant only to distinguishing town from country in very particular textual structures, which, in turn, are parts of a much wider ideological enterprise. Ultimately such idealizations have to be explicated, not as singular misrepresentations, but in relation to a structure of representations and images, implicated in historically specific texts, institutions and practices. (Converse representations and images of rural idiocy need similar treatment). Part of this dismantling of the structure may entail exposing the gross inaccuracies of geographical and historical detail, and it would be unnecessarily self-defeating to make it impossible to correct such falsity from historical research, for example, just because it is in the history books for children. Some relevant advances might have been made within the academic discipline of history since the writing of many of these textbooks, and it would be odd to ignore these when considering the textbooks' representations of the Peasants' Revolt or the industrial revolution. But it would be mistaken to reduce our analysis to the procedure of comparing school history with academic history. Fitzgerald (1980) argued that the academic community was, regrettably, the last group to influence the content of textbooks in the United States and that such books were more subject to all the popular pressures and superficial pedagogic fashions. Fitzgerald's reactions, however, say little about how those textbooks worked to create their sense of reality, with or without the authority and power of the academic discourse. Accuracy of detail is only one aspect of realism. The texts studied, for all their fanciful images of life in places of great historical and geographical distance, used a number of devices or 'conventions of portrayal' (Ellis, 1982, p. 6) to attach those images to things the child-readers were thought to know in common sense and everyday experience. Through the frequent device of the breakfast table, for example (p. 150), so often used to 'bring home' the reality of Imperial and Commonwealth trade to the reader, the idealized labour on the sugar plantation could be as 'real' as the sugar in one's tea. In an odd way, too, some of the books used a form of 'self-reference', by which they, as books used in schools, described lessons in imaginary schools. For example, in *Longman's Ship Series — Pictorial Geography Readers*, Book IV (1900) the perfect teacher and her perfect pupils are introduced to us:

> The afternoon session had just commenced in a school situated in one of our coast towns. The teacher was about to give a geography lesson and the class was looking forward to the lesson with pleasure. (p. 29)

Summary

The above discussion may well be thought to have a number of negative effects for the possibility of intervening or changing the dominant form and content of contemporary school knowledge. This difficulty seems to be given added significance by the way contemporary debate between epistemological Marxists and their adversaries has been conducted, especially around the concept of ideology. To some writers it would appear that, to be able to act, to influence policy, or take one's part in revolutionary practice, one must use the concept critically, although there is little agreement on the basis of that critical force. For some there is a reliance on science, for others a belief in the ultimate universal consciousness of a class which has 'nothing to lose but its chains'. For writers like Perry Anderson and Alex Callinicos the political (and, by implication, educational) implications of foregoing Marxist epistemological certainties are disastrous (Callinicos, 1982, chapter 1; and Anderson, 1983). Meanwhile those on the other side reject any reliance on epistemology as the decider of truth, believing that, in the end, it amounts to tautology, privilege, and aprioristic notions of knowledge production (Hindess and Hirst, 1977). The debate can appear to result only in the production of dark and forbidding choices. For some the whole post-Althussarian development could appear as a decline into an ineffective self-indulgence, where the exposure of the devices of realism degenerate into providing a place only for the individual, clever, mental anarchists, who keep their reason while those around them lose theirs. Some of Callinicos's commentary on what he calls the 'Nietzschean challenge' to Marxism by Foucault and Deleuze, for example, may be taken in this way (Callinicos, 1982, p. 3). For others, no doubt, the certainties of scientific Marxism and the laws of tendency, expressed by the Party and state schools against ideological allcomers, are even less attractive.

As far as curricula and educational change is concerned then the position adopted in this volume does seem to rule out certain strategies, judgments and justifications and yet allow and encourage others:

1   It does mean that one cannot decide on what should be included or excluded in educational texts on the basis of certain content being the expression of the ideology of a class or apparently functional to a class. Take, for example, claims that some curriculum content dehistoricizes or naturalizes in order to legitimate the ruling class — a view which might be derived from the use of Parekh's notion of ideology as apologia (Parekh, 1982). But as McCarney points out, this can hardly be accepted, either as a necessary part of bourgeois ideology or ideology in general:

> This may be all the more obvious if one is concerned to have a concept of ideology suited to the needs of contemporary social theory. We live in a relatively self-conscious and historically conscious age in which intellectuals generally have assimilated something of the lessons of Marx and of the shocks which the bourgeois order has suffered since his time. It would be a simple matter to find defenders of that order who, far from supposing that it is eternal because grounded in human nature, are well aware that it is a historical product to be sustained by deliberate and strenuous effort. (McCarney, 1985)

Furthermore, such views can bring one back to what Poulantzas called the 'number plate' theory of class ideologies

(Poulantzas, 1973, pp. 201–6) with all its shortcomings and/or the conviction partly shared by Poulantzas, that proletarian experience of work makes the class somehow revolutionary.

Notions of a radical, popular proletarian curriculum, however disguised, is thereby made highly problematic.

2   The position adopted in this volume also appears to make it impossible to reject the content of some textbooks as mere pre- or non-scientific ideological illusion, as this so often assumes a position of epistemological and political authority outside of ideology which has the appearance, at least, of arrogant scientism.

But *positively*, having argued against any absolute distinction between material and immaterial, (symbolic and real), this does enable one to take schooling as an important and inescapable locus of power and representation. Not reducing the school curriculum to the expression of some (economic) practice elsewhere does mean that one must take the mode of representation seriously, especially when the implications of power within discourse is made clear. As Frow notes in an article which was not concerned with schools but which clarified the significance of such institutions when the so-called epistemological guarantees have been rejected:

> The decisive criterion of analysis could thus no longer be the relation between discourse and a reality which would be external to it . . . Instead the relevant criterion would be that of the relations between discourse and power, the intrication of power *in* discourse. We would be specifically concerned with the institutions, the forms of transmission and diffusion, and the pedagogical forms which impose and maintain discourses and which contain dissenting or marginal positions within certain limits. (Frow, 1985, p. 200)

In a certain way, rejecting any appeals to an extra-discursive reality may lead to a theorizing which treats schools more like other institutions, but not by any functionally-based homologies or correspondence.

Secondly, the development of curriculum materials will be enhanced by an appreciation that, although 'findings' from research and academic disciplines can be used to correct previous, child-like historical or geographical misconceptions, this still means that such knowledge comes from, in these cases, referential discourses, and not from an extra-discursive reality. Thus the position makes inescapable the necessity of pedagogic (and political) calculations about inclusion and exclusion.

A third positive point it is that once the production of subjects is seen as internal to the discursive practices and their texts then some of the superficialities implied in the 'correction of bias' approach to curriculum change can be avoided. Again, providing the element of power and minimal contexting is not excluded, then this could constitute a useful advance in fields such as multiracial education.

Lastly, consideration of the place of the subject *within* the texts forces one to consider one's own position in any alternative texts, however radical might be the content. It demands an explicit consideration of power and closure which may be implicated in, for example, the production and consumption of the radical curriculum text.

But in the end an analysis which does not lead directly to curriculum innovation, which does not provide another parallel historical narrative or geographical travelogue, which refuses to place all its emphasis, at least, on solving problems via the provision or censorship of texts *for children*, is not necessarily flawed. Too many of the pedagogues and educationalists who have written for children have seen in them the means to a better world, and too few have considered the effects *on adults* of writing as they did for children. It would be a simple arrogance to believe that one is analyzing, in the case of this volume, the books read by one's own generation and by the generation before it merely to inform the production of books for the next. *We* must have partly and contradictorily accepted the invitations to be educated, and British, and all that went with that, to be now thinking that it matters much to look back at how it happened. If contradictory and 'decentred' conceptions of the subject and the social formation make it more difficult to sustain pedagogic convictions they also make it more difficult to claim privilege and to dominate.

Notes

1 In *The Human Sciences and Philosophy* (1969, p. 103) Goldmann made a distinction between ideology and world view wherein the former was related to a declining class.
2 I am more persuaded by the position on power and resistance represented by the work of Foucault. To use Smart's description of that position, it maintains that, 'the very existence of power relation pre-supposes forms

of resistance … as an inherent feature of the power relation … Thus broad cleavages in the social order, massive binary divisions, constitute at best possible fleeting moments in a history of a society amidst a plurality of irregular resistances' (Smart, 1983, p. 90).

3   Rural Origins and National Progress

An initial reading of history textbooks published in the first half of the twentieth century would confirm some contrasting images of the country and the town. The country appears as peaceful, clean and domestic. It is a place of beauty, where people work *with* nature under a sunny sky and then enjoy their simple village pleasures. There is always smoke curling up from the cottage chimneys where mother does her baking. In the school-book pictures the vantage point is always from above, showing the three field system or perhaps the great house. The rural location is, in essence, a human settlement surrounded by hills and woods. The town by contrast is usually viewed from within; it is a dirty street in which bustling life exists. Labour is divided, first by the guilds and then by factories. Smoke from dark houses or factory chimneys lingers above the human mass which passes its foggy days in toil or gossiping in taverns. If occasionally some apprentices play games in the street urban children are, more often, to be found up those very chimneys or in those factories, at work, suffering the beatings of their employers, waiting to be rescued at last by free state schools where they can learn about 'our past'.

Such images and contrasts certainly may be taken as confirming that generations of young readers have been guided into a non- or anti-industrial English culture (Wiener, 1981). But, as we have attempted to argue, the acceptance of this interpretation would mean that the engagement of this research with the textbooks could only be one of adding up the confirming instances of ruralism or anti-industrialism. What is to be attempted here, however, is some analysis of *how* the general dualities of town and country, pre- and post-industrial, are produced by the *particular* types of texts being studied. The interpretation which relies on conceptions of ruralist national culture would tend to ignore the changing social-locational differences within that mass of 'English school children' which would so affect the receiving of the messages as to help make such holistic cultural analysis problematic. In particular the approach overlooks the struggle by the texts to produce and delineate that which is too easily taken for granted, i.e. English childhood. This has been a struggle (a) with the contemporary contexts of the lives of urban, rural and suburban child-readers of different classes, sexes and races; and (b) with the academic discourses and their representations of past urban and rural lives which have, at times, been differently presented.

What is being attempted here is a move away from an account of the way textbook writers expressed the values of their class or of the class above them to a pre-given childhood. Instead the following analysis of school history textbooks for young children tries to be more concerned with questions of production; how a set of conventions became established and dictated what could be said; how the adjective 'English' was filled with meaning; how, in the attempted definition of national identity the images of the rural and urban evolved. Reversing the notions expressed in numerous prefaces and introductions found in the history textbooks themselves, these texts are not just to be read and understood by English school-children but the English child is also to be read, understood, and constructed by the texts.

Before going on to look in detail at both the static signs of country and town life and the conventional signs of the emergence in the texts of the urban and the industrial in these national narratives we must consider when, how, and in what contexts the rural-urban contrasts appeared in the first place. Why was it thought useful and important to describe to children the town and the country at different historical periods?

There is a sense in which a rural past is a universal past. Textbooks in all literate societies *could* include contrasts between rural locations, original rural existences and subsequent urban development — yet they may not. The relative exclusion of rural life and conditions may occur in the construction of a 'national past'[1] for a number of reasons. It may have been a time of slavery or dependence, and a memory best forgotten. In a so-called 'under-developed' country the rural past may be too much like the rural present, and if a particular kind of national progress is to be denoted then towns and city life may be the key locations to be represented. Furthermore, a previous colonial power may have used old 'traditions' to rule such a country and so created the need for a break (Ranger, 1984). Past city cultures, such as those of the Indus or the great cities of the ancient Ganges, for example, may be seen to constitute culture and movement, whereas the countryside was, and is, 'timeless'. Ferro has noted how, in Indian history textbooks, for example, the ancient city life of the Sind is used to show how clever the people of India were so long ago (Ferro, 1984, pp. 34–5). In other contexts 'the urban' has been associated with tradition and the rural-nomadic with radical challenge (Zubaida, 1985).

More likely, perhaps, in view of the problems of recent rapid urbanization in such societies, the ideological task has been seen as combining a commitment to progress with a sense of national continuity, and so the country and the town have to be held together in an uneasy relationship.

Less fancifully, there have been internal and external reasons why urban-rural contrasts were not always drawn in English history textbooks. Historical events may have occurred in rural and urban places, yet the locations had no significance. As history was seen only as a series of events, the actions of great men, or just dated military and political occurrences, then the locations had no meaning. Towns fell, the countryside was laid waste, people took news from one place to another, but that was all.

In fact, town and country, as contrasts, entered children's history only with certain other abstractions. It came about when 'the everyday life of ordinary people' was thought worthy of inclusion, and when social changes in general came to be considered. The period in which this first occurred coincided with the development of mass state schooling. One may presume, therefore, that it had something to do with attempts to recruit the ordinary child into national membership by including, if only in the shadows and as features in the landscape, his or her ancestors. Looking at children's history books just before and at the very beginning of the period studied (1880–1960) we can see that, where these were not just a list of events, then they were given over to following Carlyle's dictum that 'the History of the World is but the biography of great men'. Lady Callcott's *Little Arthur's History England* (1834), made one or two generalizations about the Anglo-Saxons, but, other than that, kept to moral stories of great actions. T.J. Livesey, in the *Granville History Readers*, justified the mixture of 'tales of noble and heroic deeds with stories of human fortitude and suffering' on the grounds that children liked them (Livesey, 1885).

In adult history, however, some consideration of the living conditions of the different classes had already been attempted by

Macaulay in chapter 3 of his *History of England*. Burke sees this, along with J.H. Green's *Short History of the English People*, as the beginning of an English 'people's history' (Burke, 1981).

One or two children's writers attempted such a thing, usually by reference to the 'manners' of previous periods. Henry Ince, for example, in *Outlines of English History* (1856 ed.) produced some fragments of a naive and strange 'social' history. In his preface he indicated that,

> As the duty of the historian does not simply consist in presenting a bare narrative of political and military transactions, notices of domestic life, the manners, arts, dress etc., of the various eras of English history are occasionally introduced ... (*ibid*, p. iii),

but this amounted to little more than judgmental parodies of the appearances and mentalities of the people of earlier times. A flavour of these can be gained from the following description of the Britons:

> The manners of the Britons, like those of other Celtic nations, were extremely simple; they lived chiefly on milk, the flesh of animals and the natural productions of the soil. They were remarkable for their size, stature and fair complexion, and excelled in swimming, running and other manly exercises. (pp. 5–6)

This text was later revised by Hassall in 1888 and in the preface the work of J.R. Green and other academic historians was acknowledged as the source of the additions and revisions. Added to the original was some attempt at a social history, but it was composed chiefly of notes on punishments, 'learning' and so on (Ince and Gilbert, 1888). Most of this text, however, as with others of the nineteenth century, was just a list of kings, their genealogies and actions, followed by a moral and medical autopsy of each, even when they proclaimed otherwise in their introductions (Taylor, 1845). In the case of the books written for use in specific examinations, as, for example, Carter's *Groundwork of English History for the London Matriculation Examination*, this form continued well into the twentieth century (Carter, 1907).

From the perspective of this study the first set of texts to create space for the production of rural and urban dualities we found was Charlotte Yonge's *English History Reading Books* (1880) for it was in Part V of this series that she turned from lists of events and characters to the social conditions of rich and poor. It is here we find descriptions of thirteenth century rural and town life (*ibid*, p. 77) and sixteenth century poverty (*ibid*, p. 141). In the light of subsequent twentieth century developments the remarkable thing about this book is its complete lack of sentimentality about rural life and its social relationships. The lack of protection of the poor in a paternal village system when the lord is grasping and rapacious is well appreciated. Town life appears as much more preferable; as a place for self-improvement and education. The illustrations, taken from previously used plates, as was often the case with nineteenth century children's books, were exclusively of towns and town life, and they ennobled the city.

It could be said, then, that 'the people' and 'the places' appear to emerge together because the stages upon which the lives of the common people are played in these histories are not the stages of national events but sociogeographical locations. People are to be found primarily in the villages and towns, living in their simple homes, working in the fields and factories and suffering the changes to those locations. They appear very infrequently as actors. In most of the books this is restricted to one event, the Peasants' Revolt. Problems arise for the production of the national narrative, not only in that circumstance, but also when the deeds of national heroes have to be separated from related changes in the landscape which cannot but be seen to be detrimental to the lives of ordinary English people of the time. It is then when national progress as the natural sequencing of events comes to the rescue. The actions of agricultural improvers like Coke and Townsend, or the much-admired inventors of industrialization, have to be both insulated from their rural or urban effects and somehow encapsulated in the story of a nation whose agricultural and industrial progress eventually helps to care for its people and protect them from their external enemies.[2]

To encourage 'our masters' to feel they have a stake in the nation as well as for pedagogical reasons the writers of textbooks for universal schooling could not but write about the everyday lives of the people, their variations and changes. The least problematic indicator of such variation and change for them, as for some classical non-Marxist sociology, was urbanization. But the construction of narrative, national narrative in this case, requires that something of what was introduced at the beginning is there at the end, so there must be both movement (preferably progress, so that the child can feel he is lucky to be alive now) AND continuity.

The following account, then, is at least partly about the difficulties, contradictions and struggles involved in telling the story of a people and their land, who started out together, so to speak, and must be kept together despite economic and political dispossession. For a brief period history seemed to be coming to the rescue of these children's historians when, in the 1950s and 1960s, it appeared in the texts as though the conflict between the wealth-providing industrial city and the English rural life was being reconciled for the people in the suburbs and new towns, and the previous hardships of industrialization were bringing their rewards for all. But this was a premature culmination to our history. We were, as it might appear now to some people, cashing in our 'national savings' too early[3] as well as excluding from national membership a growing number of urban children, many of whose ancestors had known quite different rural origins.[4]

'The Country Air': Physical Aspects of Town and Country

What static physical features have signified life in the country and life in the town within school history textbooks over the period under consideration?

What has become clearest in the analysis of rural and urban images from Yonge's text onwards through this century is that a fundamental aspect of country life was taken to be its proximity to nature. To her, Merrie England was spoiled by its coarseness (Yonge, u.d., Part V, p. 141) but subsequent writers made more and more of the naturalism of pre-industrial and non-urban life. For T.F. Tout, writing two years into this century (Tout, 1902, Book II), the primitive but sensible life of our Anglo-Saxon forefathers was full of charm and naturalness:

> The country was very scarcely peopled, and most of the countryside was still taken up with waste, forest, moor and fen ... Nearly everybody lived in the country, and most free Englishmen possessed a plot of land. The English were therefore a nation of farmers and herdsmen delighting in a simple out-of-door life. (pp. 51–2)

We shall return to this book and its construction of national identity but in this context the contrast between the natural spatial existence of early Englishmen and their later cramped and vulgar lives in towns is well made. Later in the text the Great Plague appears associated with the 'bad government and wanton luxury of the court' (p. 291) and the subsequent development of manufacturing is regarded as a mixed blessing because it brought with it a growth and concentration of population.

It was these aspects of the town which so obsessed the late Victorians and early Edwardians, and they came to dominate the visual and verbal images of the textbooks. Constant references are made to the disposal of human and other waste within the confines of the towns and to the misery of life without the benefit of 'air'. These conventions, once established, remained until the 1960s, and, in some cases, beyond. Outside of education, investment is still tempted out of London by describing a town like Kings Lynn as 'a place to live, work and breathe' (Burgess, 1982).

Fresh rural air seemed to have a particularly healing and beneficial effect. It was like a balm to the rural worker, making his labours less onerous and more invigorating. Even on the very rare occasions when children are depicted as doing rural work (they are usually seen as 'helping' as though in a suburban garden, unlike their urban counterparts) then it is being outside which makes it easier for them. Realistically describing the labour of rural children who lived 150 years ago Wragg concludes 'but at any rate the farm children worked in the open air. Perhaps the saddest little boys in England in those days were those hired out as chimney sweeps' (Wragg, 1949, p. 148).

The association between being free ('free as the air'), self-sufficient and living and working in the open comes across in Warner's contrast between the Anglo-Saxon peasant and conditions in 1912:

> Of course he was without many things that the man of today has but then he did not know them or want them. He had no anxiety about employment. His house let in water but it let in air and it was his *OWN* house.... He had a garden; he worked for himself and not for wages.... (Warner, 1912, p. 8)

Town air, on the contrary, was always foul, regardless of the period described. Priestley (no enemy of the urban himself) writes of medieval Leicester as follows:

> Below, in the houses and the shops the ceaseless clatter of industry goes on. Even worse than this are the smells which the wind wafts everywhere. Towns are not the most healthy of places, for the stables and pigsties are very near to the houses and down the middle of the street runs the main drains, often clogged with filth and decaying matter. (Priestley, 1949, p. 96)

In a chapter called 'Town Life in the Days of Henry VII and Henry VIII' Spalding and Wragg (1914) accompany their reader on a journey to London but find that 'once within the city we can hardly breathe for evil smells rising from the streets ...' (Spalding and Wragg, 1914, Book V, p. 18). Historical London, the usual city to represent urban life in general in these books, was frequently associated with drains, rubbish and problems of sanitation (for example, Marsh and Parks, 1958, p. 5; and Larkin, 1953, Book I, p. 73) and even when the writer refuses to idealize early rural existences the town is almost always equated with filth (viz Lord, 1951, p. 39). This is taken to such lengths that the Great Fire was thought a blessing (Elliot, u.d., p. 86) and the sequence of Plague and Fire is given by Bowman (1926) and others an almost biblical flavour: 'When winter came the trouble abated and a great fire cleansed the highways and swept away the old buildings' (*ibid*, p. 126).

Thus when it came to depicting The Fall — the movement of the dispossessed rural folk into the towns—the effect on them of that particular 'change of air' was striking:

> What a contrast village people must have found in their new conditions of life! They had lived in little houses dotted about here, there, and anywhere; in the new industrial towns the two-storied workmen's dwellings ran in long parallel rows, and one house was just like another. Instead of the large gardens to which they had been accustomed they had to be satisfied with tiny flagged forecourts and small back-gardens. In place of the square-towered ivy-clad churches of their villages, with spacious churchyards where grew the yew, cypress or cedar and where they could hear peals of bells chiming out on the restful Sabbath, they had to worship in churches built of wood and roofed with corrugated iron, or in red-bricked, unshapely buildings. Neither was the air as pure as that on the country hillsides. Instead of the ruddy glow which distinguishes the country farmer, the factory-workers' faces soon became pale and pasty. (Claxton, 1949, Book 5, pp. 150–1)

A quite perceptive writer of history for children, George Guest, who was determined to show the full range of conditions of life on the basis of the classes the people came from, could not help but make the conventional contrast between the picturesque and healthy rural existence and the urban life. Of the urban industrial workers he wrote:

These toilers, instead of enjoying the pure country air, the green fields and brown ploughlands as workers had formerly done, were now residents in the neighbourhood of the mills and factories where was their daily labour.... (Guest, 1913, pp. 176–7)

It is true that pollution by smoke in London had been complained about since the thirteenth century because of the type of coal used and the variety of fumes given off by brewing, dying and brick-making in the city (Thomas, 1983, pp. 242–43). The interesting point is how features of some towns at some periods are constructed as universals, with important effects, and how physical pollution has been associated with moral pollution.

During the first fifty years of our period these writers were not all unaware of the fact that, for all the improvements in sewage disposal that had been accomplished, most of their readers were by then living well away from nature and except, perhaps, for the very occasional holiday or school visit, there seemed little hope that many could return to a contact with the countryside. Certainly in the earlier period they seemed to appreciate implicitly that smoke and squalid housing in the shadows of factories was still the lot of many children who would read their books. Thus these writers were careful not to bring up to date their narrative of national progress with any lengthy consideration of contemporary town life as such. When wanting to make the differences between contemporary urban and earlier existences Spalding and Wragg came back more than once to what had been taken as the key characteristic of town living, *and they accepted it as given* —

Nowadays by far the largest number of people live in big towns, where they can but seldom see fields or woods or wild flowers. In those days (the 1480s) people either lived in villages where the fields and woods were close at hand or they lived in little towns so small that they could walk into the green fields in ten minutes. (Spalding and Wragg, 1914, Book V, p. 1)

Later they observed that, 'It takes us long to reach the land of unspoiled fields and woods' (*ibid*, p. 14).

After World War 2, however, that key aspect of urban life, distance from nature, and all the squalor which seemed to go with it, suddenly became a particular and contained 'middle' period of the life of the nation. It was inserted between England's original rural roots and its subsequent culmination in a planned compromise between town and country. One cannot help noticing that, by the 1940s and 1950s, and regardless of the living conditions experienced by many child-readers, the narrators felt convinced enough about the social democratic improvements coming to all that they could ask children to contrast the urban past with their own seemingly universal suburban present.

I am not suggesting that any simple periodization can be found in the development of the representation of the rural and urban. Original contrasts and simplifications, initially constructed in the Victorian and Edwardian periods, remained, but a key difference was that the physical squalor of previous urban conditions became increasingly explained in terms of a lack of 'planning'. This idea came to carry the burden of explaining why the growth of towns brought such a deterioration in the conditions of the nation's people.

One of the first examples of the use of this term in children's history is to be found in a pre-war book by Williams-Ellis and Fisher (1936, vol. 4). Here the rapid building of poor quality houses which accompanied industrialization was blamed on a lack of town planning (p. 32). Later they declare,

> This growth (of population) of course brought its own problems. The badly planned towns became bigger and more crowded. It became more difficult for town children to get out into the country. (p. 69)[5]

The implication is that the important rural contact for children could have been maintained if planning had been possible. In post-war Britain this was seen as the reality for all, and reference to planning can be found in a whole variety of texts. Lack of such planning in previous city development was sometimes innocently blamed on the need to meet demand quickly (Boog-Watson and Carruthers, 1951, p. 101) but Turnbull came out in his condemnation of the pursuit of private gain as the evil behind slums and urban sprawl (Turnbull, 1953, Book 8, p. 26). After a very bland and accepting history of industrialization in Book 7, in keeping with the spirit of the title of the series (*The Golden Mean Histories*) he declared that the slums were an insult to the British people, being as they were such a nation of home lovers (p. 26, Book 8), and inter-war ribbon development was equally condemned:

> It was good for the builders who made big profits, but it spoiled the appearance of the countryside, because it turned attractive open country roads into straggling streets. (p. 30)

It was not just the *industrial* towns which were seen to have suffered from the lack of planning. Some writers criticized the builders of medieval England. Reeves, in his book on *The Medieval Village* (in the *Then and Now Series*, 1953) asked the children pointedly:

> Do you think people should be allowed to build just where and how they pleased, so that towns and villages grow up all higgledy-piggledy? Or do you think town councils ought to make plans for homes, schools, factories etc and stick to them? (p. 80)

The confidence which these writers had in the post-war period of national reconstruction is nowhere better expressed than in the much-used *Mayflower Histories*. There Kelly and Stewart declared, in 1962, that

> In towns the dirty slums are disappearing and the new houses are built in wide, well-paved streets. Many of them have their own gardens. There are fine public parks too, where people can enjoy games and pleasant walks. (Book II, p. 121)

The pictures in this text depict both the usual scenes of back-to-back houses, with small, dark and indistinct figures making their way through puddled streets in Victorian England but also the strangest of scenes. In the foreground of one picture old dilapidated factories are shown as falling and being pulled down and behind them the still smoking chimneys of the remains of post-war British industry. But behind that, in the rural distance, glowing like the rising sun, we can see what looks very much like the public housing of a new town. In the foreground a child proclaims this new dawn with his arms out-stretched.

It is difficult now to appreciate the extent to which a particular form of post-war urban development should be seen as such a fundamental change. What has to be appreciated is that the expectations for a better Britain constructed by town planning had been building up since well before the War within such groups as the more socially aware history teachers in London and the big cities.[6] There is evidence of this, for example' in a book put together by some teachers in S.E. London as early as 1929 called *A Handbook for History Teachers* (Dymond 1929). In a course which they devised (with the help of R.H. Tawney) for a girls' school in Deptford, time was given to a consideration of the then new housing estate of Downham, 'whose houses, small though they are, allow of a personal cleanliness and privacy in sleeping arrangements unknown to the two-roomed Deptford homes' (*ibid*, p. 227).

The aims of this course were to give a climax to the pupils' historical studies in the consideration of such things as 'the housing problem'. In the project the children were asked to act as town planners themselves and to commit rows of houses to destruction and to plan new kitchens and bathrooms. 'Most of the girls', they add, 'who had heard of Mr Baldwin's Franchise Act, said that they would vote for people who would give them better homes' (p. 230).

For so many of the history textbook writers after the War, the new towns, new suburbs and housing estates heralded, not only better homes, but a complete escape for all, and an England with town and country reconciled. In celebration of a new universal suburbanization we find a writer like Turnbull describing the 'beautiful new housing estates' (Turnbull, 1953, Book 8, p. 31) and the 'practical and beautiful' new towns (*ibid*, p. 35). Wright expressed the belief that garden suburbs and garden cities could at last preserve a balance between country and town, and that such sensible planning could stop the loss of agricultural land. He even saw new towns as a means of repopulating the country (Wright, 1961, Book II, p. 43).

A.H. Hanson's *The Lives of the People* (1950) has numerous references to good and bad planners, from the Romans to Nash and Wren. His enemies are the speculative builders and his saviours the planners:

> The point is that the arts of building and town planning can now give you all these things (open spaces, proximity to the countryside, etc). For the first time in history they can now be given to *all* people and not just a favoured few. (*ibid*, p. 125)

Invitingly he addresses his young readers:

> These problems you must discuss among yourselves, for you are the ones who are going to live in the replanned Britain and it is up to you to decide what you want. (p. 125)

If, in a previous stage of national progress, the Great Fire had temporarily cleansed the City then good now also came from the evils of Hitler's bombs.

Purton in 1958, wrote

> Undoubtedly one of the best things that Hitler did for our cities was to destroy much of the slum property though it is a great tragedy that the only way slum clearance could be speeded up was with such a heavy loss of life and personal property. (Purton, 1958, p. 205)

Many histories of the 1950s end with such conclusions. *The Pilgrim Way* completes its national story in the living room of the White family, with mother praising all the new devices in her council house and comparing it with their previous home which was bombed in the war (Hume, 1953, Book II, p. 150).

Certain representations of town and country had become, within the conventions of history textbooks for children, the means of acknowledging material differences or divisions between the peoples of the nation. These material differences were, in a way, 'natural' differences; some had contact with nature itself, and fresh air to breathe. In the 1940s and 1950s those very differences and divisions came to be presented as a thing of the past. The process of suburbanization, long used as a means of social escape by the class to which both the textbook writers and the town-planners belonged, was represented in the books as a possibility for all, and even the urbanites of Deptford or Bethnal Green could, apparently, recreate the old domestic cosiness of home and garden in the estates of Essex or Hertfordshire.

Rural Locations, People and Their Ways of Life

If an essential physical feature of the representations of the original rural life was that it was undivided from nature, then it also seemed to lack other unpleasant divisions. Useful labour and a cosy, unified domesticity has been so often associated with the 'natural' conditions of our rural ancestors that the effect has been to naturalize both agricultural labour and patriarchal family forms. I want now to investigate this part of the imagery and attempt to show that history textbook writers presented urbanization as much more than a 'loss of air' and a change from agricultural occupations. It was also the loss of the natural habitat for both workers and their children, and, it would appear, the partial eclipse of both family life and community. The images suggest that country people live fundamentally different, better and more wholesome lives, and their activities have a charm and innocence rarely found in the towns. Not only that but *village* life has been presented, within the national narrative, as something essentially English, as the true home of English people. When introducing a chapter on the English village the anonymous author of *Highroads of History* began by associating 'home' with village life as follows:

The dearest word in the English language is the word 'home'.
No other language has a word which means exactly the same

thing. Whatever fortune may bring us we cannot think of home without tender thoughts.... The word 'home' carries with it the idea of a family bond. Now let us see what it has to teach us about our forefathers in the days of long age. (*Highroad*, 1911, p. 55)

By this strange evocation of the power of the word the author introduces children to old English place names and old English settlements as our ancestral homes.

The point has been made elsewhere (Barrell, 1980) that rural labour in eighteenth century English landscape painting was often 'naturalized' by being shown as just part of the physical scene. This has frequently been the case in history textbooks of this century. Rural labour, for example, has been shown as part of the very seasons themselves. Pedagogically, of course, the aim might have been to suggest the dependence of previous country people on the passing of the seasons; their nearness to the cycles of nature. But, like all naturalisms, any appreciation of the relative hardships of men and women in different classes is lost in the acceptance of activities which seem perfectly functional to the demands of the elements. The use of contemporary visual images in these books gave both a useful authenticity and suggested the blending of men, women and nature. The use of the contemporary calendars to depict seasonal labour, for example, was very common, as in Milliken's *Saxon and Viking* (1944, p. 27, 29, 31), and in the series *Men of Work* (Lay, 1951, pp. 6 and 7). Similar illustrations are also to be found in Priestley (1949, Book I, p. 48) and in Hitchcock and Hitchcock (1955, Book IV).

The business of maintaining life in Anglo-Saxon or medieval villages has been given a charm and naturalness, safely enclosed by nature, where everybody seems to perform their tasks in an easygoing way. The following description of such a village attempts to bring history alive, to make it 'real', but in a very particular sort of way:

The cowherd and the shepherd are probably lying under a tree watching the animals or sleeping. Why are the sheep and cattle so important? Down by the stream the little goose-girl is paddling as she guards the geese and ducks. Near the stream, where the ground is damp, the grass is growing tall and thick in the hay meadow, and close by you can see the watermill, with its big wheel turning round and round in the water as it grinds corn. It belongs to Sir William ... If you look further away still, beyond the fields and the cattle, you will see dark woods nearly all round the village. Somewhere under those trees the pigs are grunting as they root about for acorns. Further still inside the woods, far away in their own secret places, the wild deer hide. (Reeves and Hodgson, 1953, p. 4)

And even if the hardships are acknowledged, then, because of the chronological method adopted, the peasants' lives and labours stand in strong contrast to those of the urban industrial workers. Kelly and Stewart accept that life was not easy for the peasant (Kelly and Stewart, 1962, Book I, pp. 107–11) but at least it was a life of cheerful, shared family labour. It is clear that historical chronology and the chronological organization of mass schooling and the discourses of child development are tied together here, for by Book II of this popular series the more mature reader is given the horrors of death, starvation and cruelty of a later historical period.

Idealization of the Rural Past

This connection between the two chronologies forces a consideration of what could be called the idealization of the rural past. There are certain periods within these national narratives where English rural life has appeared *particularly* idealized, and this would appear to be based more on the ideological demands of constructing the nation's past for children than either on any historical evidence about the changing fortunes of the nation's agriculture or on a national, cultural ruralism. It will not be the task of this volume to decide whether the history textbooks were supported by academic historical research in judging some periods of agricultural history to be periods of growth or decline. Instead it is necessary to look at how country life has been both generalized and acknowledged in the texts in ways that permit comparisons with urban life, and how particular periods of rural existence have been signified. Such generalizations are, of course, bound to be problematic in their attempts to answer the imagined general questions from the notional pupil, such as: 'What was life like in Anglo-Saxon or Elizabethan England?', 'How was their work different from that of my parents?'. What is of interest here, however, are the special constructions of the past, which cannot be fully penetrated by merely suggesting that Merrie England was probably quite miserable for many people a large part of the time. The most consistently idealized period of textbook history is one of the earliest to be portrayed — that of Anglo-Saxon village life. The ideological reasons for this are, it appears, two fold. Because almost all these series of history books offer a chronological history of the nation for children of 7 to 11 or 13 years then the earlier the period, the younger the child. The text addresses a young, innocent reader who was presented with a picture of the world which was free from strife or unhappiness; a primitive, natural and homely world, with which the unformed and unsocialized subject can identify. One writer clearly indicates his reasons for thinking that the Anglo-Saxon period (and the Vikings) is somehow perfect and perfectable for young children:

> ... for young children few periods offer a more attractive blend of romantic incident and practical detail ... The simple homeliness of Anglo-Saxon life, the adventurous spirit of the Vikings, and even the crudities of both races present the child with something he can readily understand and heartily appreciate. (Milliken, 1944, Introduction)

And he goes on to present the Anglo-Saxons as the true ancestors of the addressed children — 'Many of our best types of Englishmen today have Saxon blood in their veins and are like them in character as well as appearance' (Milliken, 1944, p. 14).

So, if Anglo-Saxon life was simple and more easily understood by the young and innocent it itself was seen as a period of national and racial innocence too, when the purity of the natural English countryside provided a living for true, ORIGINAL people. 'The Saxons were our forefathers and our present names of many things to do with the land came from the Saxons' (Smith and Lay, u.d., Book IIIA, p. 25). Ambler and Coatman (1936, Book III, p. 47) asked the child-readers whether they were 'Anglo-Saxon types'. Children were frequently told of the importance of understanding the Anglo-Saxons on the grounds that they were the 'first of us'. Little, in the series *England's History* (1937) explicated this in the following way after a quote from J.R. Green:

> It will help us to understand the history of England if we try to discover what the men (sic) from North Germany who settled in England were really like. They were fierce and bitter fighters, and were also brave and proud, but we shall get a wrong idea of these people if we learn no more about them, for they had many fine and noble qualities ... These men were homelovers ... These Englishmen, though warlike, were

really farmers. When they had fought and secured land for their families they delighted to work it. They were no townsmen; they did not wish to dwell in cities, but liked to plough, sow, reap, look after cattle and do all a farmer's work. It was their hatred of towns which made them destroy many Roman buildings. (*ibid*, pp. 36–7)

Similarly, child-readers were invited into the English family with the following passage in the series appropriately called *The House of History* (1931):

> We Angles or English are a mixed people. We inherit something from the earliest civilized people who lived in Britain — the Celts. But our blood and our institutions are very largely Saxon, and the Saxons were lovers of the open air and the country. (Book I, p. 10)

It is interesting to note that the more recent humanistic texts seem happy to take their idealizations back to the life of the cave people. Kelly and Stewart (Book I, 1962) give us an idyllic picture of peaceful life in pre-history, with the domesticity of the cave not too incongruent with that of Dunroamin, complete with its perfect sex-stereotyping (*ibid*, pp. 7–8). For the less than humanistic writers, however, concerned narrowly with the racial aspects of our national origin, cavemen and the Ancient Britons were regarded with some suspicion. As a result the Anglo-Saxon village has been given to children as the site of an original life of plenty, the ancestral home and the English Garden of Eden.

Perhaps the most perfect example of this particular construction is to be found in the *Homeland Histories* by William Claxton (1949). In Book I the racial origins are established in a chapter called 'The Ploughmen Arrive' with reference to what good farmers the Aryans were (*ibid*, pp. 44–5). But early peoples are regarded as too similar to contemporary primitives to be made into the true forefathers of England (*ibid*, p. 63). This part is given to the Saxons, at least one of whose characteristics, their love of the countryside, is taken as highly significant by this and other writers, and is seen as distinguishing them from the Romans:

> We read how the Romans were lovers of towns. The Saxons could not bear to dwell in towns. Many village people of today say that they could not possibly live in towns such as London, Liverpool and so on. They like the wide open spaces;

they love to hear the songs of the birds; to smell the wild
flowers; to see the farmer at his work . . .
So it was with the Saxons. They belonged to a race of
people who were bold, strong and fierce. They would never
live in a walled city. (*ibid*, p. 14)[7]

There follows a very full description of village life and the activities of
the Saxon farmer, using adaptations of early pictures of ploughing,
sowing and harvest time to show a happy rural past. Village life of the
time is called 'one big help-one-another society' (Book II, p. 39) with
independent farmers giving a hand to their neighbours in the business
of ploughing and gathering in the crops. It was also a truly democratic
society — 'the Saxon plan was to work from the bottom upwards',
(p. 102) and quite unlike the Norman system which replaced it.[8]
George Guest, a writer of textbooks for children, developed this
contrast in a WEA book for post-World War I agricultural workers
(Guest, 1920). For him Anglo-Saxon communities worked together,
but by degrees, king, noble and priest exercised increased control over
the mass of inhabitants (p. 13).

Indeed, in Claxton's account of historical change, things were
never quite the same again. His Book III on the Middle Ages includes
reference to rural poverty. The houses then were 'mean, dirty hovels,
quite unfit for human beings to occupy' (*ibid*, p. 95), and later he
shows a full appreciation of the conditions of the rural work-force in
the nineteenth century. Only at the end of the story does the condition
of rural people seem to receive the same idealizing treatment as that
given to the Anglo-Saxons. In Book IV (Age of Science) he devotes a
whole chapter to the Small-holdings and Allotments Acts which, it
would appear, were about to usher in a new rural paradise. Of the
Allotments Act Claxton writes: 'The peasant's wife would not have to
pay so much of her husband's wages away to the local greengrocer
and they would be more independent' (*ibid*, p. 73). Earlier in the series
(Book III, chapter 11) he had already indicated what he thought of the
conditions of the contemporary agricultural worker:

They get along quite comfortably. Most of them live in nice
little cottages which have large gardens where they grow
nearly all the vegetables they need. (*ibid*, p. 103)

Clearly enough the tied cottages had yet to be perceived as a problem.
The social classes were accepted as the way *we* divide *our* society, and
were no longer seen as constituting a problem as they had in Norman
times, when the Anglo-Saxon Community was cruelly replaced.

'Nowadays we divide our people into three main classes — the upper, middle and lower classes. There is no clear division between these classes' (*ibid*, Book II, p. 103).

It should be admitted that this series by Claxton was specifically written for rural children. It was intended to answer the calls made by teachers in rural schools in the 1930s for school books which would deal with village life. This might explain the relative concentration on country matters and it may also explain how Claxton was able to be quite realistic about the periods of rural life between Anglo-Saxon England and contemporary rural conditions. He wanted to indicate the *improvement* in the lives of rural people for whom his book was intended. To other writers this was perhaps not quite so necessary. They could keep alive, for their mainly urban and suburban readers, the general, continuing soundness of the nation's rural roots. Thus, along with the conventional, favourable picture of the Anglo-Saxon period, non-industrial and non-urban life could be idealized *in general*, with just one or two breaks (viz, chapter IV).

Even against the general idealization of rural existence the particular appreciation of Anglo-Saxon life has been persistently outstanding during this century, but it was not always so. By contrast earlier writers of history for children had, perhaps, different illusions. Miss Corner (1851, p. 19) had recognized the Saxons as 'our ancestors' but thought them lacking in civilization and cruel. Before the respect for the primitive and an interest in racial origins combined to re-present them, Victorian textbook writers frequently used the adjective 'rude' to describe the Saxon way of life, and they were unfavourably compared to the Romans and Normans. The author of *Chambers History of England* (1901) admitted that, 'our forefathers gave no promise in those days that the British would in course of time become the foremost trading people on the face of the globe' (p. 42). Ransome (1896) and Morgan (1880) strongly disapproved of the Saxon destruction and neglect of Roman towns. The following quote, with its concern for the continuity of urban civilization, contrasts strongly with the way the later texts dealt with this episode:

> They did not even preserve the beautiful city of Bath, for it is known that a wild duck built her nest in one of the Roman baths. Chester, too, perished utterly. It was only some of the larger towns, as London and York, which managed to preserve a continuous life, and by degrees, as the English became more civilized, a taste for town life sprang up ... (Ransome, 4th ed, 1896)

It would appear that the special respect for the Anglo-Saxons began at the turn of the century, and developed steadily. Archer (1896) and Tout (1902) shared the view that, as the latter put it,

> Though life was rude there was plenty of meat and bread, ale and mead and our ancestors loved feasting and good cheer. (p. 52)

In time, as the adjective 'rude' changed its common meaning and the belief emerged that it was appropriate for children to have a knowledge of and feeling for natural, simple lives, then the images of Anglo-Saxon life became more and more positive (viz Warner, 1912; Hounsell and Hilton, u.d. 1920; and Lay 1951) culminating in what was, perhaps, the most influential of the post-war series where Unstead portrays Anglo-Saxon home life as a family camping holiday (Unstead, 1953, Book I, p. 43). The story of the Anglo-Saxons, their love of country and home life, their quiet existence in the midst of a generous English landscape, their original racial purity and their great King came to occupy a very special position in English children's history. The parallel with the genetic myths of people, which these writers would regard as primitive, cannot be avoided.

But one interesting and partial exception should be mentioned, however. Even if the Anglo-Saxons held a special place in these histories, textbook writers with an interest in racial origins have sometimes told English children that their origins are mixed, and that they have inherited some aspect of their national character from such a mixture. Gasquet (1902–3) for example, in a section called 'Origin of the Normans' (Book II) expounded a theory that their particular combination of 'French manners' and robust sea-faring spirit helped in the construction of the English. It was Fletcher and Kipling's *A School History of England* (1911) — a bloodthirsty, nationalistic book — which developed such a thesis to an extreme. It turned to the Anglo-Saxons as the source of the nation's fearlessness, but saw them also in need of considerable discipline:

> The Saxon Englishman was a savage, with the vices and cruelties of an overgrown boy; a drunkard and a gambler, and very stupid. (*ibid*, p. 28)

If they loved freedom, 'it is possible to have too much freedom' (*ibid*, p. 31). If they had rights, they 'often talked a lot of nonsense about them' (*ibid*, p. 28).

The authors followed this outburst with one of Kipling's poems which made the point that without Norman discipline the Anglo-Saxons were but spoiled children —

England's on the anvil hear the hammers ring—
Clanging from the Severn to the Tyne!
Never was a blacksmith like our Norman King —
England's being hammered, hammered, hammered into line.
(*ibid*, p. 46)

To these imperialists Anglo-Saxon childishness was like that of other nations who needed a hard, matured country to discipline them, just as the Normans had disciplined us.

In the construction of national identity within this text an imperial, historical narrative may have to find an original racial ferocity rather than peaceful, communal, agrarian roots. But this does not mean that it surrenders the image of England as a rural paradise worth fighting for. Fletcher and Kipling give a somewhat dismissive description of the agricultural life of the Saxons — 'Tilling the fields was the Saxon's real job; he was a plough-boy and a cow-boy by nature ...' (p. 31) — far too much like those people in need of British protection. All the same the book ends with that typical view of England as a garden, quoting Kipling's poem that begins: 'Our England is a garden that is full of stately views ...' and ends:

So when your work is finished, you can wash your hands and pray
For the glory of the garden that it may not pass away!
And the glory of the garden it shall never pass away!

Yet if the more general idealizations of Anglo-Saxon labour can be seen as occupying a particular place in the conventions of the national narrative because of their occurrence within the chronologies of nation and child, then some other periods of pre-industrial rural life have also received very favourable treatment. Day to day feudal England, described in the first or second book of history textbook readers, or visually represented as in the series of pictures published by Wheaton (Elliot and Hartley, n.d.) has often been portrayed with great affection, though the lack of freedom has bothered some writers. (Anglo-Saxon slavery was more often forgotten.) Priestley's text (1952) preserved some illusions about feudalism yet indicated the later freedoms of being a wage labourer. This produced some difficulties of expression, as in the following:

Thus many of the villeins although almost unfree and often

> not allowed to leave their village, were quite prosperous.
> (Priestley, 1952, p. 93)

As these are mainly histories of the English people which culminate in their twentieth century freedoms of wage labour, parliamentary democracy and, in the case of the later texts, the planned welfare state, then feudal England has to be acknowledged as having drawbacks. Once national and racial origins have been established the story of national progress can accept its shortcomings in order that contrasts may be made with the present. In *Newnes Narrative Histories*, where the first series is devoted to 'The Story of Our People' and tells of their increasing power, feudalism as a system can be portrayed as a questionable contract between king and thanes:

> ... so they protected the king and the king protected them, and the man who really paid the price was the man who ploughed the soil and reaped the crops. (Harland, 1951, p. 128)

On the other hand Englishmen had some control of their land and this appeared as a positive feature (for example, Wood, 1939, Book 2, p. 16). Spalding and Wragg in Book V of the *Piers Plowman* series conjured up the usual set of comfortable domestic images of village life with its combination of the labours of woodcutter, swineherd and shepherd, and they acknowledged possession:

> We can see the farmers at work on the hay, each cutting his own little patch. (*ibid*, p. 5)

As shall be shown later in a section on the enclosures, although the balance in these books is clearly in favour of the national gains made in the freedom of wage labour and the efficiency of agriculture, the losses of dispossession could never be completely excluded from such problematic narratives.

But besides the serious issues of feudal possession much is also made of the innocent fun of simple people, enjoying themselves around the maypole, collecting primroses and violets, or feasting at Christmas. These activities are especially represented in the descriptions of the later period of 'Merrie England' which, in one or two texts, challenge Anglo-Saxon England as the time when the nation was together in peaceful, rural community (viz Power, u.d., Book I; Priestley, 1952, Book II; and Spalding and Wragg, 1914, Book V). The latter construct the scene thus:

Village life was a happy life when Charles I became King, for folks were friendly with each other. On summer evenings the women sat spinning at the cottage doors and the men sat on the long benches outside the alehouse and talked about the crops. The young men and boys wrestled and leaped, and played many quaint old games; or boys and girls sang the old country songs and danced the old country dances together on the green. (Spalding and Wragg, 1914, Book V, p. 89)

In other areas of the curriculum too, teachers tried to re-create this world. In music, until the 1950s, much class teaching centred around the contents of Sharp and Baring-Gould's *English Folk Songs for Schools*. Country dancing spread too, encouraged originally perhaps by Ruskin at Whitelands College, where he presented the prize to the student teacher May Queen, (Marsh, 1982, p. 12), and many old dusty spinning wheels and looms in craft cupboards testify to educators' earlier fascination for the peasants' crafts.

Notes

1 The notion of a 'national past' is being used in the sense expounded by Patrick Wright (Wright, 1984, pp. 46–55). The ideas in this volume on 'national narrative' etc. suggest the distinction between 'history' as an enterprise concerned with the investigations of evidence, the discourses of academics, and 'the past' as described in this reference.
2 A number of texts saw agricultural improvements helping the nation in the Napoleonic Wars and ultimately in World War 2, and British industrial strength similarly coming to the aid of its people.
3 W.C.J. Field, in *From Serf to Citizen*, presented national history as the history of a family business, built up by 'our forefathers', and he warned that 'the fine results won by the fathers in the past may be ruined by the sons who have taken on the work' (Ward, 1940).
4 The point is made in an evocative way in Paul Harrison's (1983) *Inside the Inner City*, pp. 26–7.
5 Annabel Williams-Ellis was the wife of Clough Williams-Ellis, the builder of Portmeiron. They had cooperated in producing *The Pleasures of Architecture* in 1924, and eight years before the publication of this textbook Clough Williams-Ellis had written a major critique of suburban architecture and a patronizing attack on those satisfied with it—'mean and perkey little houses that surely none but mean and perkey little souls should inhabit with satisfaction' (quoted in *Dunroamin* by P. Oliver, I. Davis and I. Bentley, pp. 34–5, from 'England and the Octopus'). He blamed the greedy builders and the values of ordinary people for the threat to the landscape of Old England.

6   A belief in the beneficial effects of town planning as an antidote to
    laissez-faire individualism went back to late Victorian and Edwardian
    social thinkers and was informed by a critique of 'muddle' (Waller, 1983,
    p. 127). Our interest here is when and how it was taken up by history
    textbook writers.

7   Contrary to all the evidence there has existed a common belief in both
    academic and popular history that there was a gap between Roman
    urbanism and the first Norman boroughs. Decaying and deserted Roman
    towns are shown in many textbooks. A relatively sophisticated history of
    urban life, *Town Life Through the Ages* by R.W. Morris in the series
    Understanding the Modern World (Allen and Unwin, 1952, 1961), for exam-
    ple, has a chapter called 'The Town in Ruins' and a picture of Saxon
    neglect, whereas the Norman town is busy and well established. For
    discussion of this view of Anglo-Saxon towns viz Loyn (1971) p. 115.

8   A full account of the development in nineteenth century historical study
    of the Anglo-Saxon 'ancestral myth' is given by Michael Banton in *The
    Idea of Race* (Tavistock, London, 1977) especially in relation to the notion
    of the 'Norman Yoke'.

4   *The National Narrative and Realism*

If there were periods of history which have been prone to an excessive idealization for the purposes of constructing national identity, there were also periods and events in the rural past which caused great problems for these narratives. Factors which are both internal and external to the texts have to be considered in an analysis of the representations of the national, rural past. The idealized representations of some eras which have been outlined can be partially understood as the celebration of the following aspects of English, if not British nationality: a togetherness of blood; a shared existence on the nation's soil; an originating and sustaining rural life. This might account for the series of images in terms of an externally derived ideological purpose — the construction of national identity — but tends to ignore the particular narrative form of the historical texts studied, the internal necessities and effects. The question of continuity is important from both the point of view of a requirement to show an unbroken chain of national integrity[1] as well as the requirements of narrative.

To the extent that English country life has been seen as honest and wholesome and one with the English land, then establishing its *continuity* has been attempted by these texts. The English village has been used to represent that necessary timelessness and has occupied an important place in national imagery, especially in times of trouble, as, for example, in British propaganda films during World War 2. As far as history textbooks are concerned we can find explicit references to this continuity. In Book II of *Marten and Carter's Histories* (in its 27th impression in 1957) the point is well made when describing the arrival of the Normans:

> No doubt when the Saxon villages had to change their old
> Saxon lords for their new Norman lords they grumbled a

good deal. But perhaps our village has changed less than anything else in our history, and many a village has a long history. (p. 41)

Perhaps the most effective illustration of the idea was given in a book written by Grant Uden, a lecturer at Alnwick Training College. The text, entitled *Farm History*, traced English agriculture back to the Saxons and began with the following verses:

> So runs the tale; and still shall run
> A thing of tears and mirth,
> While one thing stands immutable,
> The strength of English earth.
> So shall it run; what e'er the sun
> Of triumph and of pain;
> For when the last tall tower has crashed
> Still shall the Land remain. (Uden, 1946, p. 1)

The whole book represented to its readers the continuity of farms, farming and the land through the nation's past. It was even suggested that there was a 'strange similarity' between the faces of a group of farm workers photographed in the 1940s and those of two ploughmen in a fourteenth century illuminated manuscript (*ibid*, p. 36).

Thus, when history takes strict narrative form, and when rural life is admired because it represents English roots and national continuity, then evident setbacks in the lives of English rural people can be incorporated within the narrative as self-contained events. But there is no easy way in which these texts can fulfil two contradictory ideological ends, of portraying national progress as well as national continuity, and at the same time justify the title of history. Two areas where these contradictions become explicit are in their accounts of the Peasants' Revolt and of the enclosures.

The Peasants' Revolt

It has already been suggested that the town, the country and the people occurred together in the history books, and that the latter were seen merely as living essentially domestic lives in the different landscapes. The Peasants' Revolt is significant because it has often been the only event in these texts for younger children which has allowed in the people — the country people at that — as actors in general.[2] That they were organized in conflict against authority and not enjoying the lord's Christmas hospitality, or quietly working in the fields, makes the event an intriguing one in the structure of the narrative of national continuity and progress.

Most of the books follow the simple but now considered mistaken view that the rebels were just serfs and bondmen, and they tend to see it as only a country affair.[3] Perhaps the idealization of the togetherness of rural life made the writers unable to accept the persistent conflicts and struggles in the villages between payers and receivers of rent, the continual antipathy towards labour services and the variety of fines and duties implicit in those particular forms of exploitation. If a long-term view is taken in the texts it is the lack of freedom (by which the authors mean freedom to be wage labourers) which is used to explain the stirrings of English countrymen, and this struggle remained unrelated to the long economic one against all the seigneurial levies on peasant production. It may be worth noting that in only one book did I find any reservations about the freedom to sell labour when discussing the Peasants' Revolt. Williams, Ellis and Fisher (1936) wrote that,

> Some who became simple labourers either in the town or the country found themselves up against the problem that always faces men who work for wages. They had to struggle hard to keep their wages high enough to buy them a living. (Vol. 2, p. 98)

In general the Revolt is accounted for by relatively isolated events and individuals' leadership; the poll tax is most often seen as the cause of the uprising and Wat Tyler is given much attention in all the books, as is John Ball. The point is that one need not deny to children that taxation and these individuals played significant parts in the Revolt but the textbooks' accounts tend to isolate the uprising in a sea of rural tranquillity. Perhaps it was because they saw the rebels as country Englishmen that we find surprisingly little criticism of these peasants in revolt. Even an early text like Meicklejohn's *A New History of England and Great Britain* (1901), praises the rebels because 'with sterling English honesty' they did not plunder! (p. 200)

Once the details of the march on London, the meeting with the king, and the death of Tyler have been recounted, numerous attempts are made to save the event for the nation and incorporate it into national progress, in spite of what must seem to many children as treachery by the monarch. In the summing up of the event it is suggested that the lords learnt that they could not treat the peasants as harshly as they had in the past, and with the inevitable increase in Englishmen's freedom, all would be well. The following are examples

of how the Peasants' Revolt has been taken into the national narrative
and show a remarkable consistency throughout the twentieth century:

> The lords of the villeins gradually found out that it was hardly
> worth the trouble for them to exact forced labour from their
> serfs, and that the work was done better by free men paid a
> reasonable wage. (Tout, 1st pub. 1902, this edn 1915, p. 153).

> But although the rebellion had failed, it did good, because it
> showed the landlords that they must treat the peasants fairly.
> Before many years had passed most villagers were rent-paying
> farmers. (Lay, 1915, Book I, p. 116)

> So the peasants seemed to have failed in getting what they
> wanted. But they had shown that they could be dangerous,
> and this taught the lords to treat them more carefully. (Elliot,
> 1937, p. 114)

> This revolt had not made the peasants free, but it had made the
> lords think. Little by little they began to find that the men
> who were not free often ran away, or worked badly, so as
> time passed they set them free of their own will. (Power, u.d.,
> Book III, p. 15)

> The lords, however, remembered Wat Tyler and the Peasants'
> Revolt. Poor men were better treated than before. In time all
> the villeins became free men. (Milne, 1959, Book II, p. 28)

In fact, rural resistance continued and may well have frustrated
attempts to further exploit the peasantry with the Statute of Cambridge, seven years later, which proved ineffective. It may not be
entirely fanciful to suggest another continuity — the continuing relative poverty of the agricultural worker may not be completely unrelated to the defeat in 1381.

The Enclosures

At least at the end of the Peasants' Revolt the English peasantry could
be seen as returning to their villages where they may enjoy the
gradual improvements which might come to them, and patiently wait
for freedom. In the case of the enclosures, however, the standard
narrative form, combined with the general ideological purpose, produces a number of special difficulties. Given their idealization of
certain periods of history and certain rural conditions, how could
these texts accommodate good English country folk to a movement

which they presented as both dispossessing them and propelling them into the evils of the town?

There can be found in the structure of these narratives numerous irreconcilable conflicts and contrary beliefs. First, enclosures appeared as good for the nation as a whole, but they distanced from the land those very people who have been used to represent the essence of Englishness — the country men and women, the yeomen, the small independent farmers. Second, it was difficult for the writers to avoid seeing the enclosures as the result of greed, and yet the farmers, and the agriculture which succeeded, had to be kept in high esteem as both the vestigial bearers of our national character and the source of security in times of war. Third, country-born virtues and physique have traditionally been seen as vital to the nation's health and vigour and could be used in its industry after enclosure, but they were also *used up* by urban life and labour (viz. the earlier section on 'country air'). Fourth, history textbook writers have sometimes shared in the English literary rural retrospect; in the *Piers Plowman Histories*, for example, the chapter on enclosures ends with lines from Oliver Goldsmith (Spalding and Wragg, 1914), but as many have been tempted by notions of invention, discovery, speed and a general modernity.

To overcome these difficulties the texts have set alongside harrowing stories of the ruin of simple country people's lives various attempts to justify the enclosures as part of a necessary national progress. This is accomplished chiefly by suggesting that even if the rural past was socially preferable it was economically inefficient.

Many writers tried to draw the attention of their young readers to the difficulties of the open fields and the related social relations as a preparation for their demise, and they did it with the morality of traditional school teachers. In a way the apparent problems of such a system were made realistic to the child-reader by oblique reference to the problems of school children in an imperfectly ordered classroom. Birnie, for example (1937, Book VI), who had written of the community of labour within previous rural villages, pointed out that, 'the ignorant farmer held back those who were more intelligent' (p. 18) — a very school-based fear — but then added that, 'it must always be a matter for regret that the old English peasantry were destroyed in the eighteenth century' (p. 19). Similarly Ambler and Coatman (1936) justified enclosures in the eyes of a diligent pupil reading the text:

Suppose you were one of those small farmers of 200 years ago ... When you wanted to plough your land you had to walk from A field to B field, then to C field. This was very

troublesome and a great waste of time. If your neighbour was
a lazy man and did not weed his patch some of his thistle seeds
would be blown onto your strip and spoil your crop. (Book
IV, pp. 88–9)

Burbridge (u.d.) thought the old open system inhibited initiative
(p. 27). Marten and Carter (u.d.) were almost unreserved in their
appreciation of enclosures for the way they enabled Britain to feed its
growing population in the Napoleonic Wars and, subsequently, in
World War I (Book IV, pp. 66–7).

'Why did the enclosures take place?', they ask, and provide the
standard reply:

Largely because the old system was so wasteful and unsatisfactory, and the new processes of farming, described in the next
chapter, were difficult, if not impossible, under the old conditions. A man, for instance, wasted much time in going from
one to another of his many scattered strips. Then there was the
great difficulty of draining such land, and if his neighbour
were an idle farmer the seeds of the neighbour's weeds would
blow freely over and spoil his clean plot. (*ibid*, pp. 67–8)

They acknowledge the difficulties of the dispossesed (*ibid*, p. 70) but
conclude that 'Perhaps the worst that can be said is that the enclosures
were made too rapidly' (*ibid*, p. 71) and they proceed to tell the story
of Turnip Townsend and Squire Coke.

If progress could not be held back, if it was accepted that the
national good was served by these changes, and if the old system
could be seen as frustrating the hardworking individual, then the
textbook writers could not forget one particular loss. For so many of
the writers referred to here to figure on which they focused their
attention and sympathy was that of the *yeoman*. This representative of
both a middle class sort of independence, and of sound, English, rural
ways suddenly became, in the national story, a tragic hero. The nature
and substance of these writers' regrets about the enclosures and subsequent industrialization cannot be properly understood without considering their views of this figure. History book writers had generally
idealized his homely, honest life.

For Lay the yeomen 'were the men who produced the best
soldiers and who were always patriotic' (Lay, 1915, Book IV, p. 83).
Writing about the yeoman in Stuart England Priestley (1952) established him as a national character, yet doomed:

He is the man on whom the wealth and life of the country depends. He has risen to a place of honour in the reign of Elizabeth, and he will keep his place until the smoke of the factory and the mine comes to deprive him of it. His very name calls to mind all the qualities of steadfastness, thrift, bravery, honesty and plain speaking which we like to think are part of the English character. He is the fount of England's prosperity because he works the land as a freeman. (Book III, p. 12)

Only much later does a new kind of 'middle England' hero emerge in Priestley's narrative and he is depicted at the end of Book IV as 'The Little Man' of Strube's Second World War cartoon in the *Daily Express*. This new hero was a meek man, who, after bravery in the First World War, 'settled down in a little home with a homely wife and brought up his family. He went to business every day ...' (*ibid*, pp. 132–3), only to serve his country again in 1940. For Spalding (1921), following Macaulay perhaps, the yeoman had played a vital role in holding the middle ground in old England, and it was the enclosures which made the crucial change in English history. They ushered in a harsher, more divided society, where the rich lost contact with the poor (Book 6, p. 24) and the latter started to agitate for equality.

These pages are an intriguing piece of rural retrospect. To some readers this might seem like an essentially petty bourgeois critique of industrial, capitalist society's decline into two warring classes and its longing for a return to the times when middle, independent people held things together,[4] yet Spalding's account of the loss and separation, for yeoman and labourer, which were seen to be caused by the enclosures, was quite effective (Spalding, 1921, pp. 58–63). 'This calamity', Spalding wrote, 'coming at the very time when the factories were killing out cottage spinning, destroyed the independence of the labourers. Who can tell what suffering ensued in the little cottages of rural England?' (*ibid*, p. 60).

Finally, should any child come to think that enclosure and dispossession was unjustifiable, Elliot (1937) reminds her reader that even a national and class hero has to bow before the laws of private property. The following well expresses some of the conflicts to be found in these national narratives:

Perhaps the saddest result of 'enclosures' was the gradual disappearance of the English 'yeoman' farmer, so typical of old

England. Until now he had managed well on his little bit of land but it was taken to make part of a large farm, and the yeoman then became a worker for someone else, and was no longer independent or free.

But we have to remember two things. First of all, the squire had a perfect *right* to do this enclosing if he wanted to, since the land belonged by law to him, and it was only old *custom* that had given the villagers leave to use the common ground and rent their strips of land from him. Secondly, and more important, although enclosure brought misery to many at first, in the end it made enormous improvements. (p. 186)

The analysis of the place given to enclosure and dispossession and the tragic hero, the yeoman, produces some acute problems for this analysis. At one level it could be taken as an unmediated expression of the class origins or class location of the textbook writers and an ambivalent petty-bourgeois understanding of national progress, marred by the loss of small property and apparent independence. This interpretation, however, would be mistaken on two counts. First, it fails to appreciate that the idealization of the life of the small producer has been shared by a wider class grouping (Thompson, 1968, chapter 16). The ways in which the enclosures are described may also be seen as related to both utopian socialism's belief in the freer peasant society, and its own idealizations of the past. As Corner (1985) notes about the late nineteenth century 'people's history':

> Ironically this foundation produced not studies of industrial society or of the tensions of nineteenth century capitalist development, but works which tended to an idealization of the past. The central point of focus was that moment when the 'people' were assumed to have lost their independence — with enclosures — and the peasant and the artisan played the major role in these histories. (p. 95)

Second, and more importantly for this book, this attribution overlooks some important internal, textual and metaphorical issues and the way the episode relates to the whole narrative of a national people in and of 'their' *land*. Expressions such as 'this land of ours' show up the dual meanings and references; land as soil (the raw material of earlier agriculture) and land, the bounded territory of the nation (what one might call the raw material of nationalism). Thus, in these particular texts, the tragic episode of rural dispossession can signify the (temporary) absence of the people from their birthright — a necessary tension within the story — and is only partially understood as expressing an external economic condition. The resolution of these difficulties in a 'property-owning democracy' may well be accommodating to the economic interests of the petty-bourgeoisie but is also a satisfying textual outcome for the readers of various class origins, which may make for contradictory locations of the self, i.e. of the city, without property, yet English.

Rural Life in Different Histories

To academic historians these children's national narratives must appear somewhat absurd in the way they simplify, exaggerate and telescope the long and complex processes of enclosure and agricultural change. Capitalist agriculture had been steadily growing alongside, and interconnected with, urban and non-urban manufacture, and continually placing small cultivators at risk. For Hobsbawm and Rude (1970) these enclosures were but a special case of a more general development (p. 36). For these texts they were a sudden intervention which they use to highlight the passing of old rural England, and to indicate clearly the decline into urban-industrial life for the ordinary people, of whom, for them, the yeoman was the most significant. Having represented a whole economic system and way of life by pictures of a simple landscape with figures, the village and the three fields with their natural labour, then the enclosures were constructed in the same mode — something happened to the countryside, and the balance of nature was upset. It is perhaps worth requoting from Williams (1975):

> ... there is a sense in which the idea of the enclosures, local-ized to just that period in which the Industrial Revolution was beginning, can shift our attention from the real history and become an element of that very powerful myth of modern England in which the transition from a rural to an industrial society is seen as a kind of fall, the true cause and origin of our social suffering and disorder. It is difficult to overestimate the importance of this myth in modern social thought. (p. 121)

But the books being examined here are not part of the English literary tradition, and nor are they books for historians. If one was intent on correcting historical error, on expanding the 'real history', then an analysis of school books would be an odd way of going about it. One's interest is in what it has been thought sensible to tell children about the past, and how it was told, so it is, therefore, necessary to be clear exactly what one's reactions are to what has been described in the previous sections as the idealizations of the rural past, and to the particular forms of pedagogical simplification used.

First, not all history books for children over the last 100 years follow what has been called the conventions of rural representation. Not exactly *all* books have idealized rural life, nor has it been only rural locations which have received such treatment. In the following section, for example, we note an almost universal admiration for the medieval guilds in their urban settings. It has been when the books depict 'the English people' as a whole, especially within a series of books taking a chronological, narrative form, that we find the consistent idealizations. The occasional school books which attempted a *world* history, for example, Higham's *Landmarks of World History* (Higham, u.d.) did not appear to depend upon such idealizations, associating civilization with the town. 'When we talk about "civilization"', he wrote, 'we are using an old word which means "living in cities". It was when men learnt to live together in large numbers that they became "civilized". For each man could do one thing and do it well' (*ibid*, pp. 9–10). In fact, very occasionally, when concepts like 'the *common* people' are used, we find them being seen as born of a long period of exploitation, rural and urban. Thus Hanson's post-Second World War celebration of better times for ordinary men and women was quite lacking in any idealization of the Anglo-Saxons. Not only was it seen as a period of decline in general, compared to the Roman period, but,

> for hundreds of years, while the houses of the rich were gradually becoming more civilized, the poor peasant farmer still went on living in his dirty, uncomfortable home. (Hanson, 1950, Book I, p. 103)

We have already mentioned Williams, Ellis and Fisher's break with the conventional view of the freedom that wage labour brought (1936). They also attempted some account of the relative riches of the different classes of the people of England in their text viz. the illustration on p. 125 of vol. 3, for example. In the illustration the burden of the rural labourer is very clear. Birnie (1937), too, appreciated the plight of the agricultural labourer (Book 6, pp. 76–8).

Other forms of history textbooks do seem to more readily allow variations in the 'reality' of lives as lived, and this is no doubt why there have been attempts to move the teaching of history away from the long chronologies. Later books which attempt either a history of the different ways of satisfying a human need or which attempt to give children some extended insight into life in one particular period, even when it is that of the Anglo-Saxons, have been promoted because they have been thought to be more 'realistic'. *The Earliest English*, by Cramp and Gummer (1963), makes a rare attempt at suggesting, for example, the fears as well as the hardships of the life of those people:

> Their lives were hard. There was always the dread of sickness, robbers and wild beasts, for bears, wolves and wild boars still roamed England then, and the people feared nameless monsters who might lurk in the forests and in the lakes. (p. 15)

And in their section on 'Life in the Village' the conditions of those of different status are well appreciated. When combined with a concern for the evidence of documents or archaeology then young children can be shown previous life in depth and yet with an uncondescending simplicity. It would appear that the beginning of the 1960s was a turning point in the pursuit of a new form of realism and coincided with a move from history 'readers' in series to history books as resources. Books like John Hamilton's *Saxon People* (1964), for example, contained strong, down to earth drawings by Alan Sorrell, emphasizing labour and 'life in the raw'. It is worth noting, however, that one aspect of the 'history from evidence' approach does not guarantee an escape from the images we have been examining. There had been various attempts to use illustrations contemporary with the period being described to bring a certain realism to the texts and teaching. In the mid-1950s the Historical Association published a series, *English History in Pictures*, which included *The Late Middle Ages* edited by Margaret Sharp (Sharp, 1955) which provided teachers with reproductions of original pictures, of which The Hunting Scene from Queen Mary's Psalter, and Ladies Travelling, from The Luttrell Psalter have been inserted in more than one textbook. At this time too the *Then and There Series* (Reeves and Hogson, 1953) was promoting the 'patch' approach and the importance of evidence and records, yet, itself, produced the most outstanding idealizations of the medieval village. The use of such contemporary illustrations was not new, having been attempted in, for example, Titterton's *From Romans to Normans* (1931), where much was made of history as a *true* story, faithfulness to facts, etc. Indeed one might say that the introduction of contemporary sources in these texts-in-use could serve to make real to children in twentieth century classrooms the illusions of the ages being studied. The *Macmillan History Picture Books* (1958) and the sets of large history wall pictures so popular in schools in the 1950s and 60s used, for example, scenes from the Duc du Berry's calendar to depict rural labour. It thus guaranteed that village life, even in the depths of winter, would seem, to both the Duc and the twentieth century child-reader, idyllic. (One of the strangest of realist techniques used in these texts was the photographing of models, as, for example, those found in the British Museum during the pre- and immediate post-War period, viz. *Life in Early Days* by Elizabeth Frazer (1932).[5])

The simple reversal of idealization is equally problematic; the so-called 'gloom and doom' history. The reaction of presenting the life of earlier people as one of relentless misery and poverty must also be rejected for at any time in history 'the people' have led a wider range of lives than that, in country and town. Rather, the central questions asked of the texts in this study are based on the following observations; that the locations of the people's lives do not necessarily dictate the happiness or otherwise of those lives; the idealizing of previous rural existences quite unnecessarily homogenizes for children the people and their existences in a protective, cautious and often sentimental retrospect. Social history can only proceed on generalization, and history for young children can only go so far in the particulars that it presents to them, but it is the kinds of simplified images which are so significant in the conventions of English history textbooks, and their places in the series of episodes of national chronology. English people in rural conditions have been seen as just figures, 'figures in a landscape', which serve, not themselves, or history, but as representatives of the original people of our nation. They are rarely seen as groups of people in relation to other people, but only to the land and nature. Often they are not even men or women, for whom, for example, the enclosures had quite different effects (viz. Hartmen, 1976, p. 49). It could be said that 'town' and 'country' are the ultimate homogenizations in these narratives, and, until the post-War social democratic reconstruction, have had to bear all the burdens for national difference and division. 'Rural idealizations', such as they regularly occurred within these texts, must be seen, therefore, not only against the findings of the discourses of academic research (which are not unimportant) but also in terms of *where* they occur in the national narratives, both for some ideological effects and because of the assumed nature of the child-readers who were to use the texts within a chronologically organized school system. This makes it very difficult to sustain a view of such representations of rural life as expressions of a national culture.

Towns Emerge — No Place for the Children

Finally, when and how have towns been mentioned in these texts, and how has urbanization been presented to the child readers? Quite strict conventions seem to have governed both the periods in which urban life has been shown and the activities which urban inhabitants have pursued.

In some books we have found that the distinctions between urban and rural are accentuated by there being separate chapters on 'town people' and 'country people' (Elliot, 1937, Book I; *Blackie's*, 1935, Book III), or by describing 'townsfolk' and 'countryfolk' (Power, u.d., Book III). In the portrayal of town life, London, for all its peculiarities, predominates as the representative city, just as it had done in the previous century's children's books (Whalley, 1974, p. 94).

In the representations of pre-industrial urban existence Roman towns do get some reference made to them, although in the more radically nationalistic books between 1900 and 1930 they are seen as foreign, and were best left alone by our Anglo-Saxon forefathers.

But because they were, at least, *planned* towns, then some writers in the post-war period do refer to them positively as such.

J.A. Thomas, in Book II of the series, *Real History* (1962) saw them as the forerunners of the new towns:

> ... the Romans were better builders than the Britons. Their carefully planned towns were neat and tidy and they were cleaner and more comfortable to live in. (p. 22)

Hanson (1950) held up the Roman, along with contemporary Scandinavian and Russian, towns as examples to the muddling English (p. 125).

In the general textbooks of national history town life gets mentioned next in descriptions of life in medieval England. We have already noted the writers' obsession with urban dirt and smell. Drains and filth are constantly referred to in the descriptions of the towns of this period, and only once have we found an attempt to redress the balance. Harland (1951) referred his readers to the usual belief that towns of the middle ages were dirty and unhealthy, but adds that, 'in reality they smelled no worse than an English farmyard of today' (Book I, p. 132). But for all its physical shortcomings it must be acknowledged that one aspect of town life in this period has been consistently well thought of. Chancellor, in *History for Their Masters* (1970) found that in her sample (history books for children from 1800 to 1914) there was surprisingly lengthy treatment of the middle ages and she thought that this was because of the influence of the Gothic Revival. This influence would appear to have become conventional-ized in the genre for, through the twentieth century, the guilds and their crafts receive respectful mention, and the medieval town appren-tices, unlike their later brothers and sisters, were generally seen as having a happy, but busy, life. Lord, (1930, Book I, p. 39), and Marten and Carter (u.d., Book II, p. 145) suggested that it was in the medieval town that an English love of freedom developed — an alternative to the more usual belief that this originated in the Anglo-Saxon villages.

Towns emerge again in Elizabethan England. Some writers attempted reconstructions for their readers and mixed vulgarity, crime and culture together in evocations of Elizabethan London. Harland (1951) describes a crowded inn-yard, with Shakespeare,

> listening with a smile to the bluster of Ben Jonson. Yonder sits George Chapman, translator of Homer. There, with pens and paper before them are the two inseparables, Beaumont and Fletcher, no doubt working on a new play. Walter Raleigh sits by them, sunburned almost black for he has just returned from a journey to the Orinoco ... Heads of traitors moulder on Temple Bar. Apple—women cry their wares. Pickpockets skulk on the skirts of the crowd. (Book II, pp. 28–9)

History book writers have also shared the stereotype of the cockney with their readers. Scotland (1953) told them that London 'was a colourful city and the people were eager and alert. They liked noise and colour and bustle' (Book III, p. 78). Priestley (1949) thought that 'their wits had been sharpened by centuries of commerce' (Book II p. 10).

There are other subsequent mentions of London; its fire and plague, its characters like Samuel Pepys and its coffee houses. There are also hints in the books about the luxury and laxity of London life during these times. But it is the images which indicate the emergence of nineteenth century urban life which are so striking, so universal and so black. *Physical* urbanization in this period, and subsequently, is represented as a process of 'swallowing up' (Robertson, 1932, Book

IV) of villages and rural land. In general, factory work, industrialization and urbanization are falsely conflated and homogenized by the texts. There is, in these accounts, no acknowledgement of the variety of forms of urbanization and there is little on the segregation and differentiation in Victorian cities which is so surprising given the books' frequent concern for London (Olsen, 1976). The apprentices and the craftsmen have disappeared, and the predominant urban characters are factory workers (most often women and children) and their cruel masters. Indeed, these urban, industrial locations seem to have had a monopoly of violence. Creating a typical scene for the child Marsh and Parks (1958) describe how,

> The children are being given their jobs by the overseer or foreman, who does not hesitate to use a stick or a strap on some poor child who is slow in setting about his task. ('Factory Children', p. 7)

Concentrating on such factory locations the textbooks quite forget, for example, the great numbers of women in domestic service and in handsewing, where they outnumbered those in the mills in the 1850s.[6]

Perhaps sharing the convention in which the social documents of the time were interpreted (viz Himmelfarb, 1973) the books show lives lived either in the factory or on the street and the people would all appear to be of one sector of the working class, the degraded urban poor, too far from the sustaining country. Such a view has been continued into books in current use. Speed (1980), in the *Oxford Junior History* (Book IV) claims that,

> The countryside is too far away for them to walk and there are no parks. All they can do is lounge around the court, gossiping, quarrelling and fighting, or else, if they have a little money, drinking in a public house. (p. 68)

But it should be mentioned that recently, perhaps through the influence of History Workshop and the 'history from evidence' movement, one or two attempts have been made to correct what has been taken as onesidedness. The small book for young children by Sallie Purkis, *At Home and in the Street, 1900* (1981) gives one alternative to the hitherto conventional images for it depicts the proud home of the respectable working class in Victorian England and the street as a positive place of life, in many ways preferable to the present car-ridden roads.

When history textbooks described previous, pre-nineteenth century, town life they tended to exclude domestic scenes or acknowledge the presence of women, in strong contrast to their presentation of rural homeliness. The impression was that home life was difficult or possibly spoiled in the town.[7] Instead, town existence was represented by commerce, taverns, the theatre, coffee houses and the street. Towns were places for men to trade and talk, yet the presence of women and children in nineteenth century urban development could not be avoided and so they were incorporated into the vision of the fall. Guest (1913) made the following explicit observation on the urban degradation of women;

> Thousands of women, also, were employed in the factories and mines where it was well-nigh impossible for them to keep clean-hearted and womanly. (p. 175)

(In case it should be thought that this was a text for Edwardian children only it is worth noting that after its first publication in 1913 it continued into its sixteenth edition by 1955, from which this quote is taken.) In the passing of Merrie England it was ordinary woman's domestic life which was thought to have been ruined, along with the simple ways of their class; 'All forgot their ancient songs and stories. The women were too tired to dance or even keep their houses clean' (Bowman, 1925, p. 104).

From both the texts and illustrations twentieth century readers can be left in no doubt that something fundamentally unnatural happened to women and children in nineteenth-century urbanization. Walvin (1982) has pointed out that the image of children in factories is seen by many as a central, characteristic one of Victorian Britain and noted how the grisly evidence of child labour heard by the 1832 Parliamentary Committee has passed into English folklore (p. 61). There can be no doubt that many a textbook description is traceable to this source, and that these books have contributed in no small degree to this folklore. The contrasts in the portrayal of childhood in town and country could not be more stark. It was as though children never had to work in the rural areas. The rural labour of children, in the gang system of the 1830s and 40s, for example, is hidden in the texts, yet was quite as horrific as factory work.

> One of the worst features of the system was the physical hardship imposed on both young and old on their journeys to and from work in all seasons and all weathers. In winter, if the task was fairly near, a two-journey day was worked; the gang set out at 7 am, returned at mid-day, and went again from 1 pm until dark. But in the summer the gang sometimes had to

walk seven or eight miles each way and work from 8.30 am to 5.30 pm making a day of intolerable length and hardship even for adults. For children of seven years of age — and some were still younger — such conditions must have involved indescribable suffering. (Pinchbeck and Hewitt, 1973, vol. II, p. 392)

Kitteringham's *Country Girls in Nineteenth Century England* (1973) described the ways women had to work in agricultural gangs if unable to obtain domestic work. It was not until 1867 and the Gangs Act that children under 8 were stopped from working in the country in this way. Children's lives in rural cottage industry under the possible tyranny of their own fathers would also seem little different from the hardships of urban work, yet these are also forgotten in the books studied here.

Perhaps the contrasts and constructions of being children in urban, industrial locations is clearest when the history books attempt to describe childhood through the ages. In the representation of the eighteenth century child he/she could still be seen as leading an innocent life in town and country. In Book III of the series *Children in History* (1961) Molly Harrison could present as charming a picture of 'Helping in the Town' as she had of 'Helping in the Country' (ch. 7 and ch. 6) partly because the urban lives of children were still in contact with the country. She notes that,

> the countryside was still close. Town children could watch farmers at work too, and even help them at busy times, for there were many farms on the outskirts of the towns. (p. 81)

Children were still *helping* in the eighteenth century — helping the merchant count his bales of cloth, helping on errands (*ibid*, p. 88). There is just the suggestion of child labour and the factories to come (*ibid*, p. 99). It is in such books as Elliot's earlier *Little Workers of Other Days* (u.d.) that we find the perfect history of the decline of childhood until its rescue by state education. 'Pel the Little Potter' of the New Stone Age, and 'Gurth the Little Swineherd' of the Middle Ages are unblemished idealizations of a child's life. The estrangement of children from their natural habitat begins with the life of 'Walter the Weaver's Prentice' and subsequently grows with 'Sammy the Sweep'. But even in his urban surroundings the latter could occasionally become a natural child again for 'as people did not have chimneys swept in the evenings Sammy had time to play in the dirty street where he lived with the Barkers' (*ibid*, p. 28). Decline is complete with 'Meg the Pit Girl' and the story of Polly and Dick at the Mill, beaten and miserable. These were good children who bore their burdens with fortitude for the sake of their parents. A very similar set of child-characters with similar fates is to be found in a series of booklets published by Hulton called *Living in Other Times* (Marsh and Parks, 1958). Text and pictures depict, 'Edgar the Saxon', living in a prototypical cottage and 'Hugh the Norman Page', living a rich and carefree life. 'Thomas the Apprentice' in Elizabethan London suffers the usual urban filth ('as Thomas goes by a woman empties her refuse from an upstairs window whilst a dog forages amongst the rubbish for food' (p. 5)), but is otherwise a happy boy. 'George, Turnip Townsend's Ploughboy' is the perfect country child. Then suddenly there is the break, with the Higgins family living in a backstreet of a Northern town, their home dirty and crowded, and the children suffering at the hands of the overseer.

In the *As We Were* series (Scarfe, 1960) the text's voice is that of the child him or herself, and the contrasts between rural and industrial childhood are laboured. In number 19 of these small books we find the child describing his miserable life within a family destroyed by industry and urban living:

> Saturday night is not a very happy time for me. Many people get drunk and there is always a lot of fighting and quarrelling. Sometimes I am frightened, especially when Father and Mother are drunk. (p. 14)

We have found no other period in the nation's history where English people's families are presented in this way. Within such histories the decline of a people comes to be halted by town planning, and the decline of their children by compulsory state education. Whilst it was true, for example, that only the 1876 Education Act did, finally, end the exploitation of children in the gang system, the texts appear over-anxious to make the point that their readers are lucky to be alive now and in the care of state and school. For Yonge, writing nearer the events, once free state education arrived then personal failing can be the only reason for misery. At the end of her *English History Reading Book* (u.d. 1892?) she sums up the progress of history:

> We have looked through English history and found that there never was a time when ability, backed by industry and uprightness, would not raise a man to full power, honour and influence. This is more than ever the case now, when the means of learning are within the reach of all and there are no

obstructions in the way ... It is not by changes in the con-
stitution that homes are made happy ... (p. 254)

For later writers like Power and Purton the state is more to be relied
upon and the way of addressing its beneficiaries is different. At the
end of a chapter called 'Sweeps, miners and factory hands' Power
contrasts a cruel past with a caring present:

> Very slowly conditions improved until today we are begin-
> ning to understand that the care of children is one of the most
> important tasks of every government. (Power, u.d., Book IV,
> p. 159)

Purton (1961) acknowledges that,

> We may sometimes feel that we do not think much of school,
> but most children will agree that they would sooner be at
> school than working twelve hours a day in a factory. The first
> money spent by government on education came in the same
> year that the changes were ordered in the factories. That was a
> very important year for children. (Book IV, p. 75)

A similar point is made in Ambler and Coatman (1936, Book IV).
After suggesting that factory work turned children into animals, the
text goes on:

> One day you must read the story of Lord Shaftesbury who
> spent his life trying to help the poor children in factories and
> mines. And if sometimes you wish you need not go to school,
> just think how much happier you are than those poor children
> were.

The intimacies and confusions of address in such passages — the 'we'
as children and the 'we' as people who care for them — appear to
struggle to establish the common membership and interests of those *in*
school and *of* the state. If, in every account of historical change, there
has been a position of author and reader which could be analyzed, in
these particular accounts of the birth of state schooling against the
background of urban-industrial child-degradation then both positions
come into complex relation. No such confusions of address were
necessary when depicting the pre-industrial child, but then this episode is a crucial point within the narrative. It announces the birth of
the enterprise in which the very texts themselves, and their subjects,
have their existence. Again the point could be made that textbook

writers have not been introducing child-readers to an anti-industrial culture, but pedagogue and child have both been 'finding themselves' in the narrative at a point of opposition to industrial institutions.

Finally, if the texts suggest that their readers have been rescued from industry by education, and, subsequently from squalid towns by planning, how do these books indicate the factor which, at one time, put so many people in danger yet can be seen now to be the perfected basis for their country's well-being? Not even the most ruralist history book can claim that the nation's wealth comes from the land, although it is true many have suggested the country's ultimate dependence on the farmer in war, viz. Birnie, 1937, Book 6, p. 65; Burbridge, u.d. 1936?, p. 39; Claxton, 1949, Book VI. Even the innocent child addressed by these texts might feel the need for an explanation as to why towns, seemingly all of a sudden, pulled people into them and so affected their lives. For the history textbook the answer lies in INVENTIONS, understood as the products of individual, clever, hardworking men.

The adulation of the inventors and their role in national development goes back a long way in children's history. Henry Ince, in 1856, (*Outlines of English History*) saw inventors as,

> more worthy of being honoured as benefactors of mankind, in the highest human sense of the word, than all the naval and military heroes of the past or present century. (p. 101)

He thought they were the saviours of their country from 'the terrible burden of our national debt'.

Macmillan's History Readers I (1895) was made up of stories of famous heroes, beginning with Hereward and ending with George Stephenson, who was used as an example of hard work and diligent study leading to greatness. 'Wonderful inventions' have been seen as solving the problems of the past and the future (Tout, 1902, p. 415), and writers like Claxton (1915) wanted to make children aware of their debt to those inventive forefathers:

> ... the young generation of a great industrial people should have some knowledge of the history of the chief handicrafts with which their own forefathers were concerned ... But it is even more fitting that they should be impressed with the special debt we owe to certain of our forefathers who have left their own individual mark on our great industries. (p. 7)

Perhaps nowhere is the single attribution of industrial development to invention more explicitly stated than by Scotland (1953) in *All Our Past*, when he wrote,

> While the war with Napoleon was being fought many changes were taking place in Britain itself. When the war started Britain was largely an agricultural country. When it finished it was the greatest manufacturing country in the world.
>
> This amazing change took place because of the inventions of a few, clever men. (Book IV, p. 34)

This was no exception. Most of the texts to which we have referred give a similar place to inventions. Turnbull (1953, Book VII) presents them as the key to changing the old habits (p. 62). Kelly and Stewart (1962, Books II and IV) announce the coming of industry by an account of Richard Arkwright, and Houseman and Marten (1932) see the latter hero as giving work to hundreds of thousands of people (Book IV, p. 98). Power (u.d.) tells the story of how 'the little boy who watched the kettle had changed the world' (Book IV, p. 131)! Horniblow and Sullivan (1954) conclude their account of Watt, with the following:

> By his wonderful invention and hard work James Watt had made it possible for the people of England to make more goods in a much shorter time than ever before. In a very few years Britain became so busy making goods to sell to other countries that she was called the Workshop of the World. (Book IV, pp. 137–8)

In *Adventures into History* (Smith and Lay, u.d.) Richard Arkwright tells his own story of hardship, but concludes,

> It is very pleasing to know that after all my hard work I have made machines which will greatly help to make England a rich country. (Book IV, B, p. 76)

As familiar as they are, these history-book accounts of Watt, Crompton's mule, Cartwright, Hargreaves' 'spinning Jenny', and their lists of many other inventors and inventions, have to be appreciated for the crucial place they have occupied in children's national history. At the very least the emphasis on invention has occupied a key place in the explanation of the generation of wealth for so many English children. It has provided a purely technological account of industrialization[8], permitting no consideration of the institutions within and upon which the particular national form of production developed, and

it excludes any other kinds of social, political and economic education. This cannot be because such things are intrinsically too difficult
for children. From some of the earliest books there has been a certain
frankness about the class system of *pre-industrial* modes of production.
In Morgan (1880), for example, there was a full description of the
'Distinction of Ranks' (p. 36) in Anglo-Saxon society, and in *Chambers* (1901). Even in those texts intended for rote-learning, the
feudal system and its class structure was revealed (Curtis, 1887).
Many of the later books continued to give quite useful, if sometimes
sentimental accounts of the feudal system, its three field system, its
methods of rent payment, its social order and its functioning in
simple terms. Little, like so many writers before and after, for
example, in the series, *England's History* (1937) could give a satisfactory
account of the feudal system in Book I; its categories of people; the
relations between them; the system's weaknesses etc. (pp. 73–5), and
in a section called 'Life on a Manor' considered the demesne, rotation
of crops and the nature of rent. But when it came to either describing
the development of capitalist farming or the industrial revolution in
Book III (which would have been read by older children) then the
accounts are purely in terms of technical descriptions of crop rotation,
the concentration of people and the inventions of individuals. Very
few texts indeed[9] have looked at the generation, holding and use of
surplus in developing capitalism, its bringing together of town and
country and its particular separation of English people.

For those concerned with the origins of contemporary English
attitudes to wealth creation (e.g. Wiener and Dahrendorf) this aspect
of the construction of the national past should be of interest. It has
continued to give the impression that such wealth is almost magically
delivered by the creativity of a few individuals — an industrial society's equivalent of the cargo cult. For our thesis the significance is in
how it relates, in a structured way, to the images of town and
country. Economic change, being signified by invention, permits a
limited critique of the past effects of capitalist development (urbanism,
child labour, family degradation etc.) in terms of temporary losses
which can be regained.

These constructions and their accompanying attitudes are not
restricted to any one period within our sample, but an interesting development is noticeable. The post-1945 affluence encouraged
history book writers to suggest that the material benefits of those
inventions had arrived for all. The earlier books use reference to
inventors, along with other heroes, more as moral examples of what
can be achieved by individual effort. These similarities and differences

can be brought out in a comparison of Purton's two popular series, *The New View Histories* (1958) and the *Junior New View Histories* (1961) with Hounsell and Hilton's *The Research Histories* (u.d. 1920?). Both try, in their slightly different ways, to give children some sense of national indebtedness and continuity with that otherwise dark period of the Industrial Revolution. Hounsell and Hilton, in their account of the Hanoverian period (Book IV) have three sub-sections. The first two are called 'Men Who Gave the People Power' (Hargreaves *et al*) and 'Men Who Gave the People Speed' (Stephenson and Hill). The third section begins,

> Clever inventors and manufacturers may cause a nation to grow wealthy, but wealth alone does not make a nation great. Its people must above all things be noble in thought and deed. (p. 131)

This section is titled 'Men Who Made the People Nobler', and includes reference to Lord Shaftesbury, the child saver, and the provision by Parliament of free education for all. Their message is clear —

> Thus, through the hard work and noble thinking of her great men, the children of today have a splendid chance of learning to be noble too. If these children, when they grow up, continue the work of the good men of the past, then England will become a nobler, and therefore a greater country. (p. 133)

Purton's books combine an approach to industrialization as invention and a high regard for modernity similar to that found in many others of the post-war period. Keen to show how much easier life is in the 1950s than it was in the 1850s he also used the notion of indebtedness to the past. For him it is a debt, not to past workers or to ennoblers of the people, or even to the Victorian entrepreneurs, but to the inventors who gave us our homely comforts. In Book II of the *Junior Series* he wrote:

> We live in an age of wonderful inventions which make life so much easier. With TV, electric light and refrigerators it is difficult to imagine how people could manage without them. Yet people of all these ages have helped to give us the kind of home we have today. (p. 160)

The last book in this series is called *Days of Discovery* and mixes up, in a confusing way, a wide variety of events and people from James Watt to the climbing of Everest. It establishes a view of discovery and invention as the finding or producing out of nothing the gifts of wealth and national glory. The people are mere passive inheritors of previous Englishmen's finds.

But in some of these celebrations of this post-war British inheritance it is interesting to find a strategy for pedagogic realism (showing a 'typical family') which could result in a host of social and educational exclusions. 'Yesterday', a book in the series *Understanding the Modern World* (Harston, 1951) follows such a typical post-war family which had previously lived in a 'a dismal little house in a dreary part of the town' (p. 1) but now occupy a council house on a new estate. Father is a mechanic, mother looks after the house, grandparents live in a bungalow, with a pension, the daughter attends a secondary modern school and the son, 'attends the new primary school on the estate. He has taken his scholarship tests this year and hopes to get a place in a grammar school' (p. 2). Much is made of the contrasts between the old city and the new life, and the two geographical locations bear the burden of signifying two apparently different economic and social orders. It is not necessary to romanticize the solidarities of working class urban communities and their effects upon childhood[10] to catch both the evaluating tone in those adjectives 'dismal' and 'dreary' and the way a certain geographical mobility (*from* the city) is used to denote an imagined social and economic revolution.

We cannot trace all these notions of industrialization, all these constructions of national narrative, to any essential ruralism. Purton himself was quite realistic about the conditions of previous non-urban life. But they are certainly not incongruent with notions of national identity built upon and dependent upon the emphasized origins of English people in a previous rural idyll. Conceptualizing the positive side of industrialization as invention in no way confronts or complicates the belief that the essence of its negative side was urbanization. Indeed, the critique of capitalist development in terms of it being part of, or expressed in, the evils of previous urbanization can happily co-exist with a view of wealth creation as invention and discovery. After listing all the good things which have come to us from industrialization — schools, electric light, clean water and so on, Marie Stuart (1951a, Book III) can still express all her reservations in a harmless, wistful, rural nostalgia:

> These improvements would hardly have been possible without the wealth which the Industrial Revolution brought. And yet we sometimes wonder whether the city life which most of us now lead brings as much real happiness as the simple open-air

country life which the majority of the people lived in the time
of Sir Roger de Coverley. (p. 123)

Within these history textbooks there has been found a persistent set of
images of rural and urban life. The problem has been how to understand such persistence. Instead of attributing them to a given national
ruralism it has been suggested that they must be considered one
against another, in some kind of structural relation. The frequency of
the individual images themselves would appear to be most easily
attributable to internal, pedagogic conventions and certain publishing
practices. In the case of visual images, for example, then adaptations
from, say, a medieval psalter or one of Gustave Doré's engravings of
London life have simply been reused over the years by different
authors and editors. Yet these conventions, for all their regrettable
repetitiveness born of the pedagogue's isolation from changing
academic scholarship on the one hand, and an obliviousness of the
social changes around the schools on the other, have to be seen as part
of an apparently shared enterprise. We have tried to present the latter
as the sometimes desperate exercise of marking out of national social-
racial space for children within the texts of state elementary and
primary schooling. In the following chapter we will consider the
contrasts between urban and rural in the delineation of national,
physical space.

Notes

1 On the necessity of continuity in the development of nationalism viz. B.
  Anderson's *Imagined Communities*, Chapter 2 (Anderson, 1983).
2 One of the very few exceptions being Harland (1951) *The Story of Our
  People* which dealt with both Ketts Rebellion and the Swing Riots.
3 Rodney Hilton, in *Bond Men Made Free* (1973) and others have maintained that between 10 and 20 per cent of the rebels were rural and urban
  craftsmen (self-employed and wage-earning) and that the Revolt was
  quite widely based (pp. 179–84).
4 In his account of the rise of the factory system in chapter VII and the
  division into capitalist and labourer Spalding (1921) attempted to justify
  the 'middle man' as vital to industrialization. It should be noted that this
  book was not an elementary textbook but was intended for use by
  teachers in those schools.
5 Some more recent textbooks for primary schools do promote the active
  study and comparison of evidence and may be seen as significantly
  different from those previous methods of introducing the materials of

historical research into a didactic regime, for example the *Focus on History Series* (Mitchell and Middleton, 1979).

6   School history textbooks have consistently put women and children together in their condemnation of factory life, with the implication that they too are in need of care and protection, viz. *The Woman's Chapter* by Catherine Ross (1984).

7   Contrary to such representations it could be argued that the availability of urban employment actually helped many families to stay together, viz. Anderson. (1971) *Family Structure in Nineteenth Century Lancashire.*

8   For a critique of the 'technological determinism' in school history viz. Mary Tasker's *Teaching the History of Technology* (1980).

9   F.W. Tickner in *A Junior Social and Industrial History of England* (1930) did attempt to explain some of the institutional conditions for the development of industrialization and the class structure (pp. 168–9 and chapter XXIII) as did George Guest in *A Social History of England* (1929–1955 edn) in section 6, although the latter's explanation of banking and trade is more a justification of the 'middle man' — 'Some people do not "make", that is "produce" anything; in other words they are what is known to the economist as "unproductive" workers, who, nevertheless, are entitled to payment for the risks they run, and for the services they give to the community, in general' (p. 152). Barker and Hammer (1962, Book IV, pp. 57–8) gave a rare description of land ownership and the rural classes of seventeenth century agriculture.

10 Viz. Carolyn Steedman's *Landscape For a Good Woman* (1986) for an illuminating commentary on the tradition of Seabrook and Hoggart (pp. 8–13).

5   Town and Country at Home

Within the period being considered the other conventional school subject which has been concerned with 'the social' and made reference to 'the people' has been geography. It is in this subject and its texts that we may expect to find the most explicit and theorized reference to the urban and rural. As far as the objects of the research are concerned then there are close parallels between the texts made available for teaching these two subjects to young children. Within the period 1920 to 1960, at least, they have come to be roughly equal in the hierarchy of the curriculum and have thus been similarly resourced by the production and purchase of textbooks. In many cases, too, that provision has been similarly organized by publishers and teachers through the use of series of books (usually four separate texts) produced to correspond with the ages of the children.

From the point of view of this volume, however, there can be seen to be both some key similarities (based on some ideologies of child development and pedagogy, for example) but also some highly significant differences. Thus, in some geography texts we find an emphasis on the 'natural' ways of teaching children the subject via observation of the seasons and the farmer's year, for example, which suggests a similarity with some history books which dwelt on the rural roots of English people. But if one were to approach the geography texts only in terms of their reflection of some national or class-cultural essence (in this case, some essential ruralism), then one would be confused, if not disappointed, for they have been at great pains to convince the pupils that their nation is the *workshop of the world*. Although they provided conducted tours of British farmland, and accorded great respect to the English farmer, when these texts have been concerned with international comparisons the rural and agricultural were much more associated with the contemporary life in foreign lands. When children have been introduced to the contrasts between 'us' and 'them', 'here' and 'there', then the urban and the industrial have been taken as the major positive distinguishing features of our life and nation. It was only when the textbooks were involved in presenting Britain to the British child that the charm of *our* countryside was dwelt upon, but never at the expense of an image of Britain as a whole, with town and country meshed together and interdependent. It may be that some content analysis of geography would show more references to rural locations and lives, but then this could be taken to have more to do with the discipline's concentration in the past on climate, the soil, and the so-called natural environment than with any national-cultural ruralism. Our interest, however, is chiefly in *how* the contrasts between rural and urban came to be made within the textbooks of these two subjects. This forces us to consider the different forms to be found and their effects, along with what might be called the raw material for the production of these texts, i.e. the academic-based theories and perspectives from non-school sources.

Later we shall examine the range of devices used. For the purposes of an initial comparison with history it is sufficient here to point out that where the narrative form was used in the history textbooks to establish the images of a national, rural past (its loss and the subsequent reconciliation, with all its particular connotations) in the geography books this has often taken the form of the travelogue.

In history, where the child might have been taken back to the beginning of history and the primitive in his own land, brought through the settled times and then the cruelties and squalor of urbanization and on into the planned present, in geography there has been another journey. Very often it has been from the 'tame rurality' (Massey, 1983) of the English suburb to the equally tamed countryside of, perhaps, an uncle's farm, to the factories and mines of urban Britain, then over the sea to the rural existences of the 'savage' or 'barbarian', and then back home again.

If one accepts that these textbooks have played their part in the maintenance of a strongly classified English school curriculum (Bernstein, 1975) then it is worth noting the ways they appear to have done this. On the one hand geography and history books have been equally penetrated by nationalist ideology, and equally influenced by available theories of child development and child learning. On the other hand they have both attempted to monopolize the different dimensions of time and space; they have held fast to their primitive, unsophisticated theories of determination, and relied on two similar forms of exposition (narrative and travelogue). Such exclusivity has increasingly come under strain, and, even in the present texts devoted to initiation into geographical methods, there are now frequent uses of historical example and contrast (*Oxford New Geography*, 1980). But in the main body of the books used here, certainly until the 1960s, very few textbooks attempted to combine the two subjects. One was by Mackinder (1906) who believed that such a combination would help children see all the nations in competition historically and thus develop a sense of perspective (Book IV). Another was Book I of the *Junior Regional Geographies* (Barker and Brooks, 1928). In explaining Britain's pre-eminence in the world there has been an occasional borrowing from the historical. For example, *Macmillan's Geography Reader*, Book III (1897) traced Britain's commerce back to the Normans, and Parkin (1892) attributed the growth of Empire to the Anglo-Saxon love of adventure (p. 18) as did Arnold (1896), but, as will be shown, most explanations of the wealth of this nation have been purely physical. It may be that it was only through a non-historical geography and a non-geographical history that the two subjects could maintain some strange complementarity in their construction of national identity. Where the one has tried to establish the security of the national people, its basis in the rural past and origins in a country-loving race, the other has struggled to show the differences with the primitive elsewhere, and the natural, functional unity of the homeland.

The Child Located

If most history books located the child at the end of a long process of national development then most geography books address their child-readers as very specifically located in space around which all other space is measured, placed and compared. Indeed, the device of an extended address has often been used to establish, for young children, that they are all placed somewhere. Book I of the *Columbus Geography Series*, for example, located an imaginary child, Tom Smiles, in a street, in Finsbury Park, London, England, the world (Brooks and Finch, 1928) and similar addresses can be found elsewhere, for example, *The Citizens Geographies*, Book I (1937) and Paul's *The Adventures of Man Series*, Book I (1954).

What has been the nature of this typical space which the pupils have been given to occupy, and how has it been constructed? In fact only rarely has it been accepted that, in reality, children from very different geographical backgrounds would have used these books, and, when it was, then the differences were purely those between town and country. A major series published in 1947 (*Johnston's New Picture Geographies*) began with some words for town and country children, asserting some very basic differences between them and their locations:

> The town boy perhaps cannot ride a pony, but he can take care of himself in a busy street. A town boy might laugh at his cousin from the country who could not find his way through the streets.
>
> Those of you who live in a village will think it strange to hear that there are many children in our big towns who have never heard the song of a bird, many who have never seen a field of wheat. If you live in a town you may not know that lots of country children have never been in a tramcar. Town life is not at all like country life. (pp. 10–11)

One of the main tasks of those books, at least until the 1960s, was to establish the *national* location of the reader. The children's home was, first of all, their nation. Books or chapters on Britain frequently have titles such as 'The British Homeland', the title of Book I of the *Golden Hind Geographies*, 2nd series (Brooks and Finch, 1939), or 'Our Island Home' where it was said that 'This free land of which the poet Tennyson has written with pride, is our home' (Mackinder, 1906, Book I, p. 1). Other children, too, are all understood as existing in their own, essentially different homelands. At the beginning of Book III of the *Golden Hind Series* called 'Britain and the British' the text looked back at the previous books which dealt with other countries and noted that, 'we have seen how the people of those homelands get their living in different ways because their homelands are different' (Finch, 1937, Book III, p. 11).

Those earlier books were quite explicit in their patriotic attempts to teach English children a love of their home country. *Arnold's Geography Readers* Book III (1896) began with 'We love England because it is our native land, and the home of our friends. And we are proud to know that our country is worthy of our love' (p. 8) and 'The British Isles' in the series, *The Pupils' Class Book of Geography*, ended with an activity for the class — to learn Sir Walter Scott's poem 'Love of Country', and it reproduced the following:

> Breathes there a man with soul so dead,
> Who never to himself hath said,

This is my own, my native land!
Whose heart hath ne'er within him burned,
As home his footsteps he hath turned
From wandering on a foreign strand. (Lay, 1914, p. 15)

British children of the textbooks have also been more specifically located than just by nation. Many textbook series adapted the so-called 'concentric plan' which Mackinder had introduced for the teaching of regional geography at the turn of the century. This suggested that 'the local district' should be studied first, then 'the homeland' and so on (Biddle, 1985, pp. 11–12). But with national textbooks provided for nationwide consumption, 'the local district' came to be defined in a special way. All child-readers were addressed as of the English suburbs and of the middle class. Sometimes this was done explicitly, where child characters were written about, their lives and homes described and illustrated. In the text, 'Children of the World' (*Visual Series*, 1920), the representatives of childhood in the British Isles, who are shown alongside other typical child representatives of their countries, are John and Mary, who feed the swans in the park and return home to hot, buttered toast, buns and fruit cake. Tom and Betty Clark, whose visits and journeys are the means of teaching geography in the *Pleasant Pathways to Geography Series* (Spink and Brady, 1950), lived in a comfortable semi-detached home in the suburbs of a south of England country town.

It may be argued that there were certain pedagogical reasons for using references to children's homes and localities as the starting points for teaching about maps, weather and so on. As early as the 1880s a manual of oral lessons adapted to the new revised code (Picton, 1885) suggested that maps be made of the area around the school, and Baker (1881) told the children,

> ... do not forget that you must first learn the geography of the place where you live. You must know the kind of land round about your house and school .... (Part I, p. 7)

The very well known writer of geography textbooks, Thomas Pickles, expressed a strong belief in teaching geography to young children as a continuation of their home lives, their walks and their holidays. 'Geography, like charity, begins at home', he declared in a chapter called 'The Home Region' (Pickles, 1929, p. 1). But the cultural continuity which many of these textbooks permitted and encouraged was a very restricted one.

Often the means of establishing the place and the people for

whom the books established continuity and identity have not been so
obvious, but may be deduced by the places the imaginary characters
visit and the ways they react to them. From quite early texts like
Book I of the *Graphic Geographical Reader* (1893) the imaginary child-
geographers of the texts frequently *visit* farms and industrial towns,
but never live there. In that text, for example, the imaginary child
holidays with his aunt and uncle on a farm and, for the first time,
learns all about the elements by living, if temporarily, in the country.
The imaginary child-character's links with the country are usually
familial; often it is an uncle who is the farmer, and being a farmer is
sometimes seen as a realistic ambition for the child characters. After a
holiday on his uncle's farm Harold Curtis, in T.H. Cook's *Life and
Work in the British Isles*, Book II (1950), returned home quite sure of
his ambition and was made to say that, 'it was hard and healthy work
and it was valuable work, helping to supply the people of Britain with
food' (p. 15). Another child-character in the book ended up with a
partnership in a market garden. When industrial towns are visited
they are more distant and alien. There are no invitations from industrial workers to the children. They are seen as people who do things
for *us*. Describing the grime and smoke of the Black Country one
writer concluded, 'Still thousands of people are willing to work hard
daily there to provide us with all kinds of iron and steel goods' (Lay,
1914, p. 72). In another book a child-character, who had travelled all
over Britain and elsewhere in his uncle's plane, reflected on those
people of his country forced to live in industrial towns:

> Most people in England now no longer *grow* things, they *make*
> things. No longer are they farmers, who live in the open air.
> Most of their work is done in factories. King Coal is their
> great helper, and so most of them have to live where King
> Coal lives — on the coalfields. I would much rather live in the
> open air, uncle. When I grow up I want to be a traveller like
> you. I should hate to work in a dark factory, where one can
> never see the green fields or breathe fresh air. (Horniblow,
> 1936, Book II, p. 235)

All travelogue presumes a home, whether it is acknowledged and
described or not. The homes of these imaginary travellers always
appear to be the suburbs of the south of England. As will become
clearer in the following sections, such travelogues may include child-
characters, or they may be just descriptions of the geographical
regions, but the suburb is the only location which is commensurate
with the observations and judgments made by the textbooks with

regard to the 'other parts' of the homeland, and, indeed, the world. In spite of that, the form of address was often intimate, and the invitation was to join 'us' on 'our' journey of discovering the other parts of Britain and the world, as exemplified in such titles as *Let's Look Geographies* (Heppel, 1920) and *Our Changing Commonwealth* (Murray, 1960). The following four titles of Mosbey and Young's series *Our World* (1949–1952) illustrate perfectly the combination of location and invitation, whereby child readers first get to know their home and family, and then their neighbours:

Volume 1 — Our Town and Beyond
Volume 2 — Our Neighbours Overseas
Volume 3 — Our Changing World
Volume 4 — Our World and Ourselves

In a most patriotic series a further device is used to give the reader a place and pride in their own land. In Book III a foreign child is used to express interest in the mother-land, as it is called, proclaiming that

These British must be the mightiest people on earth. Nearly a quarter of the whole world owns their sway. What a great country the Mother-land of this vast Empire must be! Come, I am eager to learn all about it. (*Royal School Series, Highroads of Geography*, 1911, Book III, p. 11)

The National Landscape and Gifts of Nature

Much of British national history told of the laying down of the nation's national-racial character which enabled its people to achieve greatness (Chapter 3). The national geographies, however, tell the nation's children about the people's natural habitat and natural good fortune. Before going on to consider the construction of town and country locations within this geography of Britain this notion of natural, national gifts needs to be clarified. It has been expressed at the beginnings of textbooks on the British Isles in a number of ways. For example, Mackinder, in 1906, gave an almost poetic account of the nation's gifts in response to the invitation to 'try and find out how so small a country can be the home of so great a people' (Book I, p. 2). His text explained this as follows:

Buried in their rocks are great stores of coal and iron so that Britain has grown rich by manufactures. (p. 3)

The Channel has given us 'the great blessings of peace and freedom at home' (p. 3) and,

> the ocean, whose waves beat upon the shores of Britain, is a great high road upon which the ships come and go carrying our trade to all the shores of the world. (p. 4)

Lay, thirty years later, posed similar problems at the beginning of Book 4 of the *Empire Geographies:*

> How has it come about that the people of this small group of islands have had such a world-wide influence? The answer is that Britain is a country favoured by nature — favoured in position, weather, soil and minerals. (Lay, 1937, Book IV, p. 3)

The geographical location of the nation has, from the earliest text-books, been seen as singularly fortunate. Geikie, in 1888, asked children to hold the globe in a certain way to show how Britain was in the middle of the inhabitable world and commented that,

> From the British Isles, as a centre, ships bear to every corner of the globe the manufacture of this country, and to the same centre they return laden with the produce of every clime. (p. 4)

This device of showing the globe in a way that placed Britain in the centre has been used by countless other textbooks and teachers. Green and Green (1939) depicted two views of the world to show how much better placed Britain was than the South Pole, and commented,

> How fortunate it is that the British Isles are in the centre of the trading nations. (Book IV, p. 12)

Pickles (1929) asked his readers to,

> Note how all the great landmasses of the world are grouped around our islands making Britain the centre of the modern world. (p. 25)

Only very rarely has it been admitted that other countries may be favoured by nature in this way.

Other writers have seen the fact that we are an island as a great fortune for it encourages trade and discourages invasion, and gives us the further gift of fish (Horniblow, 1936, Book 3, p. 79). But as far as the non-industrial and non-urban side of Britain's identity was concerned it was our *climate* which has been thought to be the most obvious and natural reason for our success as a people, being neither too hot nor too cold, and having great seasonal variety. Whereas later we shall consider the importance of this in the comparison with other lands and other races, here it is useful to look at how an ideology of child development embedded in the practices of age-based schooling and its artefacts has come to be combined with a certain nationalism, both to teach some simple geographical concepts and to construct an image of the British landscape.

Few texts which introduced geography to the young have failed to take very seriously this British landscape and the farmer as a key figure associated with it. It has been within their construction of the images of the British countryside that a number of naturalistic strands intertwine. Some such strands arise from early ideas about the import-ance of experiences of nature for the development of the child, and some from the naturalistic geographical determinism indicated in those ideas of 'nature's gifts'. One may summarize the ways in which these strands work together as follows. If geography has been defined as the study of the natural, environmental effects on the peoples of the world then the way of understanding '*our*' particular national life has been as indicated above, i.e. in terms of the availability to the British people of some gifts of nature. One of the major, tangible gifts which can be experienced directly by children must be the climate and its effects on the land, and so this warrants particular attention being given to farming. Therefore, in order that they really can appreciate these environmental effects some children have to be transported out into nature and the country, either imaginatively, in the texts, or by suggested walks, visits and, later, by geography field courses.

We find the use of country walks in one of the earlier books referred to — the *King Geographical Readers* No. I (1901). Here two children accompany their uncle on such a walk. The text abounds with sentimental anthropomorphisms and poems but has the purpose of introducing the children to simple geography, the points of the compass, the seasons etc. The only difference with later texts is that the gifts of nature are traced back to the gifts of God:

Little children look around
Flowers in all the fields abound;
Every running stream is bright,
And the orchard trees are white.
Turn your eyes to earth and heaven;
God for us the spring has given.

Little children, gladly sing
Praise to Him who sends the spring. (p. 45)

It is clear that, to the extent that the authors were conscious of the different locations of their readers, then the city child would come to be seen to be at a grave disadvantage in that view of learning geography. Using the word 'suburban' to refer to a location which seems more like that which we would now call inner city Olive Garnett, a lecturer in geography at Froebel College, wrote as follows in her preface to Book I of the *Discovery Books*:

> For thousands of children now growing up in our poor sub-urbs the daily walk to school leads from the paved yard of a tenement house along built up streets to an asphalt play-ground, often without a glimpse of a patch of earth, an open space or even of a tree ... School studies in geography, history, literature and scripture assume an acquaintance with things of the earth, the sights and sounds, seasonal changes and activities familiar to country children. A background of this kind is the birthright of children and their natural inclina-tion leads them in search of it. (Garnett, 1949–51, Book I, p. xiii)

Almost as an antidote to urban life this book takes children into a world of farming and gardening through the seasons. For autumn there are pictures of horse-drawn ploughs and pipe-smoking old gardeners. In *Things to Do* the child-readers are told to look for a field being ploughed (p. 15). Country life in spring has children running through the fields (p. 38).

Such books may have been seen by their authors as a kind of compensatory education for some, but at the same time they con-structed the images of childhood and countryside together and gave invitations and commands to the apparently deprived children which they could not accept:

> Go into an orchard on a warm, sunny day at blossom time,

wrote Glover and Young over fifty years after the publishing of the *King Readers*, referred to above, and in a more secular age,

> Listen. You will hear the soft humming sounds of bees visiting the flowers. (Glover and Young, 1961, Book II, p. 53)

In the books of this latter series the children were invited to have their adventures in a garden-world. The seasons were introduced in an existence of predominantly rural pleasures, all spaced out within the landscape and the elements.[1]

In most of these texts it is impossible to distinguish an implicit legitimation of suburban childhood as the correct and proper child-hood, and an ethnocentric view of our nation's natural fortunes from what appears to be commonsensical pedagogic justifications for ruralizing geographical learning situations. Hardingham, for example, whose worship of nature, as represented in the English seasons, knew no bounds in his 1935 text (Book III (a) of the series, *Foundations of Geography*) found *pedagogical* reasons why rural locations are most useful in the exposition of the methods for studying 'The Home Region' or one's own neighbourhood:

> Generally it will be better for those who live in a city to choose a piece of country away from the crowded streets and buildings which hide what the ground is really like. (p. 13)

So often in other texts too the village was taken as the ideal subject to introduce localities and maps; its brook, school, church and station (viz. *McDougall's Geographical Primer* u.d. 1936?; Stembridge, 1948). To learn geography, then, town children must be taken out into their nation's countryside so that they can be put into contact with its soil and climate. They must also learn to appreciate the dependence of the townspeople on the country and on the key figure, the farmer. Echoing a persistent fear felt by urban teachers over the years that their pupils may not know where milk came from[2] Hardingham (1957–60) wrote,

> Behind the appearance of the milk on our doorsteps or at school there are a great many people at work — dairymen, lorry drivers, railwaymen, the Milk Marketing Board, and so on, but behind them all is the British farmer and some of the richest land in Britain. (p. 49)

Other texts too have suggested the dependence on the farmer. *Black's New Grade Geographies* (u.d., Book 4, pp. 79–80) makes the point particularly strongly and some books attempt to redress what was thought to be an imbalance. For example the skill of the 'countryman' was compared favourably with that of the urban dweller in *Johnston's New Picture Geographies* (1937, Book III, p. 53).

Like many history books 'the farmer' was usually indistinguish-able from the farm worker — a conflation rarely made in the case of the urban worker. The farmer was, in many ways, an elemental figure, and quite unlike the industrialist. He worked patiently *with* nature, the soil and the climate (viz. Glover and Young, 1960, Book II, p. 51; and Hardingham, 1957–60, p. 24) and was the guardian of the British land:

> 'Besides getting food and other things from the land', wrote Brooks and Finch (1939), 'farmers do a great deal to keep Britain beautiful'. (Book I, p. 79)

Finally, given the travelogue form, showing children their homeland via 'tours' was bound to give special attention to the rural scenes, particularly when the geological features of Britain predominated in the texts. Picturesque Britain was emphasized by *Black's New Graded Geographies* (u.d.), Green and Green (1939), the *Visual Series* (1920) and Walter (1935) and some others.

Our Towns and Our Industry

It was by telling children about another gift of nature that the textbooks have shown them the other side of Britain and that which gives their nation its distinct place in the world. As Horniblow (1936) expressed it, 'Plenty of coal is one of the greatest gifts that Nature has given to Our Own Lands' (Book III, p. 79). It was laid down for us thousands of years ago and can now be extracted by another national hero — the miner. In some of these texts mining and farming were presented alongside one another (Brooks and Finch, 1939, Book I, pp. 48–9) and the miner and the farmer were long seen as the two key figures of national economic life (for example, Stamp and Herdman, 1938, Book II, p. 118). Accounts of coal mining were taken as the means of introducing industrial and urban Britain. Acknowledging that most people in the homeland live in towns Brooks and Finch (1939) refer to coal to explain this concentration, and the development of industry:

> In Ireland there is very little coal, which largely explains why there are more farmers than manufacturers in the 'Green Isle' — and more country-folk than town-folk. (Book I, p. 122)

Sometimes in the human form of 'King Coal' coal was shown as determining where people live and what they did. At the end of his travels with his uncle, Tom, in Horniblow's *Land and Life Series* (1936) reflected on his own nation and its people:

Most people in England now no longer *grow* things, they *make* things. No longer are they farmers, who live in the open air. Most of the work is done in factories.

King Coal is their great helper and so most of them have to live where King Coal lives — on the coalfields. (Book II, p. 235)

As far as the structure of explanation is concerned coal occupies a very similar place in the geography books to that of invention in the children's histories.

It is because of the great number of coal mines that we have, and the number of ways which we use our coal, that today our country is an industrial country. A hundred and fifty years ago ours was not an industrial country. Most of the people were farmers. There were few big towns. But today most of the people live in the towns. The work of most of them really depends on coal. (*Wheaton's Vivid Geographies*, 1946, Book IV, p. 64)

In another of Wheaton's geography series, the *Golden Mean Geographies* (1949), inventions and coal are brought together, and the latter given primacy:

Britain is one of the world's biggest workshops. Our people work hard in mills and factories. We have wonderful machinery to help us make things. We have clever people who have invented many tools to make work easier and quicker. But perhaps most important of all is that we have plenty of coal. (Midgley, 1949, Book II, p. 38)

But unlike many history textbooks, however, labour, in this case the work of the extraction of coal, has never been omitted in school geography. Often through photographs and drawings the conditions of work have been fully portrayed, and 'our' indebtedness to the miners' bravery and hard work have been noted (Green and Green, 1939, Book IV chapter 4; Lay, 1937, Book 4, p. 39; *Black's*, u.d., Book 4, part 3). In general, labour has been acknowledged but the relations between labour of different kinds have been shown as geographical only, in the sense that people's work was determined by their location alone.

Coal, then, has been used to explain our good fortune in being the workshop of the world, even if, at times, the predominance of

133

manufacture and urban life was seen with a tinge of regret, and at some distance. Industrial towns have been visited by the imaginary travelling children of these books, and we can find many accounts of the processes of steel production, cotton manufacture and so on, often presented as awe-inspiring. The *Macmillan Geography Class Pictures* (1959), for example, gave children a very positive view of British industry, with pictures of a clean, sunny pithead and glowing blast furnaces. Accompanying very similar pictures in one of his textbooks Horniblow (1936) described these furnaces as 'very wonderful places' (1936, Book III, p. 90). Furthermore, in spite of the fact that most children in twentieth century England would, because of their own extra-school lives, not need it, the textbooks frequently reminded themselves and their readers that most British people lived in towns and by manufacture. The message was frequently repeated that,

> In the main we who live in the British Isles are *makers* and not *growers*. Millions of our people work in factories, making such things as cotton and woollen clothes, steel goods, boots and shoes, pottery and machinery, chemicals and railway engines.
> A great deal of this we send abroad to people who, unlike us, are growers and cannot provide such things for themselves. (Bushell, u.d., Book III)

There can be no mistaking that Britain is an industrial nation and, because of the repetitive nature of these textbooks they tend to show Britain as the ONLY industrial country. One is tempted to see Geikie's grand overview of the nation's natural basis for its singularity in this respect as establishing a convention which has persisted through times when such Victorian optimism became increasingly out of place. All was in place and for the best in his perception of Britain:

> Hence the various national industries in which steam machinery plays a leading part have tended to establish themselves on or near to the supplies of coal. The thousands of workers who gain their livelihood by these industries have consequently been drawn together to the different manufacturing centres. Districts which a century ago were entirely rural and thinly populated are now densely inhabited and murky with the smoke of hundreds of steam engines. And thus by the grouping of the hills and the plains, and by the arrangement of the minerals underground, the present distribution and avocations of the people have been powerfully influenced. (Geikie, 1888, p. 15)

Throughout the sample, then, we find few explicit examples of out-right anti-industrialism or anti-urbanism, except for the usual observations about smoke and pollution, but what is important is the way industrial Britain is shown to the child and the way the child-reader is located in relation to it. Although a part of the nation and its existence in nature, it is still a place *elsewhere.* Other people live and work there, in difficult conditions bravely born. To return to Tom, the child subject of the *Lands and Life Series.* He had flown over the Black Country and the smoke had made his eyes ache (Horniblow, 1936, Book II, p. 113). He appreciated the work done there, but it was not for him. It was better to travel in distant lands than to arrive in an English factory. English towns are visited in these texts. They are understood in terms of their products, and their localities are seen as the result of natural occurrences; coal deposits, crossing places of rivers. The processes of production are fully illustrated. But industrial towns are treated with great reserve.

Only one town has received constantly favourable treatment, and that was London. Children have been taught about its centrality and its administrative functions through a variety of corporeal–national imagery.[3]

> London, the capital of the British Isles, and the heart of the British Empire, is now, with its suburbs, the largest human settlement in the world. (Brooks and Finch, 1939, Book I, p. 163)
>
> You may like to think of London as the heart of the British Isles ... You may like to think of London as the brain instead of the heart. The brain receives messages and sends out commands ... (*Black's* u.d., Book 4, p. 144)

London, the children are reminded,

> is the home of our King. It is in London too that many of our laws are made. (*Johnston's* 1937, Book I, p. 40)

And although its growth has often been referred to, and sometimes its suburbs, it has tended to be seen as very much a tourist's London, a London for the visitor from the country town. Its inhabitant, the cockney, is contrasted with the slower but sturdy countryman. In a book which reproduces all the national caricatures called *Our Islands and Ourselves* by Clark (Book 4 of *Wheaton's Vivid Geographies,* 1946) we find the following contrasts:

> The Londoner is quick, merry and very, very knowing. He

can tell you how to cross busy streets quickly and carefully. He knows where to find the best shops and which streets have thousands of people living in them. He knows all about motor cars and railway engines. He can play exciting games in rather dismal streets and little playgrounds. (p. 5)

This was contrasted with the Northern Scotsmen:

London is a strange, queer place to them. But to them belong the sharp, salt winds that the old Vikings loved.

Britain as a Whole

Given that the geography of these texts has been so much concerned with the presentation of national land and life, how has the often celebrated geographical variety of the British Isles, and the distinctiveness of the urban and rural been brought together and connected? Have there been similar structures to those of the history books' narratives of a people or race travelling through time together? We may get a clue from the book just referred to at the end of the previous section. After a brief outline of the different regional stereotypes the very geographical and racial variety of the British was seen as distinguishing this nation's individualized people from the black Africans, who were thought to look all the same:

Suppose we were negroes living in a wild jungle in the middle of Africa. All our friends would have our dark, close-curled hair, the same brown eyes and thick nose, the same coloured brown skin. We should all look like each other because our fathers and mothers had married people that looked like themselves. (*Wheaton's*, 1946, Book IV, p. 8)

And six pages later the diversity of the locations of the lives of English children was noted, for although the British Isles may seem a small area in the globe,

Yet in these islands live millions of boys and girls in millions of homes. There are farms in the mountains, farms in the plains. There are lonely houses by the sea, and thousands and thousands of homes muddled together in the big towns. (*ibid*, p. 14)

Like many of the texts this one then proceeded to show the interrelatedness of all the geographical variety, and especially of the differ-

ences between town and country, by tracing different products back
to their origins. The journey of milk in the children's milk bottles was
illustrated. Other things were treated similarly. Vegetables, coal, fish
and so on were traced back to the *other people* who produced them and
it was shown how they were brought to *us*. The geographical variety
within a nation, the differences between town and country, were
comprehended within the satisfaction of our needs.

In this section it is necessary to analyze how the national unity
out of diversity has been established for children in the recent past,
and how, in particular, the distinctions between town and country
and between the regions enabled the texts to unite the people and the
territory of the nation. On occasions the intentions have been openly
expressed. Walter, in a text which was first published in 1935 and
which was in its twelfth reprint by 1956, showed what she had in
mind in the Preface to the book devoted to Britain in the series *Life in
Many Lands*. It was,

> to give an account, not a geographical abstraction which might
> well be thousands of miles away, nor of a 'homeland' which,
> in spite of that name, is felt to be very remote, but of real,
> intimate Britain today — the beautiful and productive
> countryside, and the busy industrial towns and cities which
> together make up a great country. (Walter, 1935, Book IV,
> p. 4)

In another Preface Hardingham claimed that, through his book,

> We shall learn that the life and work of each region are linked
> with those in other regions, so that our country is one living
> whole made up of many parts, and that the closer the links are
> between the various parts of Britain, the more happy and
> prosperous our lives will be, and the better able we shall be to
> fill our part in the life of our country. (Hardingham, 1957–60,
> Book III)

Other texts used appropriate metaphors and analogies. Sometimes it
was the metaphor of the body of the nation. As we have seen this was
used to explain the centrality of London or as a means to express the
natural, functional interconnectedness of all the different parts of Britain — the Pennines being the nation's backbone and so on (*Royal*,
1911, Book III; Lay, 1937, Book IV, p. 7). The image of the nation as
home or family was common in a variety of texts, and thought
particularly suitable for children (McIntosh, 1984, p. 237). In one text
the ever-present metaphor of the national territory as house and home

became an *explicit* analogy, and exposed all the ambiguities in the process:

> Just as there are different rooms in a house so there are different regions ... We all know that, for example, the kitchen is a different kind of room from a bedroom. It contains different furniture, and is put to different use. Just in the same way a region contains things which are different from those in other regions, and people who work in different ways. (Hardingham, 1935, Book III, p. 68)

The ways in which the textbooks presented the material, their pedagogic devices, also had the effect of relating different locations. Green and Green (1939) employed the device of railway journeys across Britain to show the contrasts. They described how,

> We begin our trip among the noise and smoke of London, but we shall end it among the fresh, green beauty of Killarney. Only by watching the changing scenes with our own eyes can we learn what a busy and wonderful land this Britain of ours really is. (1939, Book IV, p. 27)

Walter's book was designed around the major roads, railways and steamer lanes which connected all kinds of people, the town and the country, the past and the present. Writing of the London to Dover road, for example, she commented,

> Humble and great, rich and poor — soldiers, sailors, pilgrims, churchmen and traders — all came to London by the Dover Road. And the story of the people who, through the ages, have travelled along this historic road is almost the whole story of England. (Walter, 1935, Book IV, p. 33)

Imaginary air travel was a perfect means of showing Britain and all its variety, laid out below for the imaginary child passenger. Chapter 3 of the second book in *Wheaton's Golden Mean Geographies* was significantly entitled 'We Fly Over the Homeland'. There, notions of nationhood were clearly established and extended by the child looking down on his land, its country and its towns:

> But although the British Isles are not very big, your ride in the plane would show you many different kinds of country. You would pass over great cities and quiet little villages. You would pass over cities partly hidden by great smoke clouds. You would pass beautiful meadows and cornland, dark green

forests and bare mountain slopes. (*Wheaton's* 1949, Book II, p. 6)

The two chief means of dividing up the locations in the British Isles have been by major natural regions and in terms of town and country. When attempting to show that the different ways of life in different areas were dependent on geographical factors whole regions of England, for example, became characterized by a single form of settlement. Specific natural gifts determined the form of labour necessary for the exploitation of those gifts, and that determined the form of settlement in whole areas. Thus, alongside descriptions of different forms of farming and the features of climate and soil which produced those differences, the books described and mapped the disposition of the coalfields and the way towns 'sprang up' there. This natural regionalization collapsed almost imperceptibly into human regions and appeared to produce in the texts two polarized human-environmental ways of life. Perhaps these are epitomized in the following descriptions of life in the peripheral areas of Britain like the Highlands and in the cotton towns of Lancashire:

> Life for these sturdy Highlanders is very hard, and the crofter and his wife must do everything they can to win a livelihood for themselves and their children ... The men, especially those of the lonely, rocky islands of the Hebrides, venture forth in their little boats to reap the harvest of the sea. (Green and Green, 1939, Book, IV, p. 18)

> The people of Lancashire are just as carefree and gay on holiday as they are industrious and perservering in their work, and it is because they work hard, and because they have made cotton the special object of their endeavours, that they have given their country such an important place in the life and work of Great Britain. (*ibid*, p. 116)

At times the geographers' contrasts of contemporary urban and rural life produced extraordinary images. In two sections called 'How the Countryman Lives' and 'How the Townsman Lives' the contrasts are drawn thus:

> ... the countryman works long hours, but he does not hurry, and takes life very quietly ... Bedtime is early, for the day starts early, and by ten o'clock most folk are asleep. (Hardingham, 1957–60, Book II, p. 132)

On the other hand, in the town,

> Most folk have their breakfast just before they go to work,
> and often get up so late that they do not have much time for
> breakfast.

After describing the town-person's evenings in milk-bars, cafes, cinemas, the comparison concludes,

> The townsman need never stay at home in the evening, and
> usually goes to bed much later than the countryman. Alto-
> gether life is much more of a rush in the town than in the
> country. (Hardingham, 1957–60, Book II, pp. 132–3)

Given the model of explanation it is clear from the above quotes, and
from all the descriptions of life in the different parts of the nation, that
what could not be ignored by traditional regionalizing geography, was
labour. The national gifts of nature have to be worked, wherever they
may be, and children must be told of the efforts of the farmers, coal
miners, deep-sea fishermen and all other categories of British, chiefly
male, labour. The essential part of that labour, in the geography for
children, however, was its regionalization, and the division between
town and country played a significant role in this. There has been a
strong emphasis on the different jobs people do and the different
places they live in. Finch, introducing the study of the British Isles
informed his readers,

> In the British Isles we shall find country and town folk;
> farmers and fishermen, miners and quarrymen, workers in
> mills, factories, shipyards ... (Finch, 1937, Book III, p. 15)

In that one passage can be found an indication of the basic differences
between types of 'folk' (urban and rural) and a list of major occupations in which co-exist at least two different positions in the social
division of labour. Again, as already noted, *farmers*, and not farm
workers, are listed alongside other workers. Only technical divisions
are visible. When Finch combined with Brooks in the production of a
series of geography books for older pupils this regionalizing of labour
was given to making different kinds of work and workers exotic yet
also, sometimes, belittled[4]. In a chapter called 'Sea Harvest' for example (Brooks and Finch, 1939, Book I) can be found reference to 'The
sea dogs of Devon' and the 'men of Cornwall' (p. 60) and to the
'Fisher-lassies' in the herring industry. Small localisms are inserted;
the miners have their 'snaps' (p. 117) and the mills are looked after by
'Lancashire lassies' (p. 148). It appears that it was thought necessary to
assure the pupils of the normality of these people,

The miner of today is generally a cheery soul, fond of the open air, proud of his home, keen on hard and vigorous sport, and a great lover of birds and animals. (Brooks and Finch, 1939, Book I, pp. 113–4)

It was also thought advisable to counteract any notions of class:

When we speak of 'workers' it is important for us to remember that anybody who earns his living is a 'worker', no matter whether he earns it by his muscles or his brains or both. The draughtsmen in the drawing office of a big shipyard who draft out the plans of a big new ship are just as much 'workers' as the riveters who toil at putting the great steel beams and plates together ... the head of a big business who plans out everything is a 'worker' just as much as those who carry out what he has planned. (*ibid*, pp. 52–3)

If with younger children, the errors of a class conscious analysis were not confronted so directly, class difference, especially the difference between wage labour and small scale entrepreneurship, could be transposed to differences between town and country life. At the end of a book which described life and work in the British towns and countryside through the use of fictional characters, the representative farmer visits his brother in Bradford, where they discuss the relative merits of town and country life. The availability within the town of the theatre, cinemas and public transport was seen as a great benefit, but the farmer could not see these as a recompense for the loss of rural life:

All the same, I shouldn't like to live here. Factory work is not as interesting as farming, and I should get very tired of the noise and smoke. I like to see the trees and fields, birds and animals just outside my window. (*Black's*, u.d., Book IV, p. 121)

His brother admitted that on sunny days, he would like to live on a farm, but,

You farmers never seem to have finished work, and you may lose money when the weather ruins your crops or your cattle die. We know exactly when we can stop work, we get our wages and our holidays regularly. (*ibid*, p. 122)

But like was not compared with like, farm worker with factory worker. The comforts of wage labour were found preferable to the problems of the owner — the history books had told the story of the evolution of their freedom to earn wages — and one social-geographical division was transposed and resolved thus:

> You see there is something to be said for and against both kinds of life. The farmer and factory worker both do very useful work, and each depends on the other. (*ibid*, p. 122)

To end this section on the representation of the homeland one must return to a comparison with some of the history books. For the latter, the developments of towns and country, after having effected a temporary division among the people of Britain, bring them together again through planning and the passage of time. For some geography texts the town and the country functionally co-exist in space, and the relations between the farmer (owner-worker) and the industrial worker is one of exchange of equivalents. For example, the book from which we have just quoted goes on to spell out the reciprocity between town and country in a money economy:

> The farmer's sprouts go to the miners of South Wales or the factory workers of Birmingham. (*ibid*, p. 124)

Ownership, as we have argued, is incorporated in the category 'farmer', who feeds the worker.

> With the money he gets for them he buys clothes from the factory workers of Leeds. They spend the money on food bought from a Yorkshire farmer. (*ibid*)

In these books a restricted view of the national economy is represented, time after time, as the exchange between country and town, farmer and factory worker or miner:

> Each part of the country shares its riches with others. The farmer sends to the coal-mining areas the produce of his fields. The busy workers of the towns send their goods to the farmer and to lands beyond the seas. There is exchange of riches, an exchange made easy by the roads and railways that are built without difficulty in our land of plains and valleys. (*Johnston's*, 1937, Book IV p. 15)

And even when the farmer as representative of ownership was added to with references to rural workers the urban-rural exchange model remained:

> . . . our farmers grow more corn than they can ever eat themselves; and our shepherds and herdsmen could not possibly eat

all the sheep and cattle. They sell to the miners, who work in the mines, to the manufacturers and factory workers who are busy making things .... (Horniblow, u.d., Book III, p. 45)

To sum up one might say that the differences between the natural and social areas and locations within the children's homeland were described in such a way to make them ultimately unified. Those distinctions depended upon notions like 'natural gifts' which had been distributed throughout the land. The chief gifts (soil and climate for agriculture and coal deposits for manufacture), in turn, determined two basic types of 'folk', mutually dependent, connected by the exchange of equivalents, and, in their differences, constituting the lovable variety of the child's homeland.

Notes

1 In many ways we can see these textbooks of the period 1930–60 as being ahead in terms of their ideas of children learning by doing but caught within, and being used for, a traditional class-teaching regime. They sometimes addressed individual children and enticed them to go out to look and learn, but they were, after all, the artefacts of the most formal classroom lessons. The result may have been that only children in certain class and geographical locations could really learn that way. The best the others could do was to look on at children in the books travelling, playing in the fields etc.

2 Such a fear, and the belief that the lack of experience of the countryside was an important part of the urban child's deprivation, lasted well beyond the examples used in this volume. London teachers involved in the EPA Environmental Studies Scheme in the early 1970s made rural experience via frequent visits to a country centre a significant part of their compensatory programme (Barnes, 1975, pp. 169–78).

3 In an earlier textbook, from which children were meant to learn by heart a series of descriptions and definitions we find London referred to as follows: 'The chief town in this group is LONDON, in Middlesex, the capital of the country, the most populous town, and the greatest seaport in the world' (Chisholm, 1898). In such traditional representations of the 'capes and bays' approach there was little room for sentiment and patriotism, for example, one sentence alone mentions England's comparative greatness in Hughes (1871).

4 A similar tendency has been noted in some approaches to multicultural education, viz. Julian Henrique, 'Social psychology and the politics of racism', in Henriques *et al* (1984) *Changing the Subject*, p. 82.

6   Foreign Lands and Labour

When children were presented with the geography of their homeland then the images of Britain as the workshop of the world were carefully reiterated and filled in. Only comparatively rarely was the national homeland represented only as a green and pleasant land,[1] even if the industrial-urban centres were seen as elsewhere and slightly odd. It was when the geographies of other countries were described that the peculiarity of the British nation may have been brought home to the young readers. Foreign urban and industrial development was, for the most part, excluded. Even as early as 1901 the representation of Britain and the rest of the world, as encapsulated in the following quote, was quite problematic:

> The Indian Squaw sews with a needle which comes from Reddich, the Siberian exile clanks a chain made at Dudley, the negro raiding a neighbouring village is armed with a Birmingham rifle, the North American trapper prepares his skin with a knife which has 'Sheffield' marked upon its blade . . . (*Pictorial Geographical Readers*, 1901, Book IV, p. 34)

Even if one accepts that the industrial development of some of the countries described at the turn of the century was still way behind that of the first industrial nation the representation of North America and Japan by climatically determined rural, national caricatures was as persistent as it was selective. For example, as late as 1937, only very belatedly did Book III of the Johnston series recognize that some other countries had been industrializing as well as busying themselves providing agricultural produce for Britain:

> Great Britain was the first country to manufacture in a big way in factories, instead of in a small way in the houses of

workers. For many years the Homeland was thus *the* Work-shop of the World, and sold to countries near and far the goods which its mills and factories had made.

But other countries also had coal and iron, and busy people who were willing to work and to learn. As time went on these countries built factories of their own to make work for their own people ... (p. 136)

This book was an exception as was Mackinder's Book 4 of the *Elementary Studies in Geography*. Writing only three years before the First World War he warned of a fool's paradise if young English readers did not see other nations prospering as we had done and he advocated a friendly competitiveness with the Germans and Americans, for, after all,

We and the Germans and Americans came of the great Teutonic stock of men ... In literature, science and engineering the Germans, the French and the Americans are away the most civilized of all mankind. (Mackinder, 1906, Book, IV, p. 250)

But most of the countries introduced to children of a far-flung Empire were not of this Teutonic family, and even when they were, because of the devices used and the preferred modes of geographical explanation, it was their landscapes rather than their industry or towns which received attention. These pedagogical devices will be considered first before looking at the ways the modes of geographical explanation helped, together, to create the images of foreign agriculture and rural life. It must be made clear, however, that just as the presentations of Britain's history and geography cannot be adequately understood as reflections of a national ruralism so the representations of foreign lands are not understandable as only biased racial stereotypes. Certainly there are biases and stereotypes, as will be all too clear, but they must be seen in terms of their relations with the representations of the homeland. How these books portrayed Africa were as much to do with showing the 'opposites' of their own national construction as it was to do with being biased about foreigners. Adapting some of the ideas developed by Sherwood in *The Psychodynamics of Race* (1980) one might say that these other lands and races, like the peripheral regions of the UK, were made into repositories for a way of natural-rural life which seemed no longer possible in most of Britain which had become the workshop of the world. Accusations of ethnocentricity can miss their target if they do not include the way the home country is portrayed alongside the foreign. As has been acknowledged (Kent,

1982, p. 17) at least this earlier geography teaching did deal with a wide scale of examples and was global in a certain limited sense. Our approach is to suggest that the ways those examples were presented was tied to internal and external practices and ideologies and at least one project of which was the construction of national identity, with all its contradictions.

Introducing Other Lands

The links between British school geography and British imperialism are most explicit in the way the early textbooks merely listed countries, their physical features, and their place in the Empire's history, perhaps including some picturesque qualities. Book VI called *The World at Home*, of the *Royal School Series* (1886) reads like an imperial, military shopping list. This approach was continued by some writers until the 1930s. Mulley's *The British Empire Overseas* (part of Nisbet's *Geography Class Books Series*, 1930) described one country after another, where it was and what it produced. The people were quickly dealt with in terms of their religion, race and 'qualities'. All the people of India, for example, were described in a few lines:

> The people vary from brown, highly civilized Hindus to dark, wild Deccan races, little better than savages. (Mulley, 1930, p. 21)

There are brief references made to caste, the Brahmin religion 'Mohammedans' and Sikhs. These formal listings had much to do with expectations about the books providing facts to be learnt; the *Royal Series* was specially prepared to fulfil the demands of the latest Code relevant to standard VI. But their content was also influenced by a geography tied in with imperialism.

When the imaginary journey became a more favoured device for presenting other countries those ties with imperialism remained, but in different ways. In *Travel through the British Empire* (in the series, *Tales of Travel*, 1916) Oates explained that the aim of the book was,

> to present the story of the British Empire in the series of adventures, retold from the journals of pioneers, explorers, and travellers, that will be read with eagerness by any boy or girl. (p. 7)

Stembridge, in his preface to *The World We Live In* (Book IV of the *World Wide Geographies Junior Series*, 1930) acknowledged his indebtedness to a Major-General Hendley for his notes on India and to Lieutenant G. Hendley Peters, RN, for his notes on Chinese life. Such influence is all too clear in the text. Stembridge takes the child reader on a meandering world journey, where the traveller passes simple lives lived in rural paradises as exemplified in the following:

> As we pass we catch glimpses of dark-skinned negroes diving for sponges for which these islands are famous. (p. 28)

The visits are typical of a British gentleman calling on what are usually British possessions:

> We land at Entebbe and then trek north-westward across Uganda, travelling over wooded plains and through forested valleys. Sometimes we pass a native village surrounded by grasslands in which we see herds of cattle feeding, while nearby there are groves of banana trees — for bananas form one of the chief foods of the dark-skinned woolly-haired natives. (p. 79)

This travelogue is completed at the end with the joy of the return to the homeland:

> How interesting it has all been. Yet we have never felt quite the same thrill as we do when we set our feet once more on England's soil.
> 　Yes it is good to be home at last in our own sea-girt land. (*ibid*, p. 159)

Pickles in another text invited the children to be travellers in strange lands and gave them all the paraphernalia of the Englishman abroad. Before visiting West Africa,

> We must take with us several thin, light-coloured suits, many changes of underwear and a sun helmet … Rubber boots, a mackintosh and an umbrella are made necessary by the very heavy rains which the region experiences … (Pickles, 1933, p. 38)

and later he tells the children what they would need before setting out big game hunting in East Africa (*ibid*, p. 9).

　The imaginary travelling child also fulfilled his or her role of the imperial visitor. Tom Franklin of Book II in the Series *Lands and Life* (Horniblow, 1936), to which references have already been made, handed out a penknife and chocolate to South African black children, and showed them how to make a model out of clay. The commentary added:

> Weren't the black boys pleased with this. They thought Tom was very clever. (p. 38)

An extreme example of such texts was a book called *Colin and Patricia in South Africa* (Rutley, 1952) in which white, middle class visitors accompany their uncle on a tour of South Africa and Southern Rhodesia.

A major series which had its first edition in 1919 and was still in use in the 1950s after thirty reprints and six different editions, used in its first book a most contrived and bizarre means to transport children from one land to another (*Philips Human Geographies*, 1919). They joined the man in the moon on his journeys and introduced him to children from different countries. One might expect that to such a distant traveller all land and peoples would be equally strange, but he had English children to make the necessary judgments for him. Strangely, children of the Arctic, the American Plains (Red Indians) the Steppes and the desert were given a natural charm and told the visitors their stories and myths, but it was the forest children (pygmies) who were singled out for special criticism.

> They care nothing for their own land or people ... They are cruel to one another. They threw stones and shot arrows.... These children do not tell one another stories. They know nothing about the past. They do not think about the future. They have no God, and they say no prayers. (*ibid*, Book I, p. 126)

Unlike the other travelogues, one people only were singled out to bear all the possible characteristics which were opposite to those expected of the English school child, i.e. unnationalized, having no sense of their society's past or their own future, godless.

The device of the travelogue was not always used in the same way. Sometimes it was in the form of extended letters written by friends or relations describing life in foreign lands, viz. *Pampas and Wilds of the South* by A.M. Baxter (no. 20 of series *Little People in Far Off Lands*, u.d.) and the two books of the series *My Foreign Correspondent* by Moss *et al* (1956). F.D. Herbertson used original explorers' letters in her book for children on the British Empire (Herbertson, 1906). Another variation was to get a much-travelled relative to describe his journeys to interested children. *Chamber's New Geographical Reader* (1891) was an early example of this where a father described his foreign adventures. Book 16 in the *Little People Series* (u.d.) used a much-travelled uncle to describe Nigeria in this way and the device was used extensively in the *Question-Time Series* by Ethel Phillips (1951–61). This series comprised of numerous small reading books for very young children and enabled 'Uncle Jack' to describe, in the different books, the origins and processing of such things as a coconut (Book I), treacle (Book II), sponge and soap (Book III) and so on.

This latter example brings us to another very common means of introducing foreign lands to English children. The device of the visit promoted the exotic and emphasized the movement of white people, even children, past the static lives of mainly rural folk in other countries, but it could not *connect* those lands and people to the homeland. The visiting children rarely had any extended contact with the lives of those visited. The connections were made only by considering '*what they sent us*'. Sometimes that was done by depicting in diagrams and maps the way the harvests of the world all came to Britain, as in Book II of *Wheaton's Golden Mean Geographies* (1949), pp. 23 and 25. Brooks and Finch in a book called *Many Things from Many Lands* (Finch, 1928) have a chapter called 'All Sea Roads lead to Britain'. In Alnwick's *Our Food and Our Clothes* (1951) we find national and racial caricatures all offering their goods with a smile.

In *McDougall's Geographical Primer* (u.d. 1936?) each country is organized in terms of what it sends to Britain, for example:

> The country in Europe which is nearest to England is France. From this country we get grapes, silk and wine. The countries from which tea comes are in Asia ... China, a large country in the East of Asia, also sends us tea. (pp. 25–6)

The first book of Lay's series, *The Empire Geographies* (1937), significantly called *Treasures From Land and Sea*, was typical in its tracing back a product like tea to its foreign origins. This section of the book began with a homely question, 'Have you ever made a pot of tea?' (p. 19) and then proceeded sequentially to show the simple life of foreign rural producers:

> The workers on a tea plantation are called coolies. Most of the pickers are women, who have very clever fingers. They handle the tender shoots with dainty care (*ibid*);

and then described the processes of production and transport to England.

A very common reality-making device was to *bring home* such ideas to the children by descriptions of the origins of the variety of food, as in West's *Geography at the Grocers* (no. 22 in A.L. *Everychild Series*, u.d.). Brooks and Finch (1939, Book III) used the breakfast to teach English children about trade and their dependence on foreign labour, but also, perhaps, about how all labour can be bought and the fruits to be enjoyed by the children of popular imperialism. They concluded that,

> To provide these, (sugar, tea, etc.) numbers of workers in far-off lands — in Australia, New Zealand, West Indies, Ceylon, the Gold Coast, Spain — have toiled in fields, farms and factories, and many others have given their services in transport, in offices, in banks, in shops to bring these to our tables.
>
> Yet each of us can enjoy our breakfast at small cost, little dreaming that it may have meant the joint services of thousands of workers in our own and in distant lands. For a few shillings we buy the united labours of thousands of people, thanks to trade and commerce and the wonderful machines that make them possible. (pp. 14–15)

Other texts using the breakfast table device include Cook (1950) Book III, p. 10; Glover and Young (1960) Book I, p. 55; *Johnston's* (1937) Book III, p. 23. Some extended it beyond credibility. Marie Bayne in Book II of *The World Around Us* (1934) had a geographically convenient, yet unlikely, meal of cocoa, milk and sugar, a roll and butter, two dates and an orange (p. 24). Book II of *Black's New Graded Geographies* (u.d.) called 'The Wonderland of Common Things' focused on a Mrs Brown, living in an English town, and determinedly consuming products from home and abroad and thus enabling the child reader to study, among other things, banana plantations, English market gardens and Ceylon tea pickers. Here, as in so many other texts, other places are mere sources for English suburban consumption.

It may be misleading to associate what are just pedagogical devices for use with young children with any particular ideology or economic system. The apparent affinity between the ways these devices are used in the texts and popular imperialism and derived notions of world trade needs some commentary. Setting aside the earlier way in which countries were listed with their physical features, races and products, which, in a sense, made no concessions to the child, it must be acknowledged that the later devices (which could claim to take into account at least one type of childhood) gave rise to problems as well as solutions.

One of the problems behind the 'breakfast table' approach was how it could show to the young the British people's *dependence* on foreign rural labour yet, at the same time, maintain the safe superiority of the homeland. One of the means of resolving this in texts for innocent children has been by moralizing the relationship between the two in a certain way. Notions of free trade were not thought suitable to introduce to the young so the foreign worker was seen as *helping us*, for which the child should be thankful. Thus we have titles such as 'How the Negro Farmer Helps Us' (Pickles, 1933, p. 47) and passages attempting to teach gratitude. At the end of a typically sequenced account of the origins and processing of cocoa and rubber, Lay (1937) wrote:

> We ought to be very thankful to the black people and the brown people who work in the hot, wet forests to supply us with cocoa and rubber. The work is dangerous for the damp and heat breed swarms of stinging and biting insects and give rise to fever germs ... Yet in spite of these, native peoples work in the forests, and Englishmen live near the plantations to look after them. (Book I, p. 25)

Book III of *Johnston's New Picture Geographies* (1947) remarked:

> What a number of distant lands have to help us before we can have our coffee, tea and cocoa, sugar and milk! (p. 23)

and went on to show clearly enough the dependence of post-war Britain on other peoples:

> In all parts of the world men and women have been at work growing the food which you have eaten. Hot lands and cool lands, forest lands and grass lands, have sent you their crops. English-speaking people thousands of miles away, black people, brown people and yellow people have all done their share ... The breakfast-table should teach us to think of this — the most important of all geography lessons — *How much we need the help of peoples in other lands.* (p. 26)

Teaching interdependence in the post-war world is one thing but in so many of the texts the steamships all bring things to us. Imports from foreign lands may appear to help equalize the differences among us, but nothing is said about other inequalities between them and us because Britain is presented as having reached, for all its dependence, an unassailable superiority. In a book as late as 1961 Vickers combined a humanistic description of the superiority of man (sic) with an account of his progress which fortunately placed Britain at the pinnacle:

> In our times we lead a much richer life than has ever been possible before. We can, even the poorer among us, buy foods grown on the other side of the world ... These blessings come as a direct result of man's use of his brain and his cooperation with his brother men. (p. 11)

It will be shown later how such superiority was given a natural basis, and how this indebtedness was resolved, and within that particular geography could never become an unbalanced and unsettling inequality.

Finally, another means by which it was thought that the child reader could come to understand the ways of life in other countries was by telling them of the lives of children in other lands. This also permitted some wider ideological connections to be made. Just as some history textbook writers thought that telling stories of child characters in history may have made history more real to contemporary children so geography books have, over a long period, described the lives of foreign children for the same reasons, notwithstanding the fact that childhood itself is both geographically and historically specific. Some chapter headings in an early book like *Little Folks of Other Lands* (in the series *The World and its People*, 1919) suggested clearly enough what the approach was: Tiny Black Folks; Little Brown Folks; Happy Little Folks; Little Folks by the Great River; Little Folks of Zululand; Little Black Fellows, and so on, all organized within a three-fold regional geography. The use of children's lives to show the differences between the regions was continued throughout the sample. In their description of Book I, of the *Looking at the World Series* (Green and Green, 1939) it was clear what was intended by the authors. Called, 'Families in Other Lands' it was said to contain

> Picturesque and detailed accounts of family life in lands which represent all the main climatic types. The chapters had been arranged to give all the full value of contrast.

Thus, only features of children's lives which showed how different it was in, say, 'the African forest' because of climate were included in these books. In a similar way Noyle (1949) explained to teachers that his *Family Life Abroad* (in the series *Adventures in Geography for Primary Schools*)

> contains eight studies, based on a simple pattern of climatic

regions in the form of attractive studies in which actual family events are seen as the natural outcome of environment.

In these ways, the characters were very much the children of nature. Boyce's *Children of Other Lands* (1961) tied most of the child-subjects to their nation's climate, and Marie Bayne's *The World's Children* (Book I of *The World Around Us Series*, 1934) organized her book through the major regions. The section called 'Children of the Temperate Lands', for example, included an account of Betje and Jan, two Dutch children who lived on a tulip farm, American Sal whose father was a farmer in Iowa, Billy the son of an Australian sheep farmer and little Jack of the Canadian Forest, who was the son of a lumberjack. It is interesting to note that not one example of these young regional representatives lived in a town except Pierre, a young Swiss waiter in a London cafe, and he was saving his money to return to the Alps where he had lived on a farm as a boy. The account was of his memories of a cosy childhood lived through the seasons in an Alpine valley. Similarly, Book I of the *Columbus Regional Geographies Series* (Finch, 1928) called *Children From Many Lands* used the lives of small national-racial caricatures (Little Otter, the Red Indian, Ali of the Great Desert, Teke of the Great Forest *et al*) to represent other lands by their most primitive and rural. English childhood was one of town life and visits to an uncle's farm (chapters 1 and 4).

This failure ever to account for any urban lives of children from other countries continued until the 1960s. The books of S.M. Walton's *First Geography Readers*, published in 1963 had all the children from rural areas, although making visits to the towns. In Book VI of the series (*Pepi of the Pampas*) the child has to go to town for schooling and the way adults think rural children are affected by urban life was given quite detailed treatment in a section called 'The touch of a town':

> Pepi was too frightened to notice more than white buildings, heat and noise ... (Walton, 1963)

We shall deal with the effects of regional geography on the representation of the rest of the world and of other races in the next section. What the device of using other children's lives within a regional approach did was not only to help portray childhood in other lands as a natural and primitive existence, but also tended to make all people of other races child-like. If lives in all the other countries were happy rural ones for the children, they were also quaint and secure for their parents. Easily satisfied, these happy, *simplified* people were, in the discourse, the products of the climate.

Climates, Races and Foreign Agriculture

A continual strand within this analysis has been the inappropriateness of exclusive models for explaining the content of textbooks. We have attempted to cast some doubt on notions of an essential English ruralist culture, and on the reduction of texts to just the expression of the class position of the writers. The well-documented reservations within these books about industrialization and the critical side of some rural retrospect should also disturb any simple model of pro-capitalist indoctrination. It is not that ideologies associated with external economic and political interests have not penetrated schooling and its artefacts, but they are best seen as active alongside what have been called the internal factors of pedagogic practices, their assumptions about the nature of childhood and about how children learn. In the previous section, for example, we looked at the use of pedagogically informed devices in relation to the external ideologies of popular imperialism — devices through which very particular images of almost universal foreign rurality were constructed. Now we must consider the ways in which regional geography within the academic discipline played its part.

The development of this regional geography was, in some ways, external to schooling,[2] but there is evidence of much interplay between pedagogic concerns and the development of the subject at the end of the nineteenth century and the beginning of the twentieth. Mackinder, for example, had encouraged teachers to regionalize their teaching of geography in the 1880s and 1890s (Biddle, 1985) and, after the systematic presentation of a developed theory of the regions by A.J. Herbertson (1905), these ideas were apparently more readily taken up by teachers in the Geographical Association than by the Fellows of the Royal Geographical Society. As Bramwell notes, within a year of the publication of Herbertson's paper two articles on the teaching of regional geography occurred in *The Geographical Teacher* (Bramwell, 1961, pp. 30–1). Herbertson was convinced that his classification would greatly aid the teaching of geography, and regional study was taken as a way out of the stultifying rote-learning implicit in the so-called 'capes and bays' approach and he involved himself in the production of school geography books (Herbertson and Herbertson, 1899; Herbertson, A.J., 1904; and Herbertson, F.D., 1906). In his adaptation of Frye's *Complete Geography* (*An Illustrated School Geography*) he introduced children to zones and set out a very clear causal chain linking climate and physical conditions to the differentiation of town and country (Herbertson, 1904, p. 55).

In the geographical education of children over 13 years of age the regional approach was dominant from 1918 until after the Second World War (Hogan, 1962). As far as elementary and, subsequently, primary textbooks were concerned then our evidence is that it was mainly through an *adapted* regional geography—its means of classification and its concerns — that the world was organized and explanations given as to why 'they' were different from 'us'. The first book we came across to expound a very simple regionalization of the world was number six of the *Royal School Series* (1886) where zones were first described before moving on to a long catalogue of different countries, their products and picturesque qualities. In this early book no attempt was made to conjecture upon effects of climate on the lives of the people and their differentiation. Indeed there was very little mention of human life at all. Subsequent use of regional geography to construct a hierarchy of climates and peoples, however, may be foreshadowed in the clear preference given to the natural gifts of the North Temperate Zone. The book claimed that,

> Nearly all those mammals most useful to man, in performing labour, or in furnishing him with food and clothing, belong to the temperate zones, as the horse, the ass, the cow, the sheep, etc ... The finest song-birds also belong to this zone though their sobre plumage contrasts with the brilliant colours of tropical birds. Here also is the home of the honey bee and of the silkworm. (*Royal*, 1886, VI)

From the point of view of this study teaching geography through the natural regions could be seen to have given in-built reasons why, when looking at other countries, there was an almost exclusive concentration on their agriculture and rural existence. To the exclusion of others, lives closest to nature were taken as representing *all* life elsewhere. So often, when 'foreign lands' were introduced via regional geography, either all the examples of human life were rural, or urban environments were added as an after-thought.

It has to be accepted that there are problems with coming to what may be regarded as 'a balanced coverage across the environments, from dominantly natural to dominantly man made' as Kent expresses it (Kent, 1982), but when those textbooks attempted to move from listing topographical details of each country to a more human geography and pedagogy then the people of those countries entered as the children of nature, arrested in their stage of development by the climate. What was distinctively geographical was this very climatic determination[3] and, in this respect, it must be distinguished from any genetically based racism. At the turn of the century it was thought that even *British* children who might be born in tropical, colonial settlements, for example, should be brought back to England for fear that their growth would be stunted (Hudson, 1977, p. 16).

It is impossible to trace the different intellectual influences on the textbook writers at the turn of the century and onwards but texts like A.J. and F.D. Herbertson's *Man and His Work* (1899), written as the first attempt to present the principles of human geography in popular form, and first published in 1899, set down the general perspective on the climatic determination of people's lives and character and, incidentally perhaps, provided the basis for an imperial hierarchy of the races. In that book, for example, it was argued that the climate could be too hard, and thus produced a people like the Aborigines, or too soft, as was that of the Brazilian forests. Without any notions of pure races the Herbertsons could secure the white man's superiority by showing the perfection of the temperate climate for human development. They thought it was the climate which

> makes life neither so easy that men degenerate, nor so severe that all their energies are absorbed in the task of keeping body and soul together. The annually returning winter, in which men can neither sow nor reap, but must depend on what they have cultivated in summer, teaches foresight and thrift. (p. 3)

Eight years before the publication of this book Barrington-Ward was showing children how differences of temperature led to particular kinds of plants and animals and to 'differences in mankind', adding that,

> These differences, however, are most likely caused only by climate and manner of life, for we believe that all men have sprung from one family. (Barrington-Ward, 1891, p. 43)

That text then followed with an adulation of the white race for its superior agriculture and trade. A clear, naturally based hierarchy was represented to children, with the Victorian family at the top and the savage at the bottom, with some people in between 'in that half savage state we call barbarous' (*ibid*, p. 45).

If many of the history books were involved in the presentation of myths of rural and racial origin then these geography texts used towns and trade as evidence of a naturally determined superiority in the present. Meiklejohn, in a textbook intended to be used by teachers in training, had detailed descriptions of the different races and organized their ways of life in descending order, linking them with the zones of the world and with a guarantee of superiority for those of the temperate climate:

> It is in the temperate zones of the world that different kinds of labour and enterprise have grown to their highest perfection. In these zones nature grants nothing without a struggle. In the torrid zone nature is lavish in her bounties, and does not compel man to work for a living. In the frigid zone the struggle is so severe that man spends the whole of his life in getting a mere living. (Meiklejohn, 1893, p. XLIX)

If these are early examples of the way regional geography viewed the differences between the races, an approach derived from these is to be found in textbooks for the next sixty years at least. Some have suggested an *adaptation* to the demands of the local climate by those who live in the different regions. Others have presented a climatic determination of racial differences which seems inexorable. Yet others left open the question of exactly how climatic region and race fitted together. Pickles, in his *Britain and Abroad* (1927, this ed 1949) organized his book by describing what he called 'a typical race in each region' and included as examples the usual Eskimoes in the Arctic, Arabs in the desert, the Kirghiz in the Steppes, and the Pygmies in the equatorial forest. Other writers attempted more explicit comparisons and hinted at an irreversible determination. Paul, in a series intended mainly for pupils of secondary age called the *Adventures of Man Geographies* (1954), contrasted the Eskimo, whose struggle for life took all his (sic) energies with the position at home, where,

> The British workman has free evenings and free weekends. After his day's work he can dig up his allotment or go for a walk or play football ... because he has energy and interest to spare after earning his living. (p. 170)

On the other hand the lazy 'savage' who lives in the jungle is 'encouraged in this laziness' (*ibid*, Book I, p. 171) as he can get whatever he wants by collection. Sixty years after the first regional geographies this book reiterated the climatic basis for both a superior life of comparative ease as well as one of endeavour. Referring to the white man the writer claimed that,

> unlike the savage of the hot, wet jungle, he has got to plan
> ahead if he is to live through the winter ... The man of the
> temperate zones is compelled to be enterprising. (*ibid*, p. 172)

In Book III of the series (*The Discovery of the World*) the different races
were shown as ideally suited to their different climates, and the old
divisions of savage, barbarian and civilized were reiterated. Of the
savage it was said,

> It is very difficult to civilize them. They find it so hard to copy
> the White Man that they lose heart. (Paul, 1954, Book III,
> p. 132)

Locating Britain and its people within a regional geography varied
from the simplistic, as in Lay's claim that 'our climate helps to make
us a strong and active race' (Lay, 1914, p. 7) to the common belief
that hard, long winters encouraged something like the Protestant
ethic, as was to be found in some of the examples mentioned above.
However elaborated was the explanation, what was secured was a
geographically determined national-racial superiority. As Nightingale
expressed it in the book on the British Isles in the *Visual Series*:

> A climate like ours is healthy to live and work in, for it is
> rarely too hot and never too cold for us to work well. We can
> make full use of the rich store of minerals in our rocks and of
> the fertile soil in our fields. People who live in hot lands or in
> the cold lands cannot make the most of all that nature has
> given them, because their climate hinders them. That is one
> reason why the British race has become more important in the
> world than the Negroes or the Eskimoes. (*Visual*, 1920, p. 2)

In the case of the Afro-Carribean peoples the descriptions of climatically determined ways of life frequently became a judgment in terms
of laziness, and contributed to the stereotype of carefree simplicity. In
Little Folks of Other Lands (1919) the imaginary teacher told her pupils
about life in the hot lands:

> The people need not work hard for their food. They live on
> fruit which grows wild, and they have only to pluck it from
> the trees. This makes them lazy. They do not like hard work.
> They love to lie in the sun doing nothing. (p. 13)

Horniblow (1936) followed a standard climatic explanation of differences between peoples and said of 'the Negro',

> He lives in a land where life is easy, for nature has been very

kind to him. He need not — and does not — work very hard, for he can easily get food and he does not require much clothing. (Book III, p. 9)

In Book I of the series this author had written into the text a happy, child-like black, who introduced himself thus:

As you will see later, I am a black man. My home is in Africa, where the sun is always very hot ... I am very proud of all my family, with their shiny, smiling faces, and their nice, black, woolly hair. (*ibid*, p. 7)

All is happiness and ease.

I think my home looks very nice. It is very comfortable inside for mummie and the girls have made many grass mats. (*ibid*, p. 14)

We negroes do not have many worries. We have plenty to eat, plenty of sport, and plenty of play, we laugh and sing and are very happy. (p. 19)

According to these geography textbooks foreign lands had debilitating climates and lazy natives, yet, as was shown in the previous section, many of those other lands were also introduced to children by the goods they produced for them to enjoy, and for which they should be grateful. From this selection of books it would appear that the crudest climatically determined stereotypes were to be found in the earliest books (the 1880s to the 1920s) and notions of *our* dependence only emerged in the 1930s and 40s. Children may have wondered how such difficult climatic conditions and inadequate peoples could have provided the homeland with such a variety of goods. The answer lay in the way the textbooks portrayed foreign agriculture.

Unlike the history textbooks there was no absence of rural, agricultural labour in the representation of life in other lands. Some texts used the varied examples of labour to teach the virtues of hard work and to show how thought and labour distinguish people from animals (Saunders, 1928 and 1945). As we have noted, through the sample there was an increasing concern for the English child to understand and *appreciate* foreign, rural labour. Texts and illustrations dealt with the work of tea-pickers in Ceylon, tapping rubber trees in Malaya, picking bananas and cutting sugar cane in the West Indies, cocoa farming in West Africa and so on. There were full descriptions of the seasons, the sowing, tending and harvesting of the crops. Barker, in Book IV of the *Queensway Junior Geography* took his child-readers through the year of a peasant farmer in Egypt and in Mexico, and through the busy day of an Indian worker on a Malayan rubber plantation (Barker, 1959, Book IV, pp. 18–38). In most text-books the work was done by smiling men and women who, compared to the white men, could happily withstand the effects of the heat. On the growing of cotton and sugar the author of *Little Folk of Other Lands* told the children that,

> It is too hot for white folks to work in the fields. Only black men and women can bear the heat. (1919, p. 16)

Hardingham's *Ourselves and Our Cousins* (Book III of *Foundations of Geography*, 1935) had an aunt telling her neice and nephew about sugar production in the West Indies:

> 'Aren't there any white people in Jamaica?' asked Jerry. 'There are a few', said his aunt, 'but it is the black people who do all the hard work. They can stand the heat better than white people ...' 'Oh', said Janet, 'Fancy having white sugar made by black people!'

In the case of foreign agriculture, also, there was not the same care to hide some of the social relations of production or the distinctions between ownership, control and labour. Surprisingly perhaps, both the technical processes of agricultural production and the institutions in which these occur were often made quite clear. The regime of the plantation in particular was accepted and shown to children. Describing Malayan rubber production T.H. Cook, who had confused the differences between the English farmer and agricultural worker elsewhere in his texts, wrote of the plantation manager in the comfort of his bungalow and the coolies in their huts:

> At 5 o'clock in the morning, before it is light, all the workers, men, women and children are sent to do weeding. They work in gangs of 20 or 30. Each gang is in the charge of a headman who sees that the workers do not idle. (Cook, 1950, Book III, p. 18)

Even child labour was acknowledged.

The foreign worker was so obviously different that the white child-reader was addressed as a potential manager and controller of black labour. Alnwick, in *Our Food and Our Clothes* (1951), in a section called 'A Crop of Bananas', invited the child to be a plantation manager, telling him, 'You will need an army of helpers on your big plantation' (p. 9). Seen as 'the white man method' (p. 55) the plantation was compared to the natives' 'patch' farming. Alnwick's account of the development of sugar plantations exactly paralleled the history textbooks' accounts of the enclosures at home:

> When the white man has land in these places he too grows sugar cane. . . . He not only does the job in a big way but in a thoughtful way; he plans to save time and labour by using machinery; he studies how to get more sugar by growing only the best kinds of sugar cane; he tries to keep the soil fertile by the use of manure and chemicals; and he teaches his workers to be clean and orderly on the plantation instead of careless and lazy on their patches. (p. 55)

Interestingly, no concessions were made in the textbooks provided in the United Kingdom for use in the Empire. In *Blackie's Tropical Readers* (u.d.) intended for children in the West Indies there is adulation of 'Mr Hood' an estate owner in Jamaica. The account ended thus:

> and now, as I see the men cutting down the long canes close to their stools for the mill, I feel glad that Mr Hood is reaping a good crop in return for all his thoughtfulness and labour. (p. 109)

Also similar to the history books' accounts of the liberation of English people from feudal vassalage was the geography books' contrasts between plantation work and slavery. The only difference was that the black worker needed supervision in spite of being a wage labourer. In a conventional description of the West African forests as a source of products 'for us' *Johnston's* (Book II) asked,

> Now what are these people in West Africa like? You can see some of them in the picture here.

(The picture, of a boy climbing an oil-palm tree, was the conventional image of effortless, joyful labour in an exotic, garden-like landscape.)

> They are, of course, black people. They are strong and brave, and, with white foremen to show them the way, they work on oil-palm and cocoa plantations.
>
> They are free people and not slaves, although this was the part of Africa from which many slaves were taken in the old, bad days of slavery. (*Johnston's*, 1937, Book II, pp. 23–4)

Similarly when describing West Indian sugar production the text contrasted the old slave system and showed the black saved by wage labour (Book III, p. 44). The unknown author of *Little Folks of Other Lands* (1919) made a comparison with the children's parents when writing of black rural labour released from slavery:

> They still work in the fields but now they work for wages, just as your fathers do. (p. 18)

(There was some potential for confusion in this text, given that five pages earlier the black's laziness had been determined by the climate.)

But, however the plantation system was described, the benefits of that method of agriculture abroad, like those of enclosure at home, accrued to 'us'. As Lay (1937) noted,

> We can buy a pound of tea for about 3/-, but before India had her great plantations a pound of tea in England cost 20/- and more. (Lay, 1937, Book I, p. 19)

No brief description of the way plantation agriculture was represented in these textbooks would be complete without special reference to the example most commonly found — the tea plantations of Ceylon (as it was then called). The production of the characteristic national beverage so far away seemed to compel all textbooks to describe the harvesting of this crop in the most idealized terms. Like the pictures still appearing on the tea packets in British supermarkets, the scene was luxurious and fantastic. Woman's agricultural labour, so ignored in accounts of farming at home, was appreciated as an exquisite contact with nature. Describing the scene in a section called 'How Ceylon helps fill the tea caddy' Cook (1950) after referring to the manager and his gang, wrote as follows:

> The pickers are busy at work. They are nearly all women and they make a beautiful picture as they move among the green bushes, the sun shining on their glossy black hair, on their gay coloured robes and their sparkling ornaments. (Book III, p. 35)

In a similar way Lay (1937) described this scene as follows:

> The workers of the tea plantation are called coolies. Most of the pickers are women who have very clever fingers. They handle the tender shoots with dainty care. You can see them in the picture busily filling their baskets, which they take to the factory to be weighed. The women are paid a certain amount of money for every pound of tea leaves they pick. (Book I, p. 19)

When the travelogue form took the child-subject close to such exotic foreign woman's labour the effects of white paternalism were troublesome. In Book IV of the *Pleasant Pathways Series* the much-travelled Tom was invited to the estate of a white manager of a tea plantation. One of the pickers was called over to show Tom the leaves she had picked:

> 'All the girls can pick fifty pounds of leaves in a day', said the Manager, 'so we must not keep any of them from their work. Off you go Monnee'.
> The girl smiled and returned to her work, whilst the car soon brought them to the centre of the estate.

But on returning to the ship where he worked as a cabin boy, Tom could not forget that particular white man's burden ...

> All the time he worked he thought of their lovely island, its very charming people with all the good things they produced. For a moment he wished he lived there. He felt he would love to manage a tea plantation. (Spink and Brady, 1950, Book IV, p. 63)

Partly because they concentrated on crops like tea, which were consumed by the children in the homeland, these books contained a highly ethnocentric view of foreign agriculture. Production by the indigenous population for their *own* consumption was either ignored or misrepresented, hence the common appearance of the women tea pickers of Ceylon yet the virtual complete absence of woman's labour in Africa, even though it has been estimated that the latter have been responsible for between 60 and 80 per cent of the work in the fields (viz. Women and Geography Study Group, 1984, pp. 107–14).

A Geography of 'Them' and 'Us'

In the last part of the previous section it has been shown that regional geography, as a development within the academic discipline, and into geography teaching in school books, both established a national confidence and, at the same time, a set of assumptions about other races. It located them firmly in their climates and in lands which inhibited their growth towards civilization. Where conditions were too difficult (the deserts, the Arctic) their lives were oddities; existences of constraint, hardship and struggle. Of more imperial significance, in the so-called 'hot lands' of the Carribean and Africa, life was thought to be too easy, there being no necessity to work hard and save. In the books there is a clear implication of a natural hierarchy by which the British are given their place in the world. It is a place which demands hard work and delayed gratification, but offers superiority.

A pure regional geography, however, had no internal reasons to make any explicit connections between 'their lives' and 'our lives'. It was a geography of natural differences and distances. Indeed we have attempted to show how, within children's regional geography, those lands and their peoples were so different from 'us' that their lives were fantasized. Young children were invited to see them as strange, the supposition being, perhaps, that children had a fascination for the peculiar, and this could be used to teach them about the world. People of those other lands were thus diminished.

One way of dealing with such images of other races, and their ways of life as represented in those regional geographies, would be to draw attention to the one-dimensional stereotypes, to suggest selections, omissions, idealizations and misrepresentations. Indications of the dehumanizing and belittling representations of other peoples have a moral force of their own, and inform both some of the previous commentary here and many of the criticisms of children's books by other writers, viz. Broderick (1973), Milner (1975), Dixon (1977). This is not an inconsequential part of the exercise, for it can be both educative and analytic. But *only* providing a humanistic critique is not satisfactory for the following reasons. First, this form of critical commentary does not always reveal the functions of such images with regard to wider, less obvious ideological enterprises, nor does it show how, for example, ideas derived from a form of geography relate to racism and the justification of imperialism. Attacks on stereotypes are usually attacks on singular descriptions and attributions. They say little about the systems in which these stereotypes work. Second, such an approach may presume that bias and prejudice can be overcome by representing to individual learners life in equatorial Africa, for example, with accuracy and precision. It is not that recent revisions to school texts are unimportant, but such an approach does appear to deal only with the surface of prejudice and presumes a very simple rational-individual transcendence of that bias via programmes of world studies, perhaps, or multicultural geography. What tends to be ignored is the fact that the presentations of *others* in the texts is tied into the location and differentiation of *ourselves*. Caricatures of the child-like, happy native create the space for the inquisitive, English, adult-to-be.[4] In a certain way, representations of the primitive,

rudimentary life of others have been built upon contrasting representations of 'our' lives as suburban and comfortable. Nowhere is
this found clearer than in the opposing visual images in the series
Children of Today (Boyce, 1957–58), where the text speaks of the
varying satisfaction of human needs and the illustrations help to define
'us' against 'them'.

In order now to move a little beyond the analysis and critique of
stereotypes an attempt will be made, first, to show how the images of
a children's regional geography could form part of an overall ideology
of popular imperialism, especially from the 1920s onwards. Secondly
it will be suggested where the dualities rural-urban, primitive-
civilized fit within a contemporary interest in the racism of some of
these texts.

Imperial Dependence on the Primitive

Alongside the concerns for enlisting geography teaching in the
training for citizenship there emerged, during the 1920s and 1930s, an
interest in using school geography to develop an appreciation of
British dependence on trade (Gilbert, 1984, pp. 67–9). Taking the
sample of texts studied here as a whole one can find a growing attention being given to trade and British dependence on the labour of
other, predominantly rural peoples. Such ideas were contained within
an unproblematic view of the world as a market-place. As Brooks and
Finch expressed it in 1939, 'The world today is like a vast shop ...'
(Book I, p. 212). Uncertainties about the security of Britain's imperial
connections, combined with pedagogic notions of beginning with the
children's experience, helped *add* a geography of trade and products to
a geography of the regions. One message intended for the consumers
of the products of those distant lands was that those happy peoples
had only to be released from slavery, and organized, to provide all the
goods which graced the breakfast tables all over England. This foreign, rural labour was presented against the background of a generous
— an over-generous — nature. The suggestion here is that a regional
geography, with its descriptions of separate, discrete climates, vegeta-
tions and peoples was, in a way, necessary to legitimate the position
of the homeland and its workers in relation to those other lands and
theirs. Children could be shown foreign rural labour, could be taught
about 'our' dependence on that labour, and sometimes given a view of
the system in which that labour was controlled. They could be told to
be grateful. Crucially important, however, was the way the images

from the regional fantasies coexisted with the attention given to trade in order to maintain the belief that those people who worked in the hot sun for 'us' could be happy with little reward. The reason was that, living in a natural paradise, their needs were few.[5] Unable to present international trade as the exchange of equivalents, as between the farmer and the industrial worker within Britain's own national boundaries it was, nonetheless, shown as stable and satisfactory to foreign worker and home consumer alike. A complete replacement of regional geography by a geography of trade and commerce as suggested by W.D. Wright (1938) in a book for training college students could not have produced such ideological effects if *international* trade was studied (p. v).

Horniblow, in the 1920s, hinted at the exchange which lay behind the simple commodities children may take for granted and suggested the presssures that Britain was under to produce that which other countries needed:

> ... the people of other countries work for us because we work for them. If we did not produce things they want and can pay for they would not let us have the things they produce. (u.d., Book I, p. 216)

Interestingly, however, there was no evidence in the texts of the use of British or any other industrial products by those people in the preceding descriptions of the regions.

Pickles, in the 1930s, gave considerable attention to Britain's dependence, for example, on West Africa. He noted that

> We at home are coming to depend more and more on the labour of the West African negro for many of our foodstuffs and raw materials. (Pickles, 1933, Book I, p. 38)

At the end of that book, in a chapter called 'Mutual Aid — The Benefits of Trade' the interconnectedness of 'us' and 'them was given an uneasy expression:

> So the white cotton planters in Queensland and the black labourers on the African farms are, in a way, partners in the Lancashire cotton industry. (p. 202)

Brooks and Finch, writing just before the outbreak of World War II, ended the third book of the *Golden Hind Geographies* (1940, Series II, Book III) with a chapter called 'The World Our Home' with the claim that, even savage peoples dwelling 'on the fringes of civilisation' now use manufactured goods which they get from traders ...

The following passage is worth quoting at some length for the ways in which it conceptualized a certain view of world interdependence; a view which combined a sense of moral indebtedness with a conception of different needs —

> More than ever the world's peoples have come to depend upon each other, often for their daily needs. *The more civilized they are the greater their needs, and the more they must depend on peoples in other lands whom they have never seen* ... (my emphasis). The world today is closely knit together by many ties, and we, like other people, find our 'home' and our 'country' closely connected with other 'homes' and 'countries'. Thus we must learn to think, not of ourselves alone, but of all those unknown to us in this and other countries who provide us with the things we need, and to remember that our work will be for others no less than ourselves. If we are good geographers we shall not look upon the world as a mass of independent and closely related countries and states, but as a living unit, in which, as the years go by, the various regions and their peoples must become more and more bound to one another by ties of understanding, sympathy and interdependence. (p. 267)

In *Johnston's New Picture Geographies* (1947, Book II) the combination of natural differences in needs with an acknowledgement of the dependence of white people on black was presented in a description of South Africa. Children were told that on the farms and in the houses all the work was done by blacks,

> In South Africa, even though it is not so hot as in the Guinea lands, it is still too hot for white people to do hard work. In Africa all hard work is done by the black man. (p. 32)

Four pages later the reader was assured that,

> The Kaffirs and the Zulus need few clothes, and use no chairs and tables such as we have. A few pots and pans are all they want, so that, with these very simple needs they can be quite happy with not doing very much hard work. (p. 36)

What views of the economic world and Britain's place within it might the pupils be left with on completion of these courses in geography?

We have already noted that it was a world of national, economic hierarchy, determined by climate and resources. To the extent that such a hierarchy was established, it was a world in which Britain, as the workshop of the world, had very few competitors. Because of the nature of regional geography, because of Britain's imperial role and the resulting emphasis in the texts on the key colonies, and because of some preconceptions about what should interest children, then establishing Britain's superiority was accomplished by an easy omission of other nations' industrial and urban existences. When towns were referred to they tended to be shown as interesting places to visit, for example, Stembridge's descriptions of New York, Cairo and Peking (1930) and Pickles (1933, p. 18). In pursuit of the odd and fascinating, Walter (1949), admitted that there were coal mines and towns in Canada '... but you can see plenty of those in England. But what you can't see loose in England are buffaloes ...' (Book III, p. 31).

A few interesting expressions of alarm can be found concerning other countries industrializing and their development as competitors, but these ideas come from outside of the structure of explanation and description; as authors' afterthoughts. In the *Pictorial Geographical Readers* (1901) the all-too-familiar educational explanation for the development of Germany is noted:

> One reason why the Germans are making such great progress is, that the German boy stays longer at school and works harder when in school than some British boys do. He learns a great deal about foreign countries, about their inhabitants and about their trade ... (Book IV, p. 10)

Johnston's, over thirty years later warned that,

> The difficulty now is that the 'young' countries we helped so much are no longer 'young'. They are growing up and manufacturing goods for themselves. (1937, Book IV, p. 182)

T.H. Cook's books quite ignored any examples of foreign manufacture or urban life, even in the section called 'Workers in Cool Lands', where he referred only to farming, fishing and forestry. Nonetheless he made a similar point after describing the origins of our food:

> But many of these countries can now make or manufacture their own 'goods', as well as grow food — and it was Britain that first taught other countries how to manufacture. In India, Japan and other lands factories with machinery for making cotton and other goods have been set up and are now making

much that they used to buy from Britain. That is one reason why Britain is a poorer country than it was 100 years ago. Another reason is that Britain has recently fought two costly worldwide wars to preserve freedom for herself and for other freedom-loving nations. (Cook, 1950, Book III, p. 14)

It appears that, even in the 1950s and 60s children would have to be of secondary age before they were introduced to the industries of the United States or Europe as, for example, in *Longman's Colour Geographies* by T. Herdman (1957).

Again this was no simple expression of a national ruralism or anti-urbanism. At least in making the difference between 'us and them', our industrialization and urbanization was the sign of our progress, albeit determined by a natural, racial superiority. But these books presented a very self-satisfied and increasingly problematic view of the world. It was a world in which our food was produced by willing, happy natives in far off lands; in which Britain had a guaranteed superiority; a world for the people of an imperial nation who could appreciate the natural, elemental existences of their simple charges, journey to see them in their natural ways, but return to a country where nature (country) and civilization (town) were in balance.

The Primitive, the Child and Racism

To move some way to understanding the *force* of the images, and not merely their biases, we must attempt to show how the texts were used within the very particular institutional context of national elementary and primary schools. Children were introduced to the simple, natural adult-children of other lands within a school system which was built on the graded pacing from childhood to adulthood. In a sense, black peoples were shown as childlike in the very institutions which turned white children into mature adults. The suggestion here is that constructions of the happy, childlike native cannot be understood as merely a mistake. It has also to be seen as fitting into the construction of the subjectivity of the English school children themselves.

Within a system of schooling based on stages of growth and chronological development these textbooks (often in graded series) were part of the defining of these stages and their human characteristics. Based on assumed knowledge about the nature of the users of the books the authors of the texts *wrote in* the characteristics of English childhood and how it should be nurtured. Children were 'naturally' inquisitive, they were attracted to, and best instructed by, simple, natural things, and therefore simple people in natural conditions would be appealing and quaint to child-readers who were (but only temporarily) like them. But even as these English children were being shown other children they were being placed within a developmental 'career' which could take them beyond these simple folk, by virtue of being in school and in Britain. They were being shown a childhood which was a climatically determined racial oddity — sets of people like Peter Pan, who can never grow up, or, at least, must have seemed very far behind.

There are clear racist implications in this whole pedagogic exercise of making other people's existences interesting and amusing to children, and this racism does not arise from any simple misrepresentation of other ways of life to given individual subjects. It may be seen to have some of its roots and sustenance in the very institutions of age-ordered national schooling and in the implicit theories of childhood, child development and motivation, and thus making it much more difficult to deal with than by any simple revision of textbook imagery. If climatic determination was the discipline-based underpinning of racist conceptions of other peoples, then preconceptions of childhood and institutions of child development provided the context for the discourse.

The dualities, rural-urban, primitive-civilized, were important insofar as they, in contradictory ways, informed the general points of comparison of states of life. The English child was addressed as within the process of moving from a natural innocence to an educated, civilized state. Other societies or peoples were presented in terms of their differences from the civilized ways of life into which the children were to be initiated. Contradictions and ambivalences were inevitable. This may be because the state of nature, like the condition of childhood, has so long been regarded ideally as both a 'pure' condition, beyond institutions, industry and urban life, and as a point in time and/or space from which to assess national progress or decline. Also important was the way in which it has been thought that a distance from the natural, elemental way of life could be sapping of strength. We have noted this aspect in some of the history books and their concern over the enfeebling effects of urbanization. Certainly one imperial interest in the primitive people of other lands was in the way they were indeed elemental creatures, instinctive, and, in that way, 'clever' in aspects of life concerned with survival. Many of the exercises of the Boy Scout movement were devoted to an emulation by youth of such primitive activities.

Some books merely listed the clever natural activities of the nations of different climates. In *People and Homes in Many Lands* (Moss, 1930) the different regions are all inhabited by clever, adaptable people. But, as Fairgrieve and Young's *Real Geography* (1939) illustrated, there were implicit ambivalences when the struggles of natural people were appreciated against a view of progress which brings ease of life. There was, in that series, a very definite adulation of the strength and cleverness of, for example, a tribe in the Amazon forest (Book I, pp. 1–9) and of a Masai boy who learnt to become a warrior (Book III, p. 7). Yet such people were seen in an order of progress. In the conclusion to Book I they wrote:

> We have learnt too that there are different stages of living. The Waiongongs and the blackfellows have a hard struggle to live at all. The Mexicans and the West Indian negroes, because they can use tools and simple machines to help them, live somewhat more easily. The Spaniards in Chile and Argentina, and the British in Australia and New Zealand, because they use bigger and better machines, live most easily of all. (p. 100)

Other writers have suggested the dangers of European city life for the native. Writing appreciatively about the primitive skills and courage of the Masai, Waldock told how their elders believe that those who go to the town schools of the European will forget the old ways of their fathers and will no longer respect their tribe nor honour their leaders. The writer adds,

> There is some truth in this belief, for many simple Africans learn only bad ways in the towns and lose the fine traditions of their own people. (*People of the World*, 1957–59)

The projection of characteristics possibly thought to have been lacking in English society added to the fantasy (viz. Henriques *et al*, 1984, pp. 88–9), but the differential effects of what has been called these invitations to national-racial membership should not be forgotten. The places offered to white children in the 1930s and 40s and 50s were comfortable ones, but for others they were very difficult to accept. The problems were most obvious for certain racial minorities who began entering the schools whilst many of these books were still in use. True, there was nothing in the theories of climatic determination which meant that black children brought up in Britain's more bracing climate would not work hard and succeed in education as in other endeavours, but the general identification of blacks within these books may have conspired against that. At best some of the indigenous white children, young adults and teachers may have adopted an indulgent view that black people had been brought to urban Britain from their exclusively rural backgrounds (a common misunderstanding regarding the origins of Afro-Caribbean people, for example) to 'help us', and we must try to help them. At worst, such texts may have encouraged a view of blacks as child-like primitives, jumping the queue of progress by helping themselves to things that the British had taken hundreds of years of hardship and delayed gratification to amass, and were only then about the enjoy in post-war social democratic Britain.

In these texts the origins of, for example, Afro-Caribbean families were re-presented back to their offspring as a paradise for happy adult-children, by words and pictures. Fairgrieve and Young (1939, Book I) for example, described the beauty of Jamaica and its people (pp. 53–63) where the 'Negroes are cheerful people and love gay things ...' (p. 59), who grow all they need in their gardens. Their ways were described as amusing, with a hint of profligacy:

> On Sundays 'best clothes' are worn. Mother squeezes her feet into tight boots or shoes, puts on a dazzling frock and hat that is loaded with flowers and ribbons. Father dons a tight jacket and a high, stiff collar and swings a cane. Whatever money the negro can spare is spent on best clothes for Sunday. (*ibid*, p. 62)

The children

> are not very fond of books and lessons; they would rather climb trees or play in the water of ponds or streams ... The children seem to stay away from school on any excuse ... (p. 62)

Similar points were made by Mason in *The Land of the Sugar Cane* (no. 25 of *Little People in Far Off Lands*, u.d.), where the 'natives' were seen as comical (p. 18) and cheerful (p. 3). The links between climatic determination, limitation of needs and racialist fantasy are perfectly shown in the following quote:

> On the the whole, the negro has a very carefree life, as his needs are simple. He requires little clothing, and rents are very low, usually about one shilling a week. He only needs fuel for cooking, not for warmth, and in the country he can simply go

out and collect it. Food is easy to get, as he can live on plantains and fruit, which can be fresh and cheap all the year round.

The native people are very kind hearted and good tempered ... (p. 3)

Thus national geography and national history could make for an impenetrable racist closure just at the time when the military and economic basis of British popular imperialism was changing. It could appear that in such a society the white, native myths of origin provided the perfect counterpart for the black British myths of return (Anwar, 1979).

Notes

1 Only one series in the sample attempted to present England as almost entirely rural and that was the *Visual Series — The British Isles* (1920). In this book, which emphasized the picturesque, possibly because it was advertised as a colouring-reading book, there were only four urban scenes out of the forty-eight depicted.
2 It is difficult to call the development of the social sciences and some social philosophy in the latter part of the nineteenth century completely external to the wider enterprise of state education. In France, for example, Emile Durkheim was deeply involved in the development of the educational system of the Third Republic and in the construction of that state's identity as an object of secular reference within moral education.
3 Gilbert (1984) notes that there is some disagreement about how deterministic Herbertson's original regional geography actually was (p. 66). We are interested here only in its manifestations in children's books.
4 In English fiction for boys, too, writers like George Henty had promoted the view of Africans as being 'just like children' viz. Green (1980) *Dreams of Adventure, Deeds of Empire* (p. 221).
5 The domestic parallel of this conception of different needs within a justification of a market system may be found in the writing of Francis Ysidro Edgeworth, who argued that the rich, within a domestic market economy, had a greater capacity for pleasure than the poor and thus derived greater utility from their extra income viz. Eatwell (1982) *Whatever Happened to Britain?* (pp. 40–1).

Summary and Conclusion

In a sense the last sections of the previous chapter have brought this book back to its starting point. If, in the past, English geography textbook writers could confidently explain the relative backwardness of other peoples by reference to their *physical* climate, so perhaps, could an American academic like Wiener explain Britain's economic ills in terms of the debilitating effects of living in an anti-industrial, anti-urban culture. Indeed for those who believe that the English state of mind has had a major effect on past economic growth, the rhetoric of 'changing the economic climate' echoes in metaphor the previous implied criticisms of other populations, except that, over the last ten years or so, the criticisms have been aimed at the mass of 'our' people. It is *they* who have become lazy, without enterprise, too easily satisfied, and in need of a more bracing atmosphere. In an economy so open to import penetration it is not surprising that some groups in Britain have also imported Wiener's explanation of the nation's decline. In Chapter 1 we attempted to trace back to its place of origin the American liberal and revisionist interest in the apparent negative influences of a family of beliefs which have been termed ruralist, and which closely resembled the elements of culture which Wiener found in Britain.

But an interest in the way rural life (contemporary or previous) has been depicted and understood in comparison with the urban, and a concern for the possible causes and effects of such representations has not been an exclusively American study. In Chapter 1, for example, we considered also the quite different approach of Raymond Williams who rejected any essential national, cultural ruralism, and searched instead for the ideological functions of different representations of the country and the city. Judgments were made by Williams in terms of the *misrepresentation* of human existence in towns and country, and the misunderstanding of capitalist relations in both places. It was this use of the concept of misrepresentation, however, which has provided a point of tension in this book and required that we consider the bases for any claim, by Williams or others, that, within the body of representations and images often called 'ruralist', was a consistent *unrealistic* representation of country life and labour. The review of some of the debates in social science and Marxism did not suggest that there was any straightforward empirical or theoretical means of correcting such (mis)representations, especially when applied to the type of texts chosen for analysis.

One of my criticisms of Williams was that his position in *The Country and the City* (1975) made for difficulties in appreciating the particular *institutional* nature of the British economy. It is possible that a similar lack of significance given to the particulars of institutionally specific discourse also lay behind the problems of applying to school textbooks any form of analysis which only proceeded by revealing errors of fact and misrepresentations of rural or urban realities. By playing upon the exceptional nature of these books Chapter 2 attempted to produce a working compromise between an interest in the realisms of these texts on the one hand and the real-institutional conditions of their production, distribution and use on the other.

Although this study was not aimed directly at the content and presuppositions of the Wiener thesis but did emerge from a concern for the possible educational derivations from it, it has shown the problems with such an approach to national or class cultures and schooling. Many of the textbooks that have been examined could be read as expressing the identifiable cultural essence of ruralism, but contrary images were also found when crossing the subject boundary between history and geography. The way the texts were read in this study suggested that they did not exist as expressions of some previous national culture, but as attempts to project or construct that upon which the whole enterprise of universal state schooling and its textbooks depended, i.e. an assumption that there was a naturally integrated distinct people existing within given boundaries. Combining with that the predominant practices and discourses of child development during the period, centred as they were on learning by progressive contact with the reality of nature, it is not surprising that images within the textbooks could be counted up and used as evidence for the thesis which explains, culturally, Britain's economic decline. But, in another approach, the contents of the textbooks could also be seen as indicating, in indirect and tangential ways, many of the *other* explanations of Britain's industrial decline, as exemplified in the recent book by Coates and Hillard (1986). There is much evidence of the over-inflated perception of Britain's world role after 1945; the dominance of its imperial past, with all the effects that had upon economic institutions, the so-called British disease of class division, and, above all, of the economic illiteracy of its people.

Finally, it is on this question of economic and social literacy that one could indicate some of the education implications of this study for contemporary conditions. In Chapters 2 to 6, it was noted that, through the forms of address and the textual location of author and reader, some children would have had difficulty in accepting the invitations both to membership of the nation offered and to the category of 'educated person'. Even in recent textbooks most closely approximating to the traditional forms of class reader, such as, for example, the *Story Line Geography Series* (Daly and Morrison, 1985) at least the cultural and locational (if not economic) diversity of the child-readers is now acknowledged. Other educational developments coming after the end of the period of this study, like Eric Midwinter's and others' advocacy of a community-based social curriculum for primary schools (Midwinter, 1971 and 1980), the initiatives in local history and geography, community and urban studies (for example, Community Service Volunteers, u.d.), have by implication at least, undermined the whole basis and possibility of nationally produced and consumed textbooks in such areas of the curriculum. But, if some of these changes have been more sensitive to the cultural origins of children, these approaches are not without their problems, especially when the question of economic and social literacy is addressed. Not only can such developments sometimes produce an enclosed localism, but learning the crafts of historian and geographer by the collecting of local evidence may do little to guarantee some satisfactory introduction to even the simplest concepts in social and economic understanding. Nor can much optimism be gained from some of the recent developments in industrial education for the age-range considered in this volume. There has been a tendency to concentrate on the technical processes of production, as, for example, in the work of the Edge Hill College Primary Industrial Education Project, and that reported in Jamieson (1984). The social-institutional nature of industrial production in this and other societies has been relatively ignored. (The work published by the Inner London Education Authority (Wagstaff, 1980) which does at last introduce the organization of labour within enterprises is an exception in the field.)

It remains to be seen whether some more widely acceptable and usable programmes in these areas could be devised, but the educational and other alliances necessary to make this possible are both complex and difficult to foresee. The spaces for such a project within the primary school curriculum have been created by a combination of child-centredness and the recent developments of multicultural education. Whilst this can bring welcome relief from the divided and simplistic determinations which have been found beneath earlier school history and geography, such developments rely on a problematic projection of a unified child–subject and a deep culturalism.[1] Furthermore the very tradition which has 'protected' children from labour, (what we have called an internal factor behind the apparent anti-urbanism of some of the textbooks) may either help exclude the excesses of vocationalism found in some secondary and further education at present, or continue to exclude *all* serious considerations of economic life. To add to the complexity, the emphasis on experience and skills, with all its empiricist pre-suppositions, are central concepts in both the rhetoric of many progressive school teachers as well as that of the proponents of prevocational education, and could have consequences for any attempt at a coherent programme of economic and social literacy. It is now clear that further constraints will be placed on such necessary curriculum development by a national curriculum and testing.

Whatever may be professionally possible for the future development of appropriate curriculum materials, this study could be taken as showing how difficult it may be to overcome the past. Looking back, as adults, at the books which were read by us as children might produce both an embarrassed humour and a confidence that at least the invitations they contained could no longer work now. Taking the way those books combined a form of address (that assumed national intimacy of 'we') with the use of the distinction between town and country, which made for a 'point of view' or centre somewhere in between these two localities, one may well believe that some sort of social time has passed them by. In view of all the ethnic, demographic and economic changes which have so characterized Britain since 1960 one may ask how that centre could possibly hold now. But, on reflection, the answer may not be so obvious, for such invitations as were given in those books have always worked more by promises and desires than by any real descriptions of that to which one was being invited.

Note

1   The Australian Social Literacy Project is an interesting attempt to use this combination in a selfconscious way, 'to fashion a social education program which is intellectually rigorous and coherent, yet which maintains the best of progressive methodology, such as learning through active inquiry, experience and negotiation' (*Social Literacy, An Overview*, u.d., p. 2).

Bibliography

General

AHIER, J. (1977) 'Philosophers, sociologists and knowledge in education', in Young, M.F.D. and Whitty, G. (Eds) *Society, State and Schooling*, Lewes, Falmer Press.

AHIER, J. (1983) 'History and sociology of educational policy' in AHIER, J., and FLUDE, M. (Eds) *Contemporary Education Policy*, London, Croom Helm.

AHIER, J. and FLUDE, M. (Eds) (1983) *Contemporary Education Policy*, London, Croom Helm.

ALTHUSSER, L. (1971) 'Ideology and ideological state apparatuses' in *Lenin and Philosophy*, London, New Left Books.

ALVARADO and FERGUSON (1983) 'The curriculum, media studies and discursivity', *Screen*, 24, 3.

ANDERSON, B. (1983) *Imagined Communities: Reflections on the Origin and Spread of Nationalism*, London, Verso.

ANDERSON, P. (1968) 'Components of the national culture', *New Left Review*, 50.

ANDERSON, P. (1983) *In the Tracks of Historical Materialism*, London, Verso.

ANWAR, M. (1979) *Myth of Return: Pakistanis in Britain*, London, Heinemann.

ANYON, J. (1981) 'Ideology and United States history textbooks', in DALE, R. *et al.* (Eds) *Education and the State Vol 2: Policy, Patriarchy and Practice*, Lewes, Falmer Press.

BARNES, J. (Ed.) (1975) *Educational Priority, Volume III*, London, HMSO.

BARNETT, C. (1972) *The Collapse of British Power*, London, Methuen.

BARNETT, C. (1978) 'The human factor and British industrial decline — A historical perspective', *Journal of the National Association of Inspectors and Educational Advisors*, 9.

BARRELL, J. (1980) *The Dark Side of the Landscape*, Cambridge, Cambridge University Press.

BARRETT, M., CORRIGAN, P., KUHN, A. and WOLFF, J. (1979) *Ideology and Cultural Production*, London, Croom Helm.

BERNSTEIN, B. (1975) *Class, Codes and Control, Vol. 3*, London, Routledge & Kegan Paul.

BIDDLE, D.S. (1985) 'Paradigms in geography curricula in England and

Wales, 1882–1972', in BOARDMAN, D. (Ed.), *New Directions in Geographical Education*, Lewes, Falmer Press.

BODY, R. (1982) *Agriculture; The Triumph and the Shame*, London, Temple Smith.

BOMMES, M. and WRIGHT, P. (1982) 'Charms of residence, the public and the past', in CENTRE FOR CONTEMPORARY CULTURAL STUDIES, *Making Histories*, London, Hutchinson.

BOURDIEU, P. and PASSERON, J-C. (1977) *Reproduction in Education Society and Culture*, London, Sage.

BOWLES, S. and GINTIS, H. (1976) *Schooling in Capitalist America*, London, Routledge & Kegan Paul.

BRAMWELL, R.D. (1961) *Elementary School Work 1900–1925*, Durham, University of Durham Institute of Education.

BRANIGAN, E. (1978) 'Foreground and background, a reply to Paul Willeman', *Screen*, 19, 2.

BRODERICK, D.M. (1973) *Image of the Black in Children's Fiction*, New York, R.R. Bowker.

BURGESS, J.A. (1982) 'Selling places, environmental images for the executive', *Regional Studies*, 16.

BURKE, P. (1981) 'People's history or total history' in SAMUEL, R. (Ed.) *People's History and Socialist Theory*, London, Routledge & Kegan Paul.

CALLINICOS, A. (1982) *Is There A Future for Marxism?* London, Macmillan.

CASTELLS, M. (1977) *The Urban Question*, London, Edward Arnold.

CHANCELLOR, V. (1970) *History for Their Masters*, Bath, Adams & Dart.

CHILDREN'S RIGHTS WORKSHOP (1976) *Sexism in Children's Books*, London, Writers and Readers Publishing Cooperative.

COATES, D. and HILLARD, J. (1986) *The Economic Decline of Modern Britain*, Brighton, Wheatsheaf Books.

COLEMAN, D.C. (1973), 'Gentlemen and players', *Economic Review*, 26, 1.

COLLS, R. and DODD, P. (1986) *Englishness, Politics and Culture 1880–1920*, London, Croom Helm.

COMMUNITY SERVICE VOLUNTEERS (n.d.) *Opening Doors*, London C.S.V.

CONNELL, I. (1978) 'Ideology/discourse/institution', *Screen*, 19, 3.

CORNER, P. (1985) 'Marxism and the British historiographical tradition' in BARANSKI, Z.G. and SHORT, J.R., (Eds) *Developing Contemporary Marxism*, London, Macmillan.

COWARD, R. (1977) 'Class, "culture" and the social formation', *Screen*, 18, 1.

COWARD, R. and ELLIS, J. (1977) *Language and Materialism*, London, Routledge & Kegan Paul.

DALE, R. (1983) 'Thatcherism and education' in AHIER, J. and FLUDE, M. *Contemporary Education Policy*, London, Croom Helm.

DIXON, B. (1977) *Catching Them Young*, London, Pluto Press.

DUGGETT, M. (1975) 'Marx on peasants', *Journal of Peasant Studies*, 2, 2.

DURKHEIM, E. (1968) *The Division of Labour in Society*, New York, Free Press.

DYMOND, D. (Ed.) (1929) *A Handbook for History Teachers*, London, Methuen.

DYOS, H.J. and WOLFF, M. (Eds) (1973) *The Victorian City, Images and Realities, Vols. I & II*, London, Routledge & Kegan Paul.

EAGLETON, T. (1978) *Criticism and Ideology*, London, Verso.

EATWELL, J. (1982) *Whatever Happened to Britain?* London, Duckworth.

ELLIS, J. (1982) *Visible Fictions*, London, Routledge & Kegan Paul.

ENGELS, F. (1935) *The Housing Question*, London, Martin Lawrence.

ENGELS, F. (1970) 'The peasant question in France and Germany' in MARX, K. and ENGELS, F. (Eds) *Selected Works, Vol. III*, Moscow, Progress Publishers.

ENNEW, J., HIRST, P.Q. and TRIBE, K. (1977) '"Peasantry" as an economic category', *Journal of Peasant Studies*, 4, 4.

ERBEN, M. and GLEESON, D. (1977) 'Education as reproduction: A critical examination of some aspects of the work of Louis Althusser' in YOUNG, M. and WHITTY, G. (Eds) *Society, State and Schooling*, Lewes, Falmer Press.

FERRO, M. (1984) *The Use and Abuse of History*, London, Routledge & Kegan Paul.

FITZGERALD, F. (1980) *America Revised: History School Books in the Twentieth Century*, New York, Vintage Books.

Formations (Series), Of Nation and People (1984), London, Routledge & Kegan Paul.

FOUCAULT, M. (1977) *Discipline and Punish: The Birth of the Prison*, London, Allen Lane.

FROW, J. (1985) 'Discourse and power', *Economy and Society*, 14, 2.

GANS, H.S. (1962) *The Urban Villagers*, New York, Free Press.

GANS, H.S. (1968) 'Urbanism and suburbanism as ways of life' in PAHL, R.E. (Ed.) *Readings in Urban Sociology*, Oxford, Pergamon Press.

GILBERT, R. (1984) *The Impotent Image*, Lewes, Falmer Press.

GITTELL, M. and SHTOP, T. (1981) 'Changing women's roles in political volunteerism and reform of the city' in STIMPSON, C.R., DIXLER, E., NELSON, M. and YATRAKIS, K. (Eds) *Women in the American City*, Chicago, University of Chicago Press.

GOLDMANN, L. (1964) *The Hidden God*, London, Routledge & Kegan Paul.

GOLDMANN, L. (1969) *The Human Sciences and Philosophy*, London, Jonathan Cape.

GORBUTT, D. (1972) 'The new sociology of education', *Education for Teaching*, 89.

GREEN, M. (1980) *Dreams of Adventure, Deeds of Empire*, London, Routledge & Kegan Paul.

GRISWOLD, A. W. (1952) *Farming and Democracy*, New Haven, CT, Yale University Press.

GUMBERT, E.B. and SPRING, J.H. (1974) *The Superschool and the Superstate: American Education in the Twentieth Century*, New York, J. Wiley & Sons.

HARRISON, P. (1983) *Inside the Inner City*, Harmondsworth, Penguin.

HARTMEN, H. (1976) 'Capitalism, patriarchy and job segregation by sex', *Signs*, 1, 3.

HEATER, D. (1980) *World Studies*, London, Harrap.

HENRIQUES, J., HOLLOWAY, W., URWIN, C., VENN, C. and WALKERDINE, V. (Eds) (1984) *Changing the Subject*, London, Methuen.

HERBERTSON, A.J. (1905) 'The major natural regions: An essay in systematic geography', *Geographical Journal*, XXV, 3.

HICKS, D. (1980) *Images of the World*, London, University of London Institute of Education Centre for Multicultural Education.

HILTON, R. (1973) *Bond Men Made Free*, London, Temple Smith.

HINDESS, B. and HIRST, P.Q. (1977) *Mode of Production and Social Formation*, London, Macmillan.

HIRST, P.Q. (1979) *On Law and Ideology*, London, Macmillan.

HOBSBAWM, E.J. and RUDÉ, G. (1970) *Captain Swing*, London, Lawrence and Wishart.

HOFFMAN, M. (1981) 'Children's reading and social values' in MERCER, N. (Ed.) *Language in School and Community*, London, Arnold.

HOFSTADTER, R. (1962) *Age of Reform*, London, Jonathan Cape.

HOGAN, M.A. (1962) *The Evolution of the Regional Concept and Its Influence in the Teaching of Geography in Schools*, unpublished MA dissertation, University of London Institute of Education.

HUDSON, B. (1977) 'The new geography and the new imperialism', *Antipode*, 9, 2.

HURST, J.B. (1981) 'Images in children's picture books', *Social Education*, 45, 2.

HUSSAIN, A. and TRIBE, K. (1981) *Marxism and the Agrarian Question*, London, Macmillan.

JAMIESON, I. (1984) *'We Make Kettles': Studying Industry in the Primary School*, London, Longman and Schools Council.

JOHNSON, R. (1979) 'Three problematics: Elements of a theory of working class culture' in CLARKE, J., CRITCHER, C.E., and JOHNSON, R. (Eds) *Working Class Culture: Studies in History and Theory*, London, Hutchinson.

JOHNSON, R. (1980) 'Cultural studies and educational practice', *Screen Education*, 34.

JOHNSON, R. (1981) *Education and Popular Politics*, Unit 1 of Open University Course E353, Milton Keynes, Open University.

JOHNSTON, C. and WILLEMEN, P. (1975) 'Brecht in Britain: The independent political film', *Screen*, 16, 4.

KARRIER, C.J., VIOLAS, P. and SPRING, J. (1973) *Roots of Crisis*, Chicago, Rand McNally.

KATZ, M. (1975) *Class, Bureaucracy and Schools*, New York, Praeger Publishers.

KEITH, W.J. (1981) 'The land in Victorian literature' in MINGAY, G.E. (Ed.) *The Victorian Countryside, Vols I and II*, London, Routledge & Kegan Paul.

KELLY, R.G. (1970) *Mother Was a Lady*, PhD dissertation, University of Iowa.

KENT, A. (1982) 'Scale and regional bias' in KENT, A. (Ed.) *Bias in Geographical Education*, University of London, Institute of Education.

KITTERINGHAM, J. (1973) *Country Girls in Nineteenth Century England*, History Workshop Pamphlet no. 11.

LARRAIN, J. (1979) *The Concept of Ideology*, London, Hutchinson.

LAWERYS, J.A. (1953) *History Text-books and International Understanding*, Paris, UNESCO.

LAZERSON, M. (1971) *Origins of the Urban School*, Cambridge, MA, Harvard University Press.

LEAVIS, F.R. (1972) 'Luddites? or there is only one culture' in *Nor Shall My Staff*, London, Chatto and Windus.

LEESON, R. (1977) *Children's Books and Class Society*, London, Writers and Readers Publishing Cooperative.

LEWIS, O. (1961) *Children of Sanchez*, London, Secker and Warburg.

LEWIS, O. (1963) *Life in a Mexican Village: Tepoztlan Restudied*, Urbana, Illinois, University of Illinois Press.

LEWIS, O. (1965) 'Further observations on the folk-urban continuum' in HAUSER, P.M. and SCHNORE, L.F. (Eds) *The Study of Urbanization*, New York, John Wiley.

LEWIS, O. (1967) *La Vida*, London, Secker and Warburg.

LEWIS, O. (1970) *Anthropological Essays*, New York, Random House.

LOYN, H. (1971) 'Towns in late Anglo-Saxon England' in CLEMOES, P. and HUGHES, K. (Eds) *England Before The Conquest*, Cambridge, Cambridge University Press.

MABEY, R. (Ed.) (1984) *Second Nature*, London, Jonathan Cape.

MACCABE, C. (1974) 'Realism and the cinema: Notes on some Brechtian theses', *Screen*, 15, 2.

MACCABE, C. (1976) 'Theory and film: Principles of realism and pleasure', *Screen*, 17, 3.

McCARNEY, J. (1985) 'Recent interpretations of ideology', *Economy and Society*' 14, 1.

McCLELLAND, D.C. (1961) *The Achieving Society*, Princeton, NJ, D.Van Nostrad.

McDONNELL, K. and ROBINS, K. (1980) 'Marxist cultural theory' in CLARKE, S. *et al* (Eds) *One Dimensional Marxism*, London, Allison and Busby.

McINTOSH, M. (1984) 'The family, regulation and the public sphere' in McLENNAN, G., HELD, D. and HALL, S. (Eds) *State and Society in Contemporary Britain*, London, Polity Press.

MARSH, J. (1982) *Back to the Land, the Pastoral Impulse in Victorian England from 1880 to 1914*, London, Quartet Books.

MARX, K. (1934) *The Class Struggle in France, 1848–1850*, London, Martin Lawrence.

MARX, K. (1953) 'Letter to Vera Zuslich' in BLACKSTONE P.W. and HOSELITZ, B.F. (Eds) *The Russian Menace to Europe*, London, Allen and Unwin.

MARX, K. (1954) *Capital*, London, Lawrence and Wishart, 3 vols.

MARX, K. (1970) 'The eighteenth brumaire of Louis Bonaparte' in MARX, K. and ENGELS, F. (Eds) *Selected Works*, London, Lawrence and Wishart.

MARX, K. (1973) *Grundrisse*, Harmondsworth, Penguin Books.

MARX, K. and ENGELS, F. (1952) *Manifesto of the Communist Party*, Moscow, Progress Publishers.

MASSEY, D. (1983) 'The shape of things to come', *Marxism Today*, April.

MAYER, P. (1963) *Townsmen or Tribesmen*, Cape Town, Oxford University Press.

MELLOR, J.R. (1977) *Urban Sociology in an Urbanised Society*, London, Routledge & Kegan Paul.

MIDWINTER, E. (1971) 'Curriculum and the EPA community school' in HOOPER, R. (Ed.) *Curriculum, Context Design and Development*, Edinburgh, Oliver and Boyd.

MIDWINTER, E. (1980) 'Community education' in CRAFT, M., RAYNOR, J. and COHEN, L. (Eds) *Linking Home and School*, 3rd edn, London, Harper and Row.

MILNER, D. (1975) *Children and Race*, Harmondsworth, Penguin.

MINGAY, G.E. (Ed.) (1981) *The Victorian Countryside, Vols. I & II*, London, Routledge & Kegan Paul.

NAIRN, T. (1977) *The Break-up of Britain*, London, New Left Books.

NIEMEYER, J.H. (1965) 'The Bank Street readers: Support for the movement towards an integrated society', *The Reading Teacher*, 18, 7.

NOWELL-SMITH, G. (1976) 'Six authors in pursuit of the searchers', *Screen*, 17, 1.

OLIVER, P., DAVIS, I. and BENTLEY, I. (1981) *Dunroamin*, London, Barrie and Jenkins.

OLSEN, D.J. (1976) *The Growth of Victorian London*, London, Batsford.

PAHL, R.E. (1965) *Urbs in Rure*, London, London School of Economics and Political Science, Geography Department.

PAHL, R.E. (1968) *Readings in Urban Sociology*, Oxford, Pergamon Press.

PAREKH, B. (1982) *Marx's Theory of Ideology*, London, Croom Helm.

PARK, R.E. and BURGESS, E.W. (1921) *Introduction to the Science of Sociology*, Chicago, University of Chicago Press.

PARK, R.E. and BURGESS, E.W. (1925) *The City*, Chicago, University of Chicago Press.

PERKINS, T.E. (1979) 'Rethinking stereotypes' in BARRETT, M. *et al* (Eds) *Cultural Production*, London, Croom Helm.

PINCHBECK, I. and HEWITT, M. (1973) *Children in English Society Vols. I & II*, London, Routledge & Kegan Paul.

PLATT, A. (1969) *The Child Savers*, Chicago, University of Chicago Press.

POULANTZAS, N. (1973) *Political Power and Social Classes*, London, New Left Books.

POULANTZAS, N. (1975) *Classes in Contemporary Capitalism*, London, New Left Books.

PUBLISHING ASSOCIATION (1981) *Sex-stereotyping in School and Children's Books*, London, Publishing Association.

PURKIS, S. (1980) 'The unacceptable face of history?' *Teaching History*, 26.

RANGER, T. (1984) 'The invention of tradition in colonial Africa' in HOBSBAWN, E. (Ed.) *The Invention of Tradition*, Cambridge, Cambridge University Press.

REDFIELD, R. (1930) *Tepoztlan — A Mexican Village*, Chicago, University of Chicago Press.

REDFIELD, R. (1947) 'The folk society', *American Journal of Sociology*, 52, 4.

REDFIELD, R. (1981) *The Folk Culture of Yucatan*, Chicago, University of Chicago Press.

REDFIELD, R. and SINGER, M.B. (1954) 'The cultural role of cities', *Economic Development and Cultural Change*, 3, pp. 53–73.

ROSE, J. (1984) *The Case of Peter Pan*, London, Macmillan.

Ross, C. (1984) 'The woman's chapter', *Clio*, 4, 3.

Sales, R. (1983) *English Literature in History 1780–1830 — Pastoral and Politics*, London, Hutchinson.

Sarup, M. (1984) *Marxism/Structuralism/Education*, Lewes, Falmer Press.

Saunders, P. (1981) *Social Theory and the Urban Question*, London, Hutchinson.

Saunders, P., Newby, H., Bell, C., and Rose, D. (1978) 'Rural community and rural community power', *International Perspectives in Rural Sociology*. Chichester, John Wiley.

Schmitt, P.J. (1969) *Back to Nature, The Arcadian Myth in Urban America*, New York, Oxford University Press.

Sharp, R. (1980) *Knowledge, Ideology and the Politics of Schooling*, London, Routledge & Kegan Paul.

Sharp, R. and Green, A. (1975) *Education and Social Control*, London, Routledge & Kegan Paul.

Sherwood, R. (1980) *The Psychodynamics of Race*, Brighton, Harvester Press.

Shoard, M. (1980) *The Theft of the Countryside*, London, Temple Smith.

Simmel, G. (1972) 'Metropolis and mental life' in Wrong, D.H. and Gracey, H.L. (Eds) *Readings in Introductory Sociology*, 2nd edn. New York, Macmillan.

Smart, B. (1983) *Foucault, Marxism and Critique*, London, Routledge & Kegan Paul.

Smith, H.N. (1950) *Virgin Land*, Cambridge, MA, Harvard University Press.

Social Literacy Project (n.d.) *Social Literacy — An Overview*, Stanmore NSW, Social Literacy Project.

Steedman, C. (1986) *Landscape for a Good Woman*, London, Virago.

Sumner, C. (1979) *Reading Ideologies*, London, Academic Press.

Tasker, M. (1980) *Teaching the History of Technology*, History Association Pamphlet 47.

Thomas, K.V. (1983) *Man and the Natural World*, London, Allen Lane.

Thompson, D. (1980) *Change and Tradition in Rural England*, Cambridge, Cambridge University Press.

Thompson, E.P. (1968) *The Making of the English Working Class*, Harmondsworth, Penguin.

Thompson, G. (1979) 'Television as text: Open University "case study" programmes' in Barrett, M. *et al* (Eds) *Ideology and Cultural Production*, London, Croom Helm.

Thompson, J.B. (1984) *Studies in the Theory of Ideology*, Cambridge, Polity Press.

Tonnies, F. (1887) *Community and Society*, New York, Harper and Row (1963 edn).

Wagstaff, S. (1980) 'Work' *People Around Us* (series), London, ILEA.

Walkerdine, V. (1984a) 'Developmental psychology and the child-centred pedagogy: The insertion of Piaget in early education' in Henriques, J. *et al* (Eds) *Changing the Subject*, London, Methuen.

Walkerdine, V. (1984b) 'Some day my prince will come: Young girls and the preparation for adult sexuality' in McRobbie, A. and Nava, M. (Eds) *Gender and Generation*, London, Macmillan.

WALLER, P.J. (1983) *Town, City and Nation*, Oxford, Oxford University Press.

WALVIN, J. (1982) *A Child's World*, Harmondsworth, Penguin.

WEXLER, P. (1982) 'Structure, text and subject' in APPLE, M.W. (Ed.) *Cultural and Economic Reproduction in Education*, London, Routledge & Kegan Paul.

WHALLEY, J.I. (1974) *Cobwebs to Catch Flies, Illustrated Books for the Nursery and Schoolroom, 1700–1900*, London, Elek.

WHITE, M. (1965) 'The philosopher and the metropolis in America' in HIRSCH, W.Z. (Ed.) *Urban Life and Form*, New York, Holt, Rinehart and Winston.

WHITING, D. (1981) 'Sex-role stereotyping and the Ladybird books', *Forum*, 23, 3.

WHITTY, G. (1983) 'State policy and school examinations, 1976–1982' in AHIER, J. and FLUDE, M. (Eds) *Contemporary Education Policy*, London, Croom Helm.

WIENER, M. (1981) *English Culture and the Decline of the Industrial Spirit, 1850–1980*, Cambridge, Cambridge University Press.

WILLEMEN, P. (1978) 'Notes on subjectivity, on reading Edward Branigan's "Subjectivity Under Seige"', *Screen*, 19, 1.

WILLIAMS, R. (1961) *The Long Revolution*, Harmondsworth, Penguin.

WILLIAMS, R. (1973) 'Base and superstructure in Marxist cultural theory', *New Left Review*, 82.

WILLIAMS, R. (1975) *The Country and the City*, St Albans, Paladin.

WILLIAMS, R. (1977a) 'A lecture on realism', *Screen*, 18, 1.

WILLIAMS, R. (1977b) *Marxism and Literature*, Oxford, Oxford University Press.

WILLIAMS, R. (1979) *Politics and Letters*, London, Verso.

WILLIAMS, R. (1981) 'Between town and city' in MABEY, R. (Ed.) *Second Nature*, London, Jonathan Cape.

WILLIS, P. (1977) *Learning to Labour: How Working Class Kids Get Working Class Jobs*, Farnborough, Saxon House.

WIRTH, L. (1964) 'Urbanism as a way of life', *On Cities and Social Life*. Chicago, Chicago University Press.

WOLFF, M. and FOX, C. (1973) 'Pictures From magazines' in DYOS, H.J. and WOLFF, M. (Eds) *The Victorian City, Images and Realities, Vols. I and II*, London, Routledge & Kegan Paul.

WOMEN AND GEOGRAPHY STUDY GROUP (1984) *Geography and Gender*, London, Hutchinson.

WRIGHT, P. (1983) 'The conscription of history', *in 1984 in 1984*. London, Comedia.

WRIGHT, P. (1984) 'A blue plaque for the Labour movement?', *Formations*.

WRIGHT, P. (1985) *On Living in an Old Country*, London, Verso.

YOUNG, M.F.D. (Ed.) (1971) *Knowledge and Control*, London, Collier-Macmillan.

YOUNG, M.F.D. and WHITTY, G. (Eds) (1977) *Society, State and Schooling*, Lewes, Falmer Press.

ZIMET, S. (1969) 'American elementary reading text-books: A sociological review', *The Record*, 70, 4.

Zubaida, S. (1985) 'The city and its "other" in Islamic political ideas and movements', *Economy and Society*, 14, 3.

History and Geography Textbooks — Bibliographical Note

The study of these textbooks was greatly helped by the cooperative textbook project of the librarians of the institutes and schools of education, whereby different libraries hold out-of-date books in different subjects. The texts referred to were found in the University of London Institute of Education Textbook Library, the University of Warwick's Westwood Library (history) and the University of Southampton Library (geography). Some of the earlier texts are in the Museum of Education, University of Leeds, and the University Library, Cambridge.

Because of the lack of research into English school textbooks no comprehensive bibliographies exist. Chancellor's list of 160 history books published between 1800 and 1914 was useful (Chancellor, 1970) as were the lists produced by Professor Batho (*History of Education Society Bulletin*, number 33) and the School of Education Library, University of Liverpool.

In general the textbooks studied were published and/or in use between 1880 and 1960. No general sub-periodization has been attempted, except for noting the obvious effects of such developments as the post-World War II reconstruction on the content of the books. The combination of the economics of educational publishing, the educators' conceptions of what was relevant and suitable for young children, and the tendency of textbook writers to depend upon previous examples within the genre, meant that developments such as the loss of Empire produced little more than a change of title and some rewriting of the conclusion in many series (viz. Lay, 1937). Where the length of life of a textbook is relevant an indication of its publishing history is given in brackets. In the case of undated texts an indication at least of the date of use is given if this could be deduced from school stamps etc. on the copy consulted.

An attempt was made to study a number of books within each decade although the numerous early texts which were merely lists of definitions and details of other countries in geography, or chronologies of each reign, in history, have not been individually referenced.

Given the changes within the educational institutions during the period of the study it has not been possible to define an exact age-range of children for whom the textbooks were intended. Attention has been concentrated upon those books used by children in elementary schools, initially, and later by those in primary schools. (Some of the major series originally published in the 1920s and the 1930s were used in both types of institution.) In effect the age-range covered is between eight and thirteen years. Given that the period of the thesis ends in 1960 most of the texts have been used in formal pedagogic regimes, with the basic form of the texts, deriving from the early 'class-readers'.

History Textbooks

Allman's Little Arthur's History (see CALLCOTT)

AMBLER, S.O. and COATMAN, T. (1936) *The Stream of Time (Series)*, London, Cassell. (rev. 1953, 14th edn 1958, 1966).

ARCHER, T. (1896) *The Raleigh History Readers (Series)* — *Book III, Early England*, London, Blackie & Sons.

BARKER, E. and HAMMER, C.L. (1962) *Queensway Junior History (Series)*, London, Evans Bros.

BIRNIE, A. (1937) *The March of Time (Series)* — *Book VI, Early Nineteenth Century to the Present Day*, London, McDougall.

Blackie's Junior Histories (Series) (1935), London, Blackie & Sons.

BOOG-WATSON, E.J. and CARRUTHERS, J.I. (Eds) (1951–2) *History Through the Ages (Series)*, Oxford, Oxford University Press.

BOOG-WATSON, E.J. and CARRUTHERS, J.I. (1955a) *Understanding the Modern World (Series)*, London, Allen and Unwin.

BOOG-WATSON, E.J. and CARRUTHERS, J.I. (1955b) 'Country life through the ages', in BOOG-WATSON, E.J. and CARRUTHERS, J.I. *Understanding the Modern World (Series)*, London, Allen and Unwin.

BOWMAN, F.L. (1925) *Craftsmen and Merchants*, London, A & C Black.

BOWMAN, F.L. (1926) *The Changing Order*, from *Britain and the World History Series, Book V*, London, Pitman & Son.

BURBRIDGE, E.W. (u.d., 1936?) *Pathways Through Time*, London, Pitman.

CALLCOTT, LADY (1834) *Little Arthur's History of England*, London, T.J. Allman.

CARTER, E.H. and WRAGG, P. (1951) *Two Paths to Freedom*, Liverpool, George Philip & Son.

CARTER, M.E. (1907) *The Groundwork of English History*, London, University Tutorial Series.

Chambers 'New Scheme' Readers (Series) History of England, (1901) London, W & R Chambers.

CLAXTON, W.J. (1915) *Our Country's Industrial History*, London, Harrap (rep. 1918, 1920, 1924, rev. 1932).

CLAXTON, W.J. (1949) *The Homeland Histories (Series): I — Our Homeland in the Dark Ages; II — Saxon and Norman Days; III — The Middle Ages; IV — Tudor and Stuart Period; V — Our Homeland During the Agricultural Revolution; VI — The Age of Science*, Redhill, Wells Gardner Darton & Co.

CORNER, MISS (1851) *The History of England*, London, Thomas Dean.

CRAMP, R. and GUMMER, J. (1963) *The Earliest English*, Leeds, Arnold.

CURTIS, J.C. (1887) *Outlines of English History*, London, Simpkin & Marshall (48th edn).

ELLIOT, M.M. (u.d., 1935?) *Little Workers of Other Days*, Leeds, E.J. Arnold.

ELLIOT, M.M. (1937) *Our Yesterdays (Series)*, Leeds, E.J. Arnold.

ELLIOT, M.M. (u.d., 1953?) *Farmers Through the Ages*, (no. 34 of Everyday Child Series), Leeds, E.J. Arnold.

ELLIOT, M.M. and HARTLEY, D.R. (n.d.) *How Medieval Folk Lived*, Exeter, A. Wheaton.

FIRTH, C.B. (Ed.) (1931) *History — Junior Course (Series)*, London, Gunn & Co.

FLETCHER, C.B.L. and KIPLING, R. (1911) *A School History of England*, Oxford, Oxford University Press.

FRASER, E. (1932) *Life in Early Days (Series)*, London, Nisbet.

GASQUET, F.A. (1902–3) *The Abbey History Readers (Series)*, London, George Bell & Sons.

GUEST, G. (1913) *A Social History of England*, London, G. Bell & Sons. (1913, rev. 1929, 16th Ed. 1955).

GUEST, G. (1920) *An Introduction to English Rural History*, London, WEA.

HAMILTON, J. (1964) *Saxon People*, London, Lutterworth Press.

HANCOCK, M.S. (1904) *King Edward History Reader (Series)*, London, Sir Isaac Pitman.

HANSON, A.H. (1950) *The Lives of the People (Series) Book I*, London, Heinemann.

HARLAND, O. (1951) *The Story of Our People, (Series I of Newnes Narrative Histories): I — The Making of the Kingdom; II — The Making of the Nation; III — The Age of Expansion; IV — Government by the People*, London, Newnes Pub. Co.

HARRISON, M. (1961) *Children in History (Series) Book III, The Eighteenth Century*, Amersham, Hulton Educational.

HARSTON, K. (1951) *Understanding the Modern World (Series)*, London, Allen & Unwin.

HIGHAM, C.S.S. (u.d., 1938?) *Landmarks of World History*, London, Longmans (3rd edn 1947, 1951).

Highroads of History (1909) (anon.) in *Royal School Series*, London, T. Nelson & Son.

HIMMELFARB, G. (1973) 'The Culture of Poverty' in DYOS, H.J. and WOLFF, M. (Eds).

HITCHCOCK, A. and HITCHCOCK, L.J. (1955) *The Pilgrim Way (Series): I — Cavemen — Early Iron Age; II — Herdsmen; III — Great People; IV — The British People*, London, Blackie.

HOBLEY, L.F. (1960) *Britain's Place in the World (Series)*, Edinburgh, Oliver & Boyd.

HORNIBLOW, E.C.T. and SULLIVAN, J.J. (1954) *The March of Time (Series)*, Glasgow, Grant.

HOUNSELL, H.E. and HILTON, J. (u.d., 1920?) *The Research Histories (Series) Book IV Our Island Story*, Huddersfield, Schofield & Sims.

HOUNSELL, H.E. and HILTON, J. (u.d, 1938?) *Pictorial History (Series)*, Huddersfield, Schofield and Sims.

House of History Series (1931) London, Thomas Nelson.

HOUSEMAN, L. and MARTEN, H. (1932) *Histories (Series)*, Oxford, Basil Blackwell.

HUME, E.G., (1953) *The Pilgrim Way (Series) II, Children Through the Ages*, London, Blackie & Son.

INCE, H. (1856) *Outlines of English History* (extended by J. Gilbert), London, J. Gilbert.

INCE, H. and GILBERT, J. (1888) *Outlines of English History*, London, W.H. Allen (rev edn).

KELLY, T. and STEWART, J. (1962) *Chambers Mayflower Histories (First course)*

(Series); I — Stories of Early Days; II — Stories of Later Days, Edinburgh, W & R Chambers.

KIRKMAN, F.B. (1938) *The History Highway (Series)*, London, Thomas Nelson.

LARKIN, P. (1953) *Your World, Past and Present (Series) Book I At Home*, London, John Murray.

LAY, E.J.S. (1915) *The Pupil's Class–Book of English History*, London, Macmillan.

LAY, E.J.S. (1941) 'Adventures into history' in *Macmillan's Easy Study Series, Junior Book IA*, London, Macmillan.

LAY, E.J.S. (1951) *Men of Work, in Three Course Histories, Easy Study Series*, London Macmillan.

LAY, E.J.S. (Ed.) (1958) *Macmillan's History Picture Books (Series)*, London, Macmillan.

LITTLE, W.B. (1937) *England's History (Series): I — Early Days to 1485; II — Days of Adventure and Expansion; III — The Modern Age*, London, Pitman & Son.

LIVESEY, T.J. (1885) *Stories from English History, no. 1 of Granville History Readers*, London, Burns and Oates.

Longmans 'Ship' Historical Readers (Series) (1893), London, Longmans.

LORD, J. (1930) *A Progressive History of Britain (Series)*, London, Rivington.

Macmillan's History Readers (Series), (1895) London, Macmillan.

Macmillan's History Picture Books, (1958), see LAY E.J.S. (Ed.) (1958).

MARSH, L.G. and PARKS, H.A. (1958) *Living in Other Times (booklets)*, London, Hulton Educational.

MARTEN, H. and CARTER, E.H. (u.d.) *Marten and Carter's Histories*, Oxford, Blackwell (27 imp. 1955).

MEIKLEJOHN, J.M.D. (1901) *A New History of England and Great Britain*, London, Alfred M. Holden. (16th edn).

MILLIKEN, E.K. (1944) *Saxon and Viking*, London, G. Harrap.

MILNE, J. (1959) *The Oaktree Histories (Series)*, London, Hamish Hamilton.

MITCHELL, R. and MIDDLETON, G. (1979) *Focus on History (Series)*, London, Longmans.

MORGAN, R. (1880) *The Oxford and Cambridge History of England For School Use*, London, George Gill & Sons.

MORRIS, R W. (1952) *Town Life Through The Ages*, London, Allen & Unwin.

Oxford Junior History (Series), (1978–80), Oxford, Oxford University Press.

POWER, R. (u.d.) *The Kingsway Histories (Series)*, London, Evans Bros.

PRIESTLEY, H.E. (1949) *The Pageant of the English People (Series): I — The Making of a Nation; II — Days of Chance; III — The Commonwealth; IV — The Machine Age*, London, Macdonald.

PRIESTLEY, H.E. (1952) *English History in Play and Picture (Series): I — In the Beginning; II — Kings and People; III — Men and Machines*, London, Macdonald.

PURKIS, S. (1981) *At Home and in the Street, 1900*, London, Longmans.

PURKIS, S. and MERSON, E. (1981) *At School and in the Country in 1900*, London, Longmans.

PURTON, R.W. (1958) *New View Histories (Series)*, London, Collins Clear-type Press.

PURTON, R.W. (1961) *The Junior New View Histories (Series)*, London, Collins Clear-type Press.

RANSOME, C. (1896) *Elementary History of England*, London, Rivington Percival & Co. (4th edn).

REEVE, J.R. (1935) *History Through Familiar Things (Series): I — Food and Tools; II — Shelter and Society*, London, University of London Press (7th imp. 1956).

REEVES, M.E. and HODGSON, P. (Eds) (1953) *Then and There Series*, London, Longman.

ROBERTSON, B. (1932) *Life in Past Ages*, Book III of WOOD, J.M. (Ed.) (1932).

SCARFE, H.G. (1960) *As We Were (Series)*, London, Longmans.

SCOTLAND, A. (1953) *All Our Past (Series)*, London, Cassell & Co.

SHARP, M. (Ed.) (1955) *The Late Middle Ages*, London, The Historical Association and George Philip & Son.

SMITH, E. (1950) *Tales That History Tells (Series)*, London, The Grant Educational Press.

SMITH, J.Y. and LAY, E.J.S. (u.d.) 'Adventures into history for primary schools' in *Macmillan's Early Study Series*, London, Macmillan.

SOCIAL LITERACY PROJECT (u.d.) *Social Literacy (Series)*, Stanmore, NSW, Social Literacy Project.

SPALDING, E.H. (1921) *The Piers Plowman Social and Economic Histories (Series)*, London, G. Philip.

SPALDING, E.H. and WRAGG, P. (1914) *Piers Plowman Histories (Series)*, London, George Philip.

STUART, M. (1951a) 'Town and country' Book II in BOOG-WATSON, E.J. and CARRUTHERS, J.I. (Eds) *History Through the Ages (Series)*, Oxford, Oxford University Press.

STUART, M. (1951b) 'Home life' in BOOG-WATSON, E.J. and CARRUTHERS, J.I. (Eds) *History Through the Ages (Series)*, Oxford, Oxford University Press.

TAYLOR, E. (1845) *England and its People (2nd edn)*, London, Houlston & Stoneman.

THOMAS, F.G. (1943) *The Story of the Countryside, (1st Series)*, Oxford, Oxford University Press.

THOMAS, J.A. (1962) *Real History (Series)*, London, J.M. Dent.

TICKNER, F.W., (1930) *A Junior Social and Industrial History of England*, London, Edward Arnold.

TICKNER, F.W. (1951) *Headway Histories (1st Series)*, (New Impression) London, Edward Arnold.

TITTERTON, A. (1931) *From Romans to Normans*, Book II of FIRTH, C.B. (Ed.) *History — Junior Course (Series)*, London Ginn & Co.

TOUT, T.F. (1902–) *Longmans Historical Series for Schools (Series)*, London, Longmans.

TURNBULL, D. (1953) *The Golden Mean Histories (Series)*, Exeter, Wheaton.

UDEN, G. (1946) *Farm History*, London, Methuen.

UNSTEAD, R.J. (1953) *Looking at History (Series)*, London, A & C Black.
WARD, W.C.J. (1940) *From Serf to Citizen (Series)*, London, Blackie (new edn 1956).
WARNER, G.T. (1912) *Tillage, Trade and Invention*, London, Blackie. (1912–26th ed.).
WILLIAMS-ELLIS, A and FISHER, E.J. (1936) *A History of English Life (Series)*, London, Methuen.
WOOD, E.G. (1939) *The Project Series of History Readers*, London, Gill.
WRAGGE, P. (1949) *The Young Citizens Social History of Britain*, London, Longmans.
WRIGHT, C.R. (1961), *An Introduction to Social History (Series)*, London, Associated Newspapers.
YONGE, C.M. (u.d. 1880?) *English History Reading Books*, London, National Society's Depository.

Geography Textbooks

A.L. *Everychild Series* (n.d.), Leeds, Arnold.
ALNWICK, H. (1951) *Our Food and Our Clothes*, London, G. Harrup.
ARKINSTALL, A. and BRINDLEY, N.V. (1961) *The Living Geography (Series): I — Living in Town and Country; II — Living in Other Lands; III — Living in Britain; IV — Living in the World at Large*, London, Chatto and Windus.
Arnold's Geography Readers (1896) London, Edward Arnold.
BAKER, W.G. (1881) *Blackie's Comprehensive School Series Geographical Reader*, London, Blackie & Sons.
BARKER, E. (1959) *Queensway Junior Geography (Series): I — About Animals; II — About Shops; III — About Britain; IV — About the World*, London, Evans Bros.
BARKER, W.H. and BROOKS, L. (1928) *Junior Regional Geographies (Series)*, London, University of London Press.
BARRINGTON-WARD, M.J. (1891) *The Child's Geography*, London, George Bell.
BAXTER, A.M. (u.d.) see, *Little People in Far Off Lands (Series)*.
BAYNE, M. (1934) *The World Around Us (Series)*, Edinburgh, W & R Chambers.
Black's New Graded Geographies (Series) (u.d.): *I — Other Children's Homes; II — The Wonderland of Common Things; III — World Journeys by Land, Sea and Air; IV — Life and Work in Britain*, London, A. & C. Black.
Blackie's Tropical Readers (u.d., 1938?), London, Blackie & Sons.
BOYCE, E.R. (1957–58) *Children of Today (Series)*, London, Macmillan.
BOYCE, E.R. (1961) *Children of Other Lands*, London, Macmillan.
BRADY, R.P. (1951) *You and the Commonwealth (Series)*, London, Educational Productions.
BROOKS, L. and FINCH, R. (1928) see FINCH (1928).
BROOKS, L. and FINCH, R. (1939) *The Golden Hind Geographies (Second Series): I — The British Homeland; II — Seeing the World; III — The Gifts of the Earth; IV — Peoples and Countries of the World*, London, University of London Press.
BUSHELL, H.H. (u.d.) see *The Look and Learn Geography Course*.

Chambers' New Geographical Readers (1891) London, W & R Chambers.

CHAPPEL, B.C. (1956) *Let's Look at the British Isles*, Edinburgh, Chambers.

CHISHOLM, G.G. (1898) *Longmans Junior School Geography*, London, Longmans, Green and Co (new edn 1919).

Citizens Geographies (1937) London, Thomas Nelson.

COOK, T.H. (1950) *Life and Work in the British Isles (Series): I — Children of Many Lands; II — Life and Work in the British Isles; III — Life and Work Oversea; IV — On the World's Highways*, London, Macdonald.

DALY, A. and MORRISON, I. (1985) *Storyline Geography*, Edinburgh, Oliver and Boyd.

FAIRGRIEVE, J. and YOUNG, E. (1939) *Real Geography (Series)*, London, G. Philip & Son.

FINCH, R. (1928) *The Columbus Regional Geographies (1st series)*, London, University of London Press (18th edn 1953).

FINCH, R. (1937) *The Golden Hind Geographies (Series)*, London, University of London Press (rep. in 1959).

GARNETT, O. (1949–51) *The Discovery Books (Series): I — Looking and Doing; II — Finding Out; III — Exploring the World; IV — Pathfinding and Pathmaking*, Oxford, Basil Blackwell.

GEIKIE, A.L. (1888) *Geography of the British Isles*, London, Macmillan.

Gill's Imperial Geography (1878) Liverpool, G. Gill & Co.

GLOVER, A.H.T. and YOUNG, I.V. (1960–63) *The New Primary Geography Series: I — Looking Around; II — Looking Further Afield; III — Understanding Britain; IV — Looking at the World*, London, University of London, Press.

Graphic Geographical Reader (1893) London, William Collins.

GREEN, W.A. and GREEN, E.G. (1939) *Looking at the World (Series): I — Families in Other Lands; II — Our Neighbours and Their Work For Us; III — The World and Its Tradeways; IV — Britain and Its Work*, London, Blackie.

HARDINGHAM, B.G. (1935) *Foundations of Geography (Series)*, London, Thomas Nelson & Sons.

HARDINGHAM, B.G. (1942) *The Citizens Geographies (Series)*, London, Thomas Nelson & Sons.

HARDINGHAM, B.G. (1957–60) *This Land of Britain (Series)*, London, Thomas Nelson & Sons.

HEPPEL, B.C. (1920) *Let's Look Geographies (Series)*, London, W & R Chambers.

HERBERTSON, A.J. (1904) *An Illustrated School Geography*, London, Ginn & Co.

HERBERTSON, A.J. and HERBERTSON, F.D. (1899) *Man and His Work*, London, A & C Black.

HERBERTSON, F.D. (1906) *The British Empire*, London, A & C Black.

HERDMAN, T. (1957) *Longmans Colour Geographies (Series)*, London, Longmans.

HODGKISON, E.G. and PREECE, D.M. (1934) *The World*, London, University Tutorial Press.

HORNIBLOW, E.C.T. (1936) *Lands and Life Human Geographies (Series)*, London, The Grant Educational Co. (9th edn).

HUGHES, W. (1871) *Elementary Class-Book of Modern Geography*, Liverpool, George Philip & Son.

HUGHES, W. (1882) *Elementary Class-Book of Modern Geography, New Edition,* London, George Philip & Son.

Johnston's New Picture Geographies (Series) (1937) Books I, II and III by MIDGLEY, C.; Book IV by WHITE, E. and SUTHERLAND, D. London, W & A.K. Johnston (rev. 1953).

King Geographical Readers (1901) London, Moffat & Page.

LAY, E.J.S. (1914) 'The British Isles' in *The Pupils' Class-Book of Geography (Series)*, London, Macmillan.

LAY, E.J.S. (1937) *The Empire Geographies (Series): I — Treasure from Land and Sea; II — Life in Canada and Australia; III — Life in British African and India; IV — Life in the British Isles*, London, Macmillan (later retitled in 1958 *The Commonwealth Geographies* and jointly edited with NOYLE, G.).

Little Folks of Other Lands (1919) London, T. Nelson.

Little People in Far Off Lands (Series), (u.d.), London, E.J. Arnold.

Longmans Colour Geographies, see HERDMAN, T. (1957).

Longmans Ship Series — Pictorial Geographical Readers (1900) London, Longmans.

Look and Learn Geography Course (Series) (u.d.) London, Elkin, Matthews & Marrot.

LYDE, L.W. (1904) *An Elementary Geography of the World*, London, A & C. Black.

MACDONALD, A.M. (1960) *Around Our World (Series)*, London, W & R Chambers.

McDougall's Geographical Primer (u.d. 1936?) London, McDougall.

MACKINDER, H.J. (1906) *Elementary Studies in Geography (Series)*, London, G. Philip & Son.

Macmillan's Geography Class Pictures (1959) London, Macmillan.

Macmillian's Practical Modern Geographies (1915) London, Macmillan.

MEIKLEJOHN, J.M.D. (1893) *A New Geography in the Comparative Method*, London, A. Holden (6th edn).

MIDGLEY, C. (1949) *The Golden Mean Geographies (Series)*, Exeter, A. Wheaton.

MOSBY, J. and YOUNG, E.W. (1949–52) *Our World (Series)*, London, Edward Arnold.

MOSS, B. *et al* (1956) *My Foreign Correspondent*, London, Meicklejohn.

MOSS, F.G. (1930) *People and Homes in Many Lands*, London, G. Harrap. (3rd edn 1958).

MULLEY, J.T. (1930) *The British Empire Overseas*, London, Nisbet.

MURCHE, V.T. (1902) *The Globe Geography Readers (Series)*, London, Macmillan.

MURRAY, A. (1960) *Our Changing Commonwealth*, London, Collins.

NEWMAN, B. (1965) *Let's Visit Malaysia and Her Neighbours*, London, Burke.

NIGHTINGALE, A. (1920) see *Visual Series*.

NOYLE, G. (1949) *Adventures into Geography For Primary Schools (Series)*, London, Macmillan.

OATES, D.W. (1916) *Tales of Travel Series*, London, George Harrap.

Oxford New Geography (Series), (1980) Oxford, Oxford University Press.

PARKIN, G.R. (1892) *Round The Empire*, London, Cassell.

PAUL, L. (1954) *The 'Adventures of Man' Series*, London, Newnes Educational Publishing.

People of the World (Series), (1957–59) Oxford, Oxford University Press.

PHILLIPS, E.M. (1951–61) *Question-Time Series*, London, Macmillan.

PHILLIPS HUMAN GEOGRAPHIES *(Series)*, (1919) London, G. Philip & Sons, (rev edn 1948).

PICKLES, T. (1929) *Britain and Abroad*, London, Blackie (rep. 1949).

PICKLES, T. (1933) *Africa, Australia and New Zealand, Vol. I of Dent's Modern School Geographies*, London, J.M. Dent.

PICKLES, T. (1945) *The Work of Men*, London, J. Murray.

PICTON, J.A. (1885) *First Steps in Geography*, London, W. Isbister Ltd.

Pictorial Geographical Readers, see *Longmans Ship Series*.

Pleasant Paths to Geography, see SPINK, H.M. and BRADY, R.P. (1950).

Pupils Class-Book Geographies (Series) (1914–24) London, Macmillan.

Queensway Junior Geography, see BARKER, E. (1959).

Royal School Series (1886) *The World At Home*, London, T. Nelson & Sons.

Royal School Series (1911) *Highroads of Geography*, London, T. Nelson & Sons.

RUTLEY, C.B. (1952) *Colin and Patricia in South Africa*, London, Macmillan.

SAUNDERS, E.M. (1928) *The Round World*, London, G. Philip.

SAUNDERS, E.M. (1945) *Geography Through Projects (Series)*, Exeter, A. Wheaton.

SPINK, H.M. and BRADY, R.P. (1950) *Pleasant Pathways to Geography (Series)*, London, Schofield & Sims.

STAMP, L.D. and HERDMAN, T. (1938) *Discovering Geography (Series)*, London, Longmans (rep. 1964).

STEMBRIDGE, J.H. (1929) *The World-Wide Geographies (Series)*, Oxford, Oxford University Press (rev. 1948 as *The New World-Wide Geographies*).

STEMBRIDGE, J.H. (1930) *The World Wide Geographies — Junior Series*, Oxford, Oxford University Press.

THRALLS, Z. (1956) *The World Around Us*, New York, Harcourt Brace.

VICKERS, S.B. (1961) *World Way Geographies (Series)*, London, Educational Publishing Co.

Visual Series (1920) London, A & C Black (rep., 1956).

WALTER, L.E. (1935) *Life in Many Lands*, London, J. Nisbet. (12th rep., 1956).

WALTER, L.E. (1949) *You Look Down On The World (Series)*, London, Newnes.

WALTON, S.M. (1963) *First Geography Readers (Series)*, Exeter, A. Wheaton.

Wheaton's Golden Mean Geographies (1949) Exeter, A. Wheaton.

Wheaton's Vivid Geographies (1946) Exeter, A Wheaton.

WHITE, P. (1951) *My Foreign Correspondent — In the British Isles*, London, Meiklejohn.

WILLIAMS-ELLIS, A. (1951) *A Food and People Geography*, London, University of London Press.

WRIGHT, W.D. (1938) *Life and Commerce in Britain*, London, Dent & Sons.

Index